The
Reference Shelf®

For Reference

Not to be taken from this room

The Supreme Court

The Reference Shelf
Volume 87 • Number 1
H.W. Wilson
Published by
GREY HOUSE PUBLISHING
Amenia, New York
2015

The Reference Shelf

The books in this series contain reprints of articles, excerpts from books, addresses on current issues, and studies of social trends in the United States and other countries. There are six separately bound numbers in each volume, all of which are usually published in the same calendar year. Numbers one through five are each devoted to a single subject, providing background information and discussion from various points of view and concluding with an index and comprehensive bibliography that lists books, pamphlets, and articles on the subject. The final number of each volume is a collection of recent speeches. Books in the series may be purchased individually or on subscription.

Publisher's Cataloging-In-Publication Data
(Prepared by The Donohue Group, Inc.)

Supreme Court / [compiled by Grey House Publishing]. -- [First edition].

   pages : illustrations ; cm. -- (The reference shelf ; volume 87, number 1)

   Edition statement supplied by publisher.
   Includes bibliographical references and index.
   ISBN: 978-1-61925-690-3 (v. 87, no. 1)
   ISBN: 978-1-61925-689-7 (volume set)

   1. United States. Supreme Court--Sources. 2. Judges--United States--Sources. 3. Constitutional law--United States--Sources. 4. United States--Politics and government--2009---Sources. I. H.W. Wilson Company. II. Series: Reference shelf ; v. 87, no. 1.

KF8742 .S86 2015
347.73/26

Cover: United States Supreme Court. Image © Catherine Karnow/Corbis

Contents

2

The Justices

3

Politics and the Court

4

Major Decisions

5

Public Perceptions of the Court

Preface

The Supreme Court

The workings of the Supreme Court of the United States today do not differ dramatically from the court's practice for more than two centuries. As openings occur, the justices are still appointed by the sitting president "with the Advice and Consent of the Senate," as prescribed in Article II, Section 2, of the U.S. Constitution. Justices still hear oral arguments, read relevant documents shedding light on the particulars of a case, are guided by precedent—the court's earlier decisions on similar matters of law—confer in private to arrive at their decisions, and issue written opinions, with concurrences and dissents, presenting the legal reasoning of the majority opinion deciding the case. Time and technology have, of course, affected some of the more external workings of the court, particularly in how it communicates with the public and other branches of the government, yet the court's procedures—for better or, in the eyes of some, for worse—have proved to be remarkably durable.

Article III, Section 2, of the U.S. Constitution presents the nature of the cases that are the proper business of the Supreme Court, regarding which "the supreme Court shall have appellate Jurisdiction, both as to Law and Fact, with such Exceptions, and under such Regulations as the Congress shall make." Under certain circumstances, the Supreme Court is to be a trial court: "In all Cases affecting Ambassadors, other public Ministers and Consuls, and those in which a State shall be Party, the supreme Court shall have original Jurisdiction." Yet what we now regard as the court's primary task—judicial review, or deciding the constitutionality of legislatively enacted laws—is not expressly enumerated in the Constitution but rather took shape as the court began functioning, when Chief Justice Marshall claimed this power for the court in *Marbury v. Madison* (1803).

If the court's primary mission has evolved over time, so has its stature. This upward trajectory is traced by Jill Lepore in "Benched: The Supreme Court and the Struggle for Judicial Independence," the essay that is presented as a prologue to this volume. Theoretically the founders regarded the judiciary as a co-equal branch of the federal government, alongside the executive branch (the president and cabinet) and the legislative branch (the two houses of Congress). But controlling neither the "sword" nor the "purse," as Alexander Hamilton memorably put it in *The Federalist, No. 78*, the court at first commanded little respect or prestige. President George Washington, as Lepore points out, was hard pressed to fill the position of chief justice. Once Marshall laid claim to judicial review, however, the court was set on the path to its current eminence. It did not quickly embark on that path, however; after *Marbury*, the court did not again declare a federal act unconstitutional until it struck down the Missouri Compromise in *Dred Scott v. Sandford* (1857), a decision deplored by Abraham Lincoln, among many others—including later justices of the court. Chief Justice Charles Evans Hughes called it a "self-inflicted wound." Still, judicial review with respect to federal laws—used sparingly for so long—was exercised with increasing frequency thereafter. (The court did fairly regularly exercise judicial review in cases involving state laws, however.)

In his concurrence in *Brown v. Allen* (1953), Associate Justice Robert Jackson famously wrote of the Supreme Court of the United States in his day: "We are not final because we are infallible, but we are infallible only because we are final." As Jackson well understood, while the Supreme Court is the nation's highest appellate court, the ultimate arbiter in any given case, and its verdict is indeed final for that case, "what seems established by one decision is apt to be unsettled by another." Witness, for example, the court's embrace of "separate but equal" in *Plessy v. Ferguson* (1896) and subsequent rejection of that doctrine in *Brown v. Board of Education of Topeka* (1954), or its finding in *Lawrence v. Texas* (2003) that consensual sexual conduct (whether heterosexual or same-sex) is a liberty protected by substantive due process under the Fourteenth Amendment, thus overturning its previous (and relatively recent) ruling in *Bowers v. Hardwick* (1986).

The Federalist, No. 78 was written in part to counter the claims of the "Anti-Federalists"—opponents of the Constitution that was to replace the Articles of Confederation as the embodiment of the nation's form of government—that the Constitution granted too much power to the judiciary, especially in extending the power of the federal judiciary over state courts. Judicial review gradually increased the court's power to heights Alexander Hamilton did not deem possible in *The Federalist,* and raising the stakes when the court did evolve in its thinking as Jackson described. Jackson worried about the court's credibility, and in fact over some of the same issues that troubled the Anti-Federalists. As Jill Lepore points out, "Historically the struggle over judicial review has been part of a larger struggle over judicial independence: the freedom of the judiciary from the other branches of government, from political influence, and, especially, from moneyed interests, which is why the Court's role in deciding whether Congress has the power to regulate the economy"—that is, the scope of the Commerce Clause—"is so woefully vexed."

***

This book explores the Supreme Court from a variety of perspectives, beginning with how the court does its work and proceeding to look at the current court: the individual justices, their complex interactions with and influences on their colleagues, their jurisprudence—that is, the principles and philosophies that govern their thinking—and how their opinions, concurrences, and dissents not only apply constitutional law but shape it. Faith in the integrity of the justices is of the utmost importance to the court's legitimacy in the eyes of the public. As the Pew Research Center's analysis has shown, citizens may approve or disapprove of the court depending on some combination of their personal circumstances—education and religious beliefs, for example—and their political persuasion. If we are to maintain a functioning democracy "under law," however, disapproval cannot spill over into a full-fledged loss of confidence in the court's legitimacy, for the court "says what the law is," as Marshall reminds us.

Therefore the book goes on to examine the pull of politics and ideology on the court: its paradoxical idealization as being above politics despite its necessarily thorough grounding in it, both because of the nature of the confirmation process and because, however subliminally, the justices are attentive to the political currents of the day. Chief Justice John G. Roberts Jr. acknowledged as much at the outset of his tenure on the court, expressing concern about the effects of numerous 5–4 decisions in important cases on the court's legitimacy in the eyes of the public. After all, nine justices cannot be expected to view a complex legal matter in precisely the same way, but if their votes (whatever their reasoning) are repeatedly nearly equally divided on closely watched cases that directly affect the lives of millions of Americans—such as the 2012 ruling on the constitutionality of the Affordable Care Act or the 2013 decision striking down the Defense of Marriage Act (both were 5–4 decisions) citizens may reasonably conclude that factors other than "what the law is" are playing a role in determining the court's decisions.

Those decisions are the focus of the next section of the book, beginning with the court's ruling in *Bush v. Gore* (2000), a watershed decision for the modern Supreme Court that effectively delivered the state of Florida's electoral votes—and hence the 2000 presidential election—to George W. Bush. The power of judicial review ensures that the court regularly passes judgment on the actions of the legislative branch, but on no other occasion has it been involved so decisively in the affairs of the executive branch. Other cases and court orders discussed in this section have far-reaching implications in the private sphere as well as ramifications for public policy. The articles presented here often return to the question of judicial activism as against a purported norm of judicial restraint with respect to precedent, ending with Richard L. Hasen's consideration of "How Justices Move the Law."

In its final section the book directly addresses public perceptions of the court and the justices. Is political polarization the "new reality of today's Supreme Court . . . in a way that parallels" the polarization of "other political institutions and the rest of society," as Norm Ornstein asserts? That question is more complex than it may at first appear. Transparency in the form of the direct access to the court's proceedings that modern technology can offer may or may not shed real light on its workings, may or may not ensure or promote the openness and judicial independence that Americans say they seek. And judicial independence, fundamental as it is to the integrity of the court, does not in itself offer a guarantee that the complex can be made simple or the shadowed clear to the satisfaction of all citizens. Laurence H. Tribe cites a "fundamental truth of our Constitution and democracy: "The most complex questions can never be answered once and for all, certainly not by nine black-robed men and women interpreting a centuries-old charter." What the justices confront is the "court's unending quest to balance conflicting rights, to distill the meaning of U.S. history, to draw a map of constitutional guarantees even as the terrain shifts beneath its feet."

Tribe wrote in response to the 2010 commencement address delivered at Harvard University by David H. Souter, in which the retired justice described the Constitution as "no simple contract." The Constitution's language, he said, "grants and guarantees many good things, and good things that compete with each other and can never all be realized, all together, all at once.

"Remember that the tensions that are the stuff of judging in so many hard constitutional cases are, after all, the creatures of our aspirations," Souter continued, "to value liberty, as well as order, and fairness and equality, as well as liberty. And the very opportunity for conflict between one high value and another reflects our confidence that a way may be found to resolve it when a conflict arises. . . . If we cannot share every intellectual assumption that formed the minds of those who framed the charter, we can still address the constitutional uncertainties the way they must have envisioned, by relying on reason, by respecting all the words the Framers wrote, by facing facts, and by seeking to understand their meaning for living people.

"That is how a judge lives in a state of trust, and I know of no other way to make good on the aspirations that tell us who we are, and who we mean to be, as the people of the United States."

Benched: The Supreme Court and the Struggle for Judicial Independence

By Jill Lepore
The New Yorker, June 18, 2012

Originally, the Supreme Court of the United States met in a drafty room on the second floor of an old stone building called the Merchants' Exchange, at the corner of Broad and Water Streets, in New York. The ground floor, an arcade, was a stock exchange. Lectures and concerts were held upstairs. For meeting, there weren't many places to choose from. Much of the city had burned to the ground during the Revolutionary War; nevertheless, New York became the nation's capital in 1785. After George Washington was inaugurated in 1789, he appointed six Supreme Court Justices—the Constitution doesn't say how many there ought to be—but on February 1, 1790, the first day the Court was called to session, upstairs in the Exchange, only three Justices showed up and so, lacking a quorum, court was adjourned.

Months later, when the nation's capital moved to Philadelphia, the Supreme Court met in City Hall, where it shared quarters with the mayor's court. Not long after, the Chief Justice, John Jay, wrote to the President to let him know that he was going to skip the next session because his wife was having a baby ("I cannot prevail on myself to be then at a Distance from her," Jay wrote to Washington), and because there wasn't much on the docket, anyway.

This spring, the Supreme Court—now housed in a building so ostentatious that Justice Louis Brandeis, who, before he was appointed to the bench, in 1916, was known as "the people's attorney," refused to move into his office—is debating whether the Affordable Care Act violates the Constitution, especially with regard to the word "commerce." Arguments were heard in March. The Court's decision will be final. It is expected by the end of the month.

Under the Constitution, the power of the Supreme Court is quite limited. The executive branch holds the sword, Alexander Hamilton wrote in the Federalist No. 78, and the legislative branch the purse. "The judiciary, on the contrary, has no influence over either the sword or the purse; no direction either of the strength or of the wealth of the society; and can take no active resolution whatever." All judges can do is judge. "The judiciary is beyond comparison the weakest of the three departments of powers," Hamilton concluded, citing, in a footnote, Montesquieu: "Of the three powers above mentioned, the judiciary is next to nothing." . . .

In 1800, the capital moved to Washington, D.C., and the following year John Adams nominated his Secretary of State, the arch-Federalist Virginian John Marshall, to the office of Chief Justice. Adams lived in the White House. Congress met at the Capitol. Marshall took his oath of office in a "meanly furnished, very inconvenient" room in the Capitol Building, where the Justices, who did not have clerks, had no room to put on their robes (this they did in the courtroom, in front of gawking spectators), or to deliberate (this they did in the hall, as quietly as they could). Cleverly, Marshall made sure that all the Justices rented rooms at the same boarding house, so that they could at least have someplace to talk together, unobserved.

Marshall was gangly and quirky and such an avid listener that Daniel Webster once said that, on the bench, he took in counsel's argument the way "a baby takes in its mother's milk." He became Chief Justice just months before Thomas Jefferson became President. Marshall was Jefferson's cousin and also his fiercest political rival, if you don't count Adams. Nearly the last thing Adams did before leaving office was to persuade the lame-duck Federalist Congress to pass the 1801 Judiciary Act, reducing the number of Supreme Court Justices to five—which would have prevented Jefferson from naming a Justice to the bench until two Justices left. The newly elected Republican Congress turned right around and repealed that act and suspended the Supreme Court for more than a year.

In February, 1803, when the Marshall Court finally met, it did something really interesting. In *Marbury v. Madison,* a suit against Jefferson's Secretary of State, James Madison, Marshall granted to the Supreme Court a power it had not been explicitly granted in the Constitution: the right to decide whether laws passed by Congress are constitutional. This was such an astonishing thing to do that the Court didn't declare another federal law unconstitutional for fifty-four years.

The Supreme Court's decision about the constitutionality of the Affordable Care Act will turn on Article I, Section 8, of the Constitution, the commerce clause: "Congress shall have power . . . to regulate Commerce with foreign Nations, and among the several States, and with the Indian Tribes." In *Gibbons v. Ogden,* Marshall interpreted this clause broadly: "Commerce, undoubtedly, is traffic, but it is something more: it is intercourse." ("Intercourse" encompassed all manner of dealings and exchanges: trade, conversation, letter-writing, and even—if plainly outside the scope of Marshall's meaning—sex.) Not much came of this until the Gilded Age, when the commerce clause was invoked to justify trust-busting legislation, which was generally upheld. Then, during the New Deal, the "power to regulate commerce," along with the definition of "commerce" itself, became the chief means by which Congress passed legislation protecting people against an unbridled market; the Court complied only after a protracted battle. In 1964, the commerce clause formed part of the basis for the Civil Rights Act, and the Court upheld the argument that the clause grants Congress the power to prohibit racial discrimination in hotels and restaurants.

In 1995, in *U.S. v. Lopez,* the Court limited that power for the first time since the battle over the New Deal, when Chief Justice William Rehnquist, writing for the majority, overturned a federal law prohibiting the carrying of guns in a school zone: the argument was that gun ownership is not commerce, because it "is in no sense an economic activity." (In a concurring opinion, Justice Clarence Thomas cited Samuel Johnson's *Dictionary of the English Language*.) Five years later, in *U.S. v. Morrison,* Rehnquist, again writing for the majority, declared parts of the federal Violence Against Women Act unconstitutional, arguing, again, that no economic activity was involved.

However the Court rules on health care, the commerce clause appears unlikely, in the long run, to be able to bear the burdens that have been placed upon it. So long as conservatives hold sway on the Court, the definition of "commerce" will get narrower and narrower, despite the fact that this will require, and already has required, overturning decades of precedent. Unfortunately, Article I, Section 8, may turn out to have been a poor perch on which to build a nest for rights.

There is more at stake, too. This Court has not been hesitant about exercising judicial review. In Marshall's thirty-five years as Chief Justice, the Court struck down only one act of Congress. In the seven years since John G. Roberts, Jr., became Chief Justice, in 2005, the Court has struck down a sizable number of federal laws, including one reforming the funding of political campaigns. It also happens to be the most conservative court in modern times. According to a rating system used by political scientists, decisions issued by the Warren Court were conservative thirty-four percent of the time; the Burger and the Rehnquist Courts issued conservative decisions fifty-five percent of the time. So far, the rulings of the Roberts Court have been conservative about sixty percent of the time.

What people think about judicial review usually depends on what they think about the composition of the Court. When the Court is liberal, liberals think judicial review is good, and conservatives think it's bad. This is also true the other way around. Between 1962 and 1969, the Warren Court struck down seventeen acts of Congress. ("With five votes, you can do anything around here," Justice William Brennan said at the time.) Liberals didn't mind; the Warren Court advanced civil rights. Conservatives argued that the behavior of the Warren Court was unconstitutional, and, helped along by that argument, gained control of the Republican Party and, eventually, the Supreme Court, only to engage in what looks like the very same behavior. Except that it isn't quite the same, not least because a conservative court exercising judicial review in the name of originalism suggests, at best, a rather uneven application of the principle.

The commerce clause has one history, judicial review another. They do, however, crisscross. Historically, the struggle over judicial review has been part of a larger struggle over judicial independence: the freedom of the judiciary from the other branches of government, from political influence, and, especially, from moneyed interests, which is why the Court's role in deciding whether Congress has the power to regulate the economy is so woefully vexed. . . .

The principle of judicial independence is related to another principle . . . much influenced by Montesquieu's 1748 "Spirit of Laws": the separation of powers. "The judicial power ought to be distinct from both the legislative and executive, and independent," Adams argued in 1776, "so that it may be a check upon both." There is, nevertheless, a tension between judicial independence and the separation of powers. Appointing judges to serve for life would seem to establish judicial independence, but what power then checks the judiciary? One idea was to have the judges elected by the people; the people then check the judiciary.

At the Constitutional Convention, no one argued that the Supreme Court Justices ought to be popularly elected, not because the delegates were unconcerned about judicial independence but because there wasn't a great deal of support for the popular election of anyone, including the President (hence, the electoral college). The delegates quickly decided that the President should appoint Justices, and the Senate confirm them, and that these Justices ought to hold their appointments "during good behavior."

Amid the debate over ratification, this proved controversial. In a 1788 essay called "The Supreme Court: They Will Mould the Government into Almost Any Shape They Please," one anti-Federalist pointed out that the power granted to the Court was "unprecedented in any free country," because its Justices are, finally, answerable to no one: "No errors they may commit can be corrected by any power above them, if any such power there be, nor can they be removed from office for making ever so many erroneous adjudications." This is among the reasons that Hamilton found it expedient, in the Federalist No. 78, to emphasize the weakness of the judicial branch.

Jefferson, after his battle with Marshall, came to believe that "in a government founded on the public will, this principle operates . . . against that will." In much that same spirit, a great many states began instituting judicial elections, in place of judicial appointment. You might think that elected judges would be less independent, more subject to political forces, than appointed ones. But timeless political truths are seldom true and rarely timeless. During the decades that reformers were lobbying for judicial elections, the secret ballot was thought to be more subject to political corruption than voting openly. Similarly, the popular vote was considered markedly less partisan than the spoils system: the lesser, by far, of two evils.

Nor was the nature of the Supreme Court set in stone. In the nineteenth century, the Court was, if not as weak as Hamilton suggested, nowhere near as powerful as it later became. In 1810, the Court moved into a different room in the Capitol, where a figure of Justice, decorating the chamber, had no blindfold but, as the joke went, the room was too dark for her to see anything anyway. It was also dank. "The deaths of some of our most talented jurists have been attributed to the location of this Courtroom," one architect remarked. It was in that dimly lit room, in 1857, that the Supreme Court overturned a federal law for the first time since *Marbury v. Madison*. In *Dred Scott v. Sandford*, Chief Justice Roger B. Taney, writing for the majority, voided the Missouri Compromise by arguing that Congress could not prohibit slavery in the territories.

In 1860, the Court moved once more, into the Old Senate Chamber. When Abraham Lincoln was inaugurated, on the East Portico of the Capitol, Taney administered the oath, and Lincoln, in his address, confronted the crisis of constitutional authority. "I do not forget the position, assumed by some, that constitutional questions are to be decided by the Supreme Court," he said, but "if the policy of the government, upon vital questions affecting the whole people, is to be irrevocably fixed by the decisions of the Supreme Court, the instant they are made . . . the people will have ceased to be their own rulers, having to that extent, practically resigned their government into the hands of that eminent tribunal." Five weeks later, shots were fired at Fort Sumter.

In the decades following the Civil War, an increasingly activist Court took up not only matters relating to Reconstruction, and especially to the Fourteenth Amendment, but also questions involving the regulation of business, not least because the Court ruled that corporations could file suits, as if they were people. And then, beginning in the eighteen-nineties, the Supreme Court struck down an entire docket of Progressive legislation, including child-labor laws, unionization laws, minimum-wage laws, and the progressive income tax. In *Lochner v. New York* (1905), in a 5–4 decision, the Court voided a state law establishing that bakers could work no longer than ten hours a day, six days a week, on the ground that the law violated a "liberty of contract," protected under the Fourteenth Amendment. In a dissenting opinion, Justice Oliver Wendell Holmes accused the Court of wildly overreaching its authority. "A Constitution is not intended to embody a particular economic theory," he wrote. . . .

Lochner led to an uproar. In 1906, Roscoe Pound, the eminent legal scholar and later dean of Harvard Law School, delivered an address before the American Bar Association called "The Causes of Popular Dissatisfaction with the Administration of Justice," in which he echoed Holmes's dissent in *Lochner*. "Putting courts into politics, and compelling judges to become politicians, in many jurisdictions has almost destroyed the traditional respect for the Bench," he warned. . . . . *Lochner*, together with a host of other federal- and state-court rulings, contributed to a surge of popular interest in judicial independence, including calls for "judicial removal": the firing of judges by a simple majority of the legislature. In 1911, Arizona, preparing to enter the union, had a proposed constitution that included judicial recall, the removal of judges by popular vote, which was also a platform of Theodore Roosevelt's Bull Moose campaign. The U.S. Congress approved the state's constitution, but when it went to the White House William Howard Taft vetoed it. He objected to recall. Before he became President, Taft was a judge. He wanted not less judicial power but more. The next year, Taft began lobbying Congress for funds to erect for the Supreme Court a building of its own.

On October 13, 1932, Herbert Hoover laid the cornerstone, at a construction site across from the Capitol. The plan was to build the greatest marble building in the world; marble had been shipped from Spain, Italy, and Africa. At the ceremony, after Hoover emptied his trowel, Chief Justice Charles Evans Hughes delivered remarks recalling the Court's long years of wandering. "The court began its work as a homeless department of the government," Hughes said, but "this monument bespeaks the common cause, the unifying principle of our nation."

In 1906, Hughes had run for governor of New York against William Randolph Hearst; as against Hearst's five hundred thousand dollars, Hughes spent six hundred and nineteen dollars. Miraculously, he won. Once in office, he pushed through the state legislature a campaign-spending limit. In 1910, Taft appointed Hughes to the Supreme Court, where, as a champion of civil liberties, he often joined with Holmes in dissent. Hughes resigned from the bench in 1916 to run for President; he lost, narrowly, to Woodrow Wilson. After serving as Secretary of State under Warren G. Harding and Calvin Coolidge, he was appointed Chief Justice in 1930.

Three weeks after Hoover laid the cornerstone for the new Supreme Court Building, F.D.R. was elected President, defeating the incumbent by a record-breaking electoral vote: 472 to 59. As the New York Law School professor James F. Simon chronicles in *F.D.R. and Chief Justice Hughes: The President, the Supreme Court, and the Epic Battle Over the New Deal* (Simon & Schuster), the President-elect immediately began lining up his legislative agenda. He met with Holmes, who told him, "You are in a war, Mr. President, and in a war there is only one rule, 'Form your battalion and fight!' "

By June of 1933, less than a hundred days after his Inauguration, F.D.R. had proposed fifteen legislative elements of his New Deal, all having to do with the federal government's role in the regulation of the economy—and, therefore, with the commerce clause—and each had been made law. Now the New Deal had to pass muster in Hughes's court, where four conservative Justices, known as the Four Horsemen, consistently voted in favor of a Lochnerian liberty of contract, while the three liberals—Louis Brandeis, Benjamin Cardozo, and Harlan Fiske Stone—generally supported government regulation. That left Hughes and Owen Roberts. In early rulings, Hughes and Roberts joined the liberals, and the Court, voting 5–4, let New Deal legislation stand. "While an emergency does not create power," Hughes said, "an emergency may furnish the occasion for the exercise of the power."

In the January 1935, session, the Court heard arguments in another challenge. F.D.R., expecting an adverse decision, prepared a speech in which he quoted Lincoln's remarks about *Dred Scott*, adding, "To stand idly by and to permit the decision of the Supreme Court to be carried through to its logical, inescapable conclusion" would "imperil the economic and political security of this nation." The speech was never given. In another 5–4 decision, Hughes upheld F.D.R.'s agenda, leading one of the horsemen to burst out, "The Constitution is gone!"—a comment so unseemly that it was stricken from the record.

On May 27, 1935—afterward known as Black Monday—the Supreme Court met, for very nearly the last time, in the Old Senate Chamber. In three unanimous decisions, the Court devastated the New Deal. Most critically, it found that the National Recovery Administration, which Roosevelt had called the "most important and far-reaching legislation in the history of the American Congress," was unconstitutional, because Congress had exceeded the powers granted to it under the commerce clause. Four days later, the President held a press conference in the Oval Office. He compared the gravity of the decision to *Dred Scott*. Then he raged, "We have been relegated to the horse-and-buggy definition of interstate commerce." But, in the horse-and-buggy days, the Court didn't have half as much power as it had in 1935.

The Supreme Court's new building opened six months later, on October 7, 1935. A pair of reporters described the place as "a classical icebox decorated for some surreal reason by an insane upholsterer." Nine Justices took their seats in the same raggedy assortment of chairs they had used in the Senate Chamber. Asked whether he wanted a new chair, Justice Cardozo had refused. "No," he replied slowly, "if Justice Holmes sat in this chair for twenty years, I can sit in it for a while."

And then the Hughes Court went on a spree. In eighteen months, it struck down more than a dozen laws. Congress kept passing them; the Court kept striking them down, generally 5–4. At one point, F.D.R.'s Solicitor General fainted, right there in the courtroom.

The President began entertaining proposals about fighting back. One senator had an idea. "It takes twelve men to find a man guilty of murder," he said. "I don't see why it should not take a unanimous court to find a law unconstitutional." That might have required a constitutional amendment, a process that is notoriously corruptible. "Give me ten million dollars," Roosevelt said, "and I can prevent any amendment to the Constitution from being ratified by the necessary number of states."

Meanwhile, the President was running for reelection. A week before Election Day, an attack on the Hughes Court, titled "The Nine Old Men," began appearing in the nation's newspapers and in bookstores. F.D.R. defeated the Republican, Alf Landon, yet again breaking a record in the electoral college: 523 to 8. In February 1937, Roosevelt floated his plan: claiming that the Justices were doddering, and unable to keep up with the business at hand, he would name an additional Justice for every sitting Justice over the age of seventy. There were six of them, including the Chief Justice, who was seventy-four.

The President's approval rating fell. In a radio address on March 9, 1937, he argued that the time had come "to save the Constitution from the Court, and the Court from itself." Then Hughes all but put the matter to rest. "The Supreme Court is fully abreast of its work," he reported on March 22nd, in a persuasive letter to the Senate Judiciary Committee. If efficiency were actually a concern, he argued, there was a great deal of evidence to suggest that more Justices would only slow things down.

What happened next is clear: starting with *West Coast Hotel Co. v. Parrish*, a ruling issued on March 29, 1937, in a 5–4 opinion written by Hughes, that sustained a minimum-wage requirement, the Supreme Court began upholding the New Deal. Owen Roberts had switched sides, a move so sudden, and so crucial to the preservation of the Court, that it has been called "the switch in time that saved nine." Why this happened is not quite as clear. It looked purely political. "Even a blind man ought to see that the Court is in politics," Felix Frankfurter wrote to Roosevelt. "It is a deep object lesson—a lurid demonstration—of the relation of men to the 'meaning' of the Constitution." It wasn't as lurid as all that; it had at least something to do with the law.

On May 18, 1937, the Senate Judiciary Committee voted against the President's proposal. The court-packing plan was dead. Six days later, the Supreme Court upheld the old-age-insurance provisions of the Social Security Act. The President, and his deal, had won.

On either side of the Supreme Court steps, on top of fifty-ton marble blocks, sits a sculpted figure: the Contemplation of Justice, on the left, and the Authority of Law, on the right. In the pediment above the portico, Liberty gazes into the future; Charles Evans Hughes crouches by her side. Inside, a bronze statue of John Marshall stands in the Lower Great Hall. Above him, etched into marble, are his remarks from *Marbury v. Madison*: "It is emphatically the province and duty of the judicial department to say what the law is."

Within the walls of that building, Dred Scott is nowhere to be found, and Lochner stalks the halls like a ghost. Portraits of the first Chief Justices, starting with John Jay, hang in the East Conference Room, and of the later Justices, in the West. A portrait of Earl Warren was installed after his death, in 1974. Beginning with the Court's ruling in *Brown v. Board of Education,* in 1954, Warren presided over the most activist liberal court in American history. "I would like this court to be remembered as the people's court," Warren said when he retired, in 1969. He was pointing to the difference between conservative judicial activism and liberal judicial activism: one protects the interests of the powerful and the other those of the powerless.

The Supreme Court has been deliberating in a temple of marble for three-quarters of a century. In March, it heard oral arguments about the Affordable Care Act. No one rode there in a horse and buggy. There was talk, from the bench, of heart transplants, and of a great many other matters unthinkable in 1789. Arguments lasted for three days. On the second day, the Solicitor General insisted that the purchase of health insurance is an economic activity. Much discussion followed about whether choosing not to buy health insurance is an economic activity, too, and one that Congress has the power to regulate. If you could require people to buy health insurance, Justice Antonin Scalia wanted to know, could you require them to buy broccoli? "No, that's quite different," the Solicitor General answered. "The food market, while it shares that trait that everybody's in it, it is not a market in which your participation is often unpredictable and often involuntary." This did not appear to satisfy.

The ruling that the Supreme Court hands down this month will leave unanswered questions about the relationship between the judicial and the legislative branches of government, and also between the past and the present. The separation of law from politics for which the Revolution was fought has proved elusive. That's not surprising—no such separation being wholly possible—but some years have been better than others. One of the worst was 2000, when the Court determined the outcome of a disputed Presidential election. The real loser in that election, Justice John Paul Stevens said in his dissent in *Bush v. Gore,* "is the Nation's confidence in the judge as an impartial guardian of the rule of law."

For centuries, the American struggle for a more independent judiciary has been more steadfast than successful. Currently, nearly ninety percent of state judges run for office. "Spending on judicial campaigns has doubled in the past decade, exceeding $200 million," [Jed] Shugerman reports [in *The People's Courts,* 2012]. In 2009, after three Iowa supreme-court judges overturned a defense-of-marriage act, the American Family Association, the National Organization for Marriage, and the

Campaign for Working Families together spent more than eight hundred thousand dollars to campaign against their reëlection; all three judges lost. "I never felt so much like a hooker down by the bus station," one Ohio supreme-court justice told the *Times* in 2006, "as I did in a judicial race."

Federally, few rulings have wreaked such havoc on the political process as the 2010 case *Citizens United v. Federal Election Commission*, whereby the Roberts Court struck down much of the *McCain-Feingold Act*, which placed restrictions on corporate and union funding of political campaigns. Stevens, in his dissent, warned that "a democracy cannot function effectively when its constituent members believe laws are being bought and sold."

That, in the end, is the traffic to worry about. If not only legislators but judges serve at the pleasure of lobbyists, the people will have ceased to be their own rulers. Law will be commerce. And money will be king.

1
The Court and Its Workings

SCOTUSblog intern Dan Stein runs the printed court ruling on Section 4 of the Voting Rights Act from the U.S. Supreme Court building to his colleagues, June 25, 2013.

Principles and Practice

The Supreme Court of the United States is notoriously reticent about its work. It observes long-established traditions and complex rules as well as the provisions of Article 3 of the U.S. Constitution, the formal legal basis for the court and its authority. The text of that section—included here—is brief in comparison with the sections establishing the other two branches of the federal government, and as a rule the court does not, or at least traditionally has not, attracted nearly as much attention as those other two branches. Periodically there have been exceptions, such as the period in the mid-1930s when the Hughes Court (under Chief Justice Charles Evans Hughes) struck down one New Deal law after another, earning the wrath of the people as well as that of President Franklin D. Roosevelt. Yet in a telling demonstration of Americans' deference to the court, Roosevelt's plan to circumvent the Hughes Court's conservatism by "packing" the court with additional justices caused the popularity of this exceedingly popular president to plummet. Remarkably, the court itself changed course, and the strategy was dropped, averting a constitutional crisis. Still, it had been made clear that the American public was unwilling to tolerate political interference in the court's work.

In recent years, as the stakes of the high-profile cases brought before the Supreme Court have risen, the Supreme Court's own profile has been rising, and scrutiny of the court and its workings has grown accordingly. There appears to be a new urgency to some old complaints, as commentators express their modern fears of political interference and raise some of the same objections to the court that have been raised since the time the Constitution was subject to ratification. Historically, these objections have focused on the justices' life tenure; the authority of the court to thwart the will of the people by invalidating acts passed by the people's representatives; the court's intervention in matters formerly left to the discretion of the states; the lack of a procedure for removing justices (short of conviction of treason, bribery, or "high crimes and misdemeanors"); and the court's "latitude," or authorization "not only to carry into execution the powers expressly given," as "Brutus" wrote in Anti-Federalist, No. 11, "but where these are wanting or ambiguously expressed, to supply what is wanting by their own decisions." It remains a source of controversy that the justices judge but are not themselves judged, except in the court of public opinion—just as Alexander Hamilton, for one, seems to have intended, for he thought judicial independence depended on insulating the justices from the political fallout of their decisions.

Some of these same criticisms have even appeared in the dissents and concurrences of the justices themselves. When Justice Robert H. Jackson wrote his concurrence in *Brown v. Allen* (1953), he deplored the tendency he saw in the court "to magnify federal, and incidentally its own, authority over the states," declaring that the court's interpretation (in this case of the Fourteenth Amendment) "will be more or less swayed by contemporary intellectual fashions and political currents." Jackson thought that the "belief is widely held . . . that this Court no longer respects impersonal rules of law. . . . Whatever has been intended, this Court also has generated an impression . . . that regard for precedents and authorities is obsolete, that words no longer mean what they have always meant to the profession, that the law knows no fixed principles." Today Jackson's words echo (less elegantly, in general) in the articles, columns, blog posts, social media messages, and radio and television commentary of a world he might scarcely recognize.

In the face of such wide-ranging criticism, the public may be forgiven for occasionally needing to be reminded that the justices' critically important role in our governmental system is not easily executed. The demands on the justices are many and little known to the public at large, which usually focuses intensively on the court only for that brief period in June of each year when the court's most important decisions are typically handed down.

How does the process that culminates on decision days work? The articles that follow begin with bedrock: Article III of the Constitution of the United States. In addition to that constitutional language so intensively parsed before and since, readers will find Alexander Hamilton's defense of the Constitution's conception of the Supreme Court, including the "good behavior" (lifetime) tenure of justices and the commanding place of the court in the nation's judicial system. Aspects of the current workings of the court include the role of the clerks in the justice's work, including legal research and the drafting of the justices' opinions; the remarkably small pool of top-flight lawyers chosen for oral argument before the court; the reasons why a case or collection of cases may be denied review; and how and why a given case may be accepted by the court from among the thousands of petitions submitted for its consideration each year. The groundwork for later discussion of the justices' jurisprudence is laid with a discussion of stare decisis, the doctrine of respect for precedent that has long been accepted by most Supreme Court justices in word if not entirely in deed; judicial activism and judicial restraint both play out in relation to this norm.

The court's own formulation of the rules governing the "generations" of its opinions appear here, for their own sake and because they bear on the court's communication with other parts of the judiciary and with the public. Opinions occasionally undergo changes between the time they are read from the bench and their incorporation in definitive form into the *United States Reports;* a discussion of the history and significance of such changes appears here, for although most such changes may be characterized as mundane, some are substantive indeed. One example cited in an article about Harvard law professor Richard J. Lazarus's revealing 2014 report on this subject is Chief Justice Roger B. Taney's addition of "some 18 pages to his Dred Scott opinion months after it was announced."

Finally, readers are invited to consider both why we should care about the inner workings of the court and what the obligations of the justices to history might be. Currently the justices' papers remain their own personal property, to be disposed of as they see fit, whereas papers and records produced by elected and appointed officials in other branches of the federal government belong to the public.

* * *

By and large, the articles collected in this section deal with the court as it is, not as it might be. The court is sensitive to public concerns about the way it does its work, however, and in recent years it has implemented changes in how it releases and disseminates opinions, if not entirely to the satisfaction of those accustomed to the contemporary climate of instantaneous communications. That the process of melding the court's traditional practices with modern technology has not been entirely smooth is well illustrated by the events on June 28, 2012, when the announcement of the Supreme Court's decision upholding the Affordable Care Act created a "genuine media drama," in the words of lawyer Tom Goldstein of SCOTUSblog.

As Goldstein recounts in "We're Getting Wildly Different Assessments," his SCOTUSblog post of July 7, 2012, the announcement proceeded according to the court's usual protocol. The court's marshal called the court to order, and the justices took their seats on the bench. The galleries for the public and the press were packed, and the atmosphere was "tense with anticipation." Printed copies of the decision were to be released to reporters stationed in the press room on the floor below the courtroom as the announcement of the decision began; additional reporters and media anchors were outside on the court steps, ready to broadcast the ruling as soon as it was conveyed to them (electronically or in hard copy) by colleagues inside the court building. "Runners"—often interns—were ready to physically carry the text from the press room to the colleagues outside.

The role of media technology—the Web and social media—in the release of the court's opinions was by now well established. The court itself formerly e-mailed its opinion after announcing it to the lawyers on both sides of a case, but by June 2012 it disseminated opinions electronically only by posting to its website.

As the chief justice started to read the opinion in the Affordable Care Act case—the last of the term's decisions to be released—a frantic effort to grasp and relay the substance of the opinion began. Millions of people simultaneously tried to access the court's website, and the site could not withstand the demand. Goldstein, recounting the events as they unfolded minute by minute, remarked that "At this moment, the website is the subject of perhaps greater demand than any other site on the Internet—ever." The court was unable to publish its own decision for a half hour, and no one not physically present at the court—including President Barack Obama—could learn the result by any means other than media reports.

If technology failed in this instance, printed copies and runners didn't. But the summary of the decision in the first few pages of the hard copy began with the rejection of the government's primary argument, that the Affordable Care Act's individual mandate that citizens purchase healthcare insurance was constitutional on the grounds of the Commerce Clause. The CNN and Fox News producers at the court seized on this statement as meaning that the act had been struck down and relayed that message to their control teams, which published their erroneous conclusion with astonishing speed through all of their outlets—websites, television networks, social media outlets such as Twitter. In fact the majority, notably including the chief justice, had accepted the government's other argument and upheld the act on the grounds that its individual mandate was within Congress's taxing power. The producers realized their error fairly swiftly, but, as Goldstein recounted in his post, they had already "pulled the trigger."

Bloomberg News, shortly followed by the wire services, scanned the decision and reported it correctly. Meanwhile Goldstein and his core SCOTUSblog team conducted a conference call with major news organizations, including the *New York Times,* the *Wall Street Journal,* and the *Los Angeles Times,* as well as the White House, while SCOTUSblog co-founder Amy Howe tended its Live Blog.

At the White House, the first news received by president himself came via the incorrect CNN and Fox reports, while his press secretary, in another office, saw those reports but was still on the SCOTUSblog conference call and monitoring the Live Blog. Goldstein, the SCOTUSblog gatekeeper, cautioned his conference call auditors and Live Blog readers that although the government had lost on the Commerce Clause, there was more to the decision. Less than a minute later, Goldstein reported that the individual mandate had been upheld. At the court, Chief Justice Roberts was still reading the portion of the opinion rejecting the Commerce Clause argument. The administration's lawyer in the Solicitor General's office at the court only then obtained a hard copy of the opinion and relayed confirmation of the SCOTUSblog report to the White House. More than five minutes after the initial CNN report, the president learned that the legislation embodying his signature domestic policy initiative had survived its court challenge.

Doubtless the technical and procedural flaws on the electronic side have been addressed, and news producers have had an object lesson in the need to take a more temperate approach to their work. But a public clamoring for changes in the court's procedures needs to be made aware that such changes do not occur easily, and the potential for disruption is great.

Bibliography

Bloch, Susan Low, Vicki C. Jackson, and Thomas G Krattenmaker. *Inside the Supreme Court: The Institution and Its Procedures.* St. Paul: Thomson/West, 2008.

Friedman, Leon, ed. *Argument: The Oral Argument before the Court in Brown v. Board of Education of Topeka, 1952–55.* New York, Chelsea House, 1983.

Goldstein, Thomas. "We're Getting Wildly Different Assessments," SCOTUSblog, July 7, 2012. http://www.scotusblog.com/2012/07were-getting-wildly-differing-assessments/

Greenhouse, Linda *The U.S. Supreme Court: A Very Short Introduction.* New York: Oxford University Press, 2012.

Johnson, Timothy R. *Oral Arguments and Decision Making on the United States Supreme Court.* Albany: State University of New York Press, 2004.

Peppers, Todd C., and Artemus Ward, eds. *In Chambers: Stories of Supreme Court Law Clerks and Their Justices.* Charlottesville: University of Virginia Press, 2012.

The Constitution of the United States: Article III

U.S. National Archives and Records Administration

Article III.

Section 1.

The judicial Power of the United States, shall be vested in one supreme Court, and in such inferior Courts as the Congress may from time to time ordain and establish. The Judges, both of the supreme and inferior Courts, shall hold their Offices during good Behaviour, and shall, at stated Times, receive for their Services, a Compensation, which shall not be diminished during their Continuance in Office.

Section 2.

The judicial Power shall extend to all Cases, in Law and Equity, arising under this Constitution, the Laws of the United States, and Treaties made, or which shall be made, under their Authority;—to all Cases affecting Ambassadors, other public Ministers and Consuls;—to all Cases of admiralty and maritime Jurisdiction;—to Controversies to which the United States shall be a Party;—to Controversies between two or more States;—between a State and Citizens of another State,*—between Citizens of different States,—between Citizens of the same State claiming Lands under Grants of different States, and between a State, or the Citizens thereof, and foreign States, Citizens or Subjects.

In all Cases affecting Ambassadors, other public Ministers and Consuls, and those in which a State shall be Party, the supreme Court shall have original Jurisdiction. In all the other Cases before mentioned, the supreme Court shall have appellate Jurisdiction, both as to Law and Fact, with such Exceptions, and under such Regulations as the Congress shall make.

The Trial of all Crimes, except in Cases of Impeachment, shall be by Jury; and such Trial shall be held in the State where the said Crimes shall have been committed; but when not committed within any State, the Trial shall be at such Place or Places as the Congress may by Law have directed.

Section 3.

Treason against the United States, shall consist only in levying War against them, or in adhering to their Enemies, giving them Aid and Comfort. No Person shall be convicted of Treason unless on the Testimony of two Witnesses to the same overt Act, or on Confession in open Court.

The Congress shall have Power to declare the Punishment of Treason, but no Attainder of Treason shall work Corruption of Blood, or Forfeiture except during the Life of the Person attainted.

*Note: Article III, section 2, of the Constitution was modified by amendment XI.

AMENDMENT XI
Passed by Congress March 4, 1794. Ratified February 7, 1795.

The Judicial power of the United States shall not be construed to extend to any suit in law or equity, commenced or prosecuted against one of the United States by Citizens of another State, or by Citizens or Subjects of any Foreign State.

The Federalist, No. 78

The Judiciary Department

By Publius [Alexander Hamilton]
Independent Journal, Saturday, June 14, 1788

To the People of the State of New York:

WE PROCEED now to an examination of the judiciary department of the proposed government.

In unfolding the defects of the existing Confederation, the utility and necessity of a federal judicature have been clearly pointed out. It is the less necessary to recapitulate the considerations there urged, as the propriety of the institution in the abstract is not disputed; the only questions which have been raised being relative to the manner of constituting it, and to its extent. To these points, therefore, our observations shall be confined.

The manner of constituting it seems to embrace these several objects: 1st. The mode of appointing the judges. 2d. The tenure by which they are to hold their places. 3d. The partition of the judiciary authority between different courts, and their relations to each other.

First. As to the mode of appointing the judges; this is the same with that of appointing the officers of the Union in general, and has been so fully discussed in the two last numbers, that nothing can be said here which would not be useless repetition.

Second. As to the tenure by which the judges are to hold their places; this chiefly concerns their duration in office; the provisions for their support; the precautions for their responsibility.

According to the plan of the convention, all judges who may be appointed by the United States are to hold their offices during good behavior; which is conformable to the most approved of the State constitutions and among the rest, to that of this State. Its propriety having been drawn into question by the adversaries of that plan, is no light symptom of the rage for objection, which disorders their imaginations and judgments. The standard of good behavior for the continuance in office of the judicial magistracy, is certainly one of the most valuable of the modern improvements in the practice of government. In a monarchy it is an excellent barrier to the despotism of the prince; in a republic it is a no less excellent barrier to the encroachments and oppressions of the representative body. And it is the best expedient which can be devised in any government, to secure a steady, upright, and impartial administration of the laws.

Whoever attentively considers the different departments of power must perceive, that, in a government in which they are separated from each other, the judiciary, from the nature of its functions, will always be the least dangerous to the political rights of the Constitution; because it will be least in a capacity to annoy or injure them. The Executive not only dispenses the honors, but holds the sword of the community. The legislature not only commands the purse, but prescribes the rules by which the duties and rights of every citizen are to be regulated. The judiciary, on the contrary, has no influence over either the sword or the purse; no direction either of the strength or of the wealth of the society; and can take no active resolution whatever. It may truly be said to have neither FORCE nor WILL, but merely judgment; and must ultimately depend upon the aid of the executive arm even for the efficacy of its judgments.

This simple view of the matter suggests several important consequences. It proves incontestably, that the judiciary is beyond comparison the weakest of the three departments of power [1]; that it can never attack with success either of the other two; and that all possible care is requisite to enable it to defend itself against their attacks. It equally proves, that though individual oppression may now and then proceed from the courts of justice, the general liberty of the people can never be endangered from that quarter; I mean so long as the judiciary remains truly distinct from both the legislature and the Executive. For I agree, that "there is no liberty, if the power of judging be not separated from the legislative and executive powers."[2] And it proves, in the last place, that as liberty can have nothing to fear from the judiciary alone, but would have every thing to fear from its union with either of the other departments; that as all the effects of such a union must ensue from a dependence of the former on the latter, notwithstanding a nominal and apparent separation; that as, from the natural feebleness of the judiciary, it is in continual jeopardy of being overpowered, awed, or influenced by its co-ordinate branches; and that as nothing can contribute so much to its firmness and independence as permanency in office, this quality may therefore be justly regarded as an indispensable ingredient in its constitution, and, in a great measure, as the citadel of the public justice and the public security.

The complete independence of the courts of justice is peculiarly essential in a limited Constitution. By a limited Constitution, I understand one which contains certain specified exceptions to the legislative authority; such, for instance, as that it shall pass no bills of attainder, no ex post facto laws, and the like. Limitations of this kind can be preserved in practice no other way than through the medium of courts of justice, whose duty it must be to declare all acts contrary to the manifest tenor of the Constitution void. Without this, all the reservations of particular rights or privileges would amount to nothing.

Some perplexity respecting the rights of the courts to pronounce legislative acts void, because contrary to the Constitution, has arisen from an imagination that the doctrine would imply a superiority of the judiciary to the legislative power. It is urged that the authority which can declare the acts of another void, must necessarily be superior to the one whose acts may be declared void. . . .

There is no position which depends on clearer principles, than that every act of a delegated authority, contrary to the tenor of the commission under which it is exercised, is void. No legislative act, therefore, contrary to the Constitution, can be valid. . . .

The interpretation of the laws is the proper and peculiar province of the courts. A constitution is, in fact, and must be regarded by the judges, as a fundamental law. It therefore belongs to them to ascertain its meaning, as well as the meaning of any particular act proceeding from the legislative body. If there should happen to be an irreconcilable variance between the two, that which has the superior obligation and validity ought, of course, to be preferred; or, in other words, the Constitution ought to be preferred to the statute, the intention of the people to the intention of their agents. . . .

Nor does this conclusion by any means suppose a superiority of the judicial to the legislative power. It only supposes that the power of the people is superior to both; and that where the will of the legislature, declared in its statutes, stands in opposition to that of the people, declared in the Constitution, the judges ought to be governed by the latter rather than the former. . . .

If, then, the courts of justice are to be considered as the bulwarks of a limited Constitution against legislative encroachments, this consideration will afford a strong argument for the permanent tenure of judicial offices, since nothing will contribute so much as this to that independent spirit in the judges which must be essential to the faithful performance of so arduous a duty.

This independence of the judges is equally requisite to guard the Constitution and the rights of individuals from the effects of those ill humors, which the arts of designing men, or the influence of particular conjunctures, sometimes disseminate among the people themselves, and which, though they speedily give place to better information, and more deliberate reflection, have a tendency, in the meantime, to occasion dangerous innovations in the government, and serious oppressions of the minor party in the community. Though I trust the friends of the proposed Constitution will never concur with its enemies,[3] in questioning that fundamental principle of republican government, which admits the right of the people to alter or abolish the established Constitution, whenever they find it inconsistent with their happiness, yet it is not to be inferred from this principle, that the representatives of the people, whenever a momentary inclination happens to lay hold of a majority of their constituents, incompatible with the provisions in the existing Constitution, would, on that account, be justifiable in a violation of those provisions; or that the courts would be under a greater obligation to connive at infractions in this shape, than when they had proceeded wholly from the cabals of the representative body. Until the people have, by some solemn and authoritative act, annulled or changed the established form, it is binding upon themselves collectively, as well as individually; and no presumption, or even knowledge, of their sentiments, can warrant their representatives in a departure from it, prior to such an act. But it is easy to see, that it would require an uncommon portion of fortitude in the judges to do their duty as faithful guardians of the Constitution, where legislative invasions of it had been instigated by the major voice of the community.

But it is not with a view to infractions of the Constitution only, that the independence of the judges may be an essential safeguard against the effects of occasional ill humors in the society. These sometimes extend no farther than to the injury of the private rights of particular classes of citizens, by unjust and partial laws. Here also the firmness of the judicial magistracy is of vast importance in mitigating the severity and confining the operation of such laws. It not only serves to moderate the immediate mischiefs of those which may have been passed, but it operates as a check upon the legislative body in passing them; who, perceiving that obstacles to the success of iniquitous intention are to be expected from the scruples of the courts, are in a manner compelled, by the very motives of the injustice they meditate, to qualify their attempts. . . .

That inflexible and uniform adherence to the rights of the Constitution, and of individuals, which we perceive to be indispensable in the courts of justice, can certainly not be expected from judges who hold their offices by a temporary commission. Periodical appointments, however regulated, or by whomsoever made, would, in some way or other, be fatal to their necessary independence. If the power of making them was committed either to the Executive or legislature, there would be danger of an improper complaisance to the branch which possessed it; if to both, there would be an unwillingness to hazard the displeasure of either; if to the people, or to persons chosen by them for the special purpose, there would be too great a disposition to consult popularity, to justify a reliance that nothing would be consulted but the Constitution and the laws.

There is yet a further and a weightier reason for the permanency of the judicial offices, which is deducible from the nature of the qualifications they require. It has been frequently remarked, with great propriety, that a voluminous code of laws is one of the inconveniences necessarily connected with the advantages of a free government. To avoid an arbitrary discretion in the courts, it is indispensable that they should be bound down by strict rules and precedents, which serve to define and point out their duty in every particular case that comes before them; and it will readily be conceived from the variety of controversies which grow out of the folly and wickedness of mankind, that the records of those precedents must unavoidably swell to a very considerable bulk, and must demand long and laborious study to acquire a competent knowledge of them. Hence it is, that there can be but few men in the society who will have sufficient skill in the laws to qualify them for the stations of judges. And making the proper deductions for the ordinary depravity of human nature, the number must be still smaller of those who unite the requisite integrity with the requisite knowledge. . . .

Upon the whole, there can be no room to doubt that the convention acted wisely in copying from the models of those constitutions which have established good behavior as the tenure of their judicial offices, in point of duration; and that so far from being blamable on this account, their plan would have been inexcusably defective, if it had wanted this important feature of good government. The experience of Great Britain affords an illustrious comment on the excellence of the institution.

1. The celebrated Montesquieu, speaking of them, says: "Of the three powers above mentioned, the judiciary is next to nothing." —Spirit of Laws. Vol. I, page 186.

2. Idem, page 181.

3. Vide Protest of the Minority of the Convention of Pennsylvania, Martin's Speech, etc.

May I Suggest a Few Revisions?

By Forrest Wickman
Slate, June 26, 2012

How Supreme Court justices—and their clerks—actually write their opinions [a Slate Explainer]:

With lots and lots of help from their law clerks. While justices are responsible for the substance of their opinions in each case, their clerks usually do the majority of the writing. These clerks follow a code of secrecy about the process of writing each opinion, but we do know how the process generally works. After oral arguments and the initial vote, the senior justice for the majority opinion chooses a judge (who may be himself or another justice) to be responsible for writing the opinion. Unless this judge is Justice Antonin Scalia, who has often taken on the task of writing opinions himself, the judge will then usually select one of his or her clerks to take the first crack at drafting the opinion. The judge will then discuss with the clerk what the opinion should say and may provide a detailed outline or just a few rough notes. Each justice is allowed to have up to four clerks—bright young law graduates, usually from Ivy League schools and often in their mid-to-late-20s—with the exception of the chief justice, who gets to have five.

Once the clerk is finished writing the first draft, which may involve painstaking research and working nights and weekends, the justice reads the draft and gives his or her revisions. These may be only a few small edits, or they may amount to a nearly complete rewrite, depending on the justice and the skills of the clerk. *Sorcerers' Apprentices,* a 2006 book on the influence of Supreme Court clerks, found that about 30 percent of the opinions issued by the Supreme Court are almost entirely the work of law clerks, with clerks responsible for the majority of the court's output. This is a relatively recent development: The Supreme Court began to institute clerks only in the 1890s, but by the mid-20th century they were already playing a significant role in drafting opinions.

After the responsible judge is happy with the opinion, it's sent to the other chambers, traditionally carried by a court messenger. Any judges who voted with the opinion will tell the authoring judge if they have any suggestions or objections to the opinion, and there may be one or more rounds of revisions—implemented with the help of clerks and secretaries—to resolve these disputes. If they don't like how the opinion turned out, and their objections are not resolvable, some judges will occasionally switch to the dissenting opinion (or write a concurring opinion), which is written at this time and circulates after the majority opinion. Otherwise they will signal that they are ready to join the opinion. Once each of the opinions is written, attorneys on the court's staff proofread it one last time and check its citations. They also write the syllabus (which is a sort of executive summary or abstract) that goes above the opinion, and this is also sent back to the judges and their clerks for review. The finished opinion goes to press and often comes out very quickly after that, at which time it's issued in the form of "slip opinions," which resemble small pamphlets or booklets. These days the slip opinions are also published online.

The fact that these important documents are sometimes ghostwritten by young clerks has not been uncontroversial. Some scholars who study the court suggest that the clerks exert a small but significant influence on the judge's decisions. In his book *Closed Chambers,* former clerk Edward Lazarus suggested that some judges function as little more than "editorial Justices." This would explain why justices tend more and more to choose clerks who share their politics, and a 2008 study found that Democratic clerks make liberal decisions more likely, and vice versa. Clerks also seem to have contributed to a decline in the quality of the court's writing. However, others have concluded that their influence is "rare and indistinct at best," and in one survey former clerks tended to agree.

Supreme Court of the United States:

Rule 10. Considerations Governing Review of Writ of Certiorari

Supreme Court of the United States
Adopted April 19, 2013, effective July 1, 2013

Review on a writ of certiorari is not a matter of right, but of judicial discretion. A petition for a writ of certiorari will be granted only for compelling reasons. The following, although neither controlling nor fully measuring the Court's discretion, indicate the character of the reasons the Court considers:

(a) a United States court of appeals has entered a decision in conflict with the decision of another United States court of appeals on the same important matter; has decided an important federal question in a way that conflicts with a decision by a state court of last resort; or has so far departed from the accepted and usual course of judicial proceedings, or sanctioned such a departure by a lower court, as to call for an exercise of this Court's supervisory power;

(b) a state court of last resort has decided an important federal question in a way that conflicts with the decision of another state court of last resort or of a United States court of appeals;

(c) a state court or a United States court of appeals has decided an important question of federal law that has not been, but should be, settled by this Court, or has decided an important federal question in a way that conflicts with relevant decisions of this Court.

A petition for a writ of certiorari is rarely granted when the asserted error consists of erroneous factual findings or the misapplication of a properly stated rule of law.

Why Did the Court Grant Cert in
King v. Burwell?

By Jonathan Adler
The Volokh Conspiracy, *The Washington Post,* November 7, 2014

Friday the U.S. Supreme Court granted certiorari in a high-profile Obamacare case, *King v. Burwell.* (Disclosure: I'm credited/blamed for being one of the folks who outlined the theory upon which this lawsuit is based.) I posted a quick comment on the case grant earlier. With this post I wanted to briefly discuss the significance of the grant and revisit some of the points I made in Monday's post on why the court might grant this case.

First a super-quick recap (so skip this paragraph if you've been following this litigation). Section 1311 of the PPACA calls upon states to create health insurance exchanges and Section 1321 requires the federal government to create exchanges in states which fail to do so (or fail to enact other mandated reforms). Section 1401 provides for tax credits for the purchase of qualifying health insurance plans in "exchanges established by the State under Section 1311." The challengers in this case argue this means what it says: that tax credits are only authorized in exchanges established by the states. The government argues that the phrase "established by the State" does not mean that the exchange actually has to have been created by the state government because other provisions establish some degree of equivalence between Section 1311 and Section 1321 exchanges and the plaintiffs' interpretation would undermine the goal of expanding health insurance coverage.

Earlier this year a divided panel of the U.S. Court of Appeals for the D.C. Circuit sided with the plaintiffs in *Halbig v. Burwell* and (on the very same day) the U.S. Court of Appeals for the Fourth Circuit sided with the federal government in *King v. Burwell.* The plaintiffs filed a petition for certiorari in *King* (which was granted today), and the government sought rehearing en banc in the D.C. Circuit (which was scheduled for December). In the meantime, a federal district court in Oklahoma also sided with the plaintiffs. A fourth case is pending in Indiana.

What does Friday's cert grant mean? Because it takes the votes of four justices to grant cert, it means at least four justices believe this case is cert worthy. Nicholas Bagley writes that Friday's cert grant likely means that at least four justices are skeptical of the government's arguments and the Fourth Circuit's decision in *King.* That may be true (and I'd like to think at least four justices will side with our arguments) but it's not that simple.

Bagley is correct that, in the usual case, the Supreme Court does not grant certiorari to affirm, particularly where there are not conflicting lower court judgments. Yet this is not the usual case and, as I explained in Monday's post ["Will the Supreme Court Grant Certiorari in *King v. Burwell*?," November 3, 2014], there are reasons four or more justices could have found *King* cert worthy apart from their views of the merits.

Under Rule 10, one of the reasons for granting certiorari is when a lower court "has decided an important question of federal law that has not been, but should be, settled by this Court." While I see *King* as a straightforward case of statutory interpretation, it unquestionably concerns an "important question of federal law," as the resolution of this case could have a significant impact on the implementation of the PPACA, particularly in the 36 states that have not established their own exchanges. Indeed, the importance of the legal issue was one of the things highlighted by the federal government and commentators in urging the D.C. Circuit to hear the case en banc.

An additional reason to take the case now is that this litigation creates substantial uncertainty about the operation of the law and, should the plaintiffs' claims be upheld, policymakers, insurance companies, and those who would otherwise be eligible for subsidies will need time to figure out how to respond. This is one of the reasons all of the lower appellate courts to consider these claims have expedited their proceedings. They recognized that there are good reasons to treat these cases as more urgent and time-sensitive than the typical case.

Further, while the D.C. Circuit's decision to rehear *Halbig* en banc vacated the original panel's judgment, the Court is aware that this is a question upon which courts are divided. Two panels on two different circuits reached different conclusions, and even the panel which sided with the government was not unanimous in its rationale. The existence of another decision rejecting the government's position provides further reasons for the justices to suspect that this is an issue that will eventually land on their lap. So, if one combines the time-sensitive nature of the litigation with the reasonable possibility that the case would end up in the Court's lap anyway, there's reason enough to take the case.

Three Recently Accepted Cases Shed Light on the Supreme Court's Process for Granting Review

By Vikram David Amar
Verdict, Justia, June 6, 2014

While many analysts this month are understandably focused on the blockbuster rulings that are due from the Supreme Court in June—the back end of the Supreme Court litigation process, if you will—in my column today I introduce and briefly analyze the front end of three cases on which the Court has granted review for the next Term, which begins this fall. Although the three disputes arrive at the Court from different kinds of lower courts and involve quite different kinds of questions on the merits, these cases taken together illustrate some nuances in the extremely important yet widely misunderstood principles that explain how the Court selects the 70–90 cases to review in full from among the thousands and thousands of requests for review each year. Quite often, the Supreme Court grants review because the lower court ruling in question (often from one of the U.S. Courts of Appeals) conflicts with other lower court rulings on precisely the same (and important) legal question, and the Court wants to provide guidance and uniformity. Indeed, one of the first things that incoming Supreme Court law clerks learn when they arrive at the Court is the fine art of differentiating true lower court conflicts from illusory ones. But the cases discussed below serve as helpful reminders that Supreme Court review involves much more than just resolving lower court conflicts.

The Boomerang of *Zivotofsky v. Kerry* and Respect for Congress

The first case in the trio is one the Supreme Court has seen before. *Zivotofsky v. Kerry* involves an effort by Menachem Zivotofsky, a U.S. citizen born in Jerusalem to U.S. parents, to have his U.S.-issued passport (and U.S.-issued Consular Report of Birth) indicate his place of birth as "Jerusalem, Israel." For many years, U.S. presidents and U.S. state departments (who issue passports and consular records) have scrupulously avoided taking an official position on the contentious question whether Jerusalem is a part of Israel. Executive branch practice concerning the birth of U.S. citizens in Jerusalem follows this policy of neutrality, and consistently has been to record the place of birth of such citizens on U.S. documents simply as "Jerusalem," without mention of any country.

In 2002, Congress passed a law that, among many other things, requires the Secretary of State, upon the request of a citizen or the citizen's legal guardian, to record the place of birth for citizens born in the city of Jerusalem "as Israel." President Bush signed the entire statute into effect, but (as he did from time to time) issued a signing statement to disclaim the legal effect of this particular part of the statute, because (he said) forcing the State Department to record Jerusalem births as being in Israel would impermissibly interfere with the President's constitutional power to formulate and speak on behalf of American foreign policy. The plaintiff in *Zivotofsky* seeks to force the executive branch to follow the terms of Congress's 2002 statute, notwithstanding the President's signing-statement disclaimer.

A few years back, the U.S. Court of Appeals for the D.C. Circuit rejected the plaintiff's efforts, but not on the ground that the Secretary of State was acting permissibly in declining to follow the statute. Instead, the D.C. Circuit held, the lawsuit presented a "political question" over which federal courts have no power to speak. In other words, the court purported not to be exercising jurisdiction to resolve the lawsuit on the merits at all, saying instead that regardless of who is right and who is wrong under the law, this kind of matter is not susceptible of judicial resolution.

The Supreme Court reversed this decision in 2012, holding that the political question doctrine does not bar review of this case. The key question whether the 2002 statute improperly invades the President's foreign affairs power to decide which countries to recognize—and is thus not a permissible exercise of Congress's power to regulate passports or any other congressional authority—is a legal one, not a political one. The Justices, rather than resolving the merits—which the Court had the power to do—then sent the case back to the D.C. Circuit to decide the merits, by "careful[ly] examin[ing] ... the textual, structural, and historical evidence put forward by the parties regarding the nature of the statute and of the passport and recognition powers."

That is precisely what the U.S. Court of Appeals for the D.C. Circuit did on remand, after which it concluded that the statute was indeed an impermissible invasion of presidential authority that he enjoys under the Constitution. Although the D.C. Circuit found the text of the Constitution less than clear, it found a strong historical record over the last two hundred years of the President asserting—and Congress seeming to allow—exclusive executive power to recognize foreign nations, which weighed heavily against the validity of the statute. And although the court conceded that Congress does have meaningful power to regulate passports, that power is not exclusively congressional in the way that the recognition power is exclusively presidential. Since the statute might be said to interfere with the President's foreign policy choice to remain neutral as to the legal authority over Jerusalem—indeed, challenging this neutrality policy was the reason Congress passed the provision—the statute conflicted with the President's foreign policy autonomy and thus could not be enforced.

Zivotofsky again sought Supreme Court review at the end of last year, and about a month ago the Justices agreed to hear the case again. Why would the Court choose to grant review on the merits, given that it consciously chose not to reach the merits in 2012? Part of the answer is that the Court in 2012 didn't have the benefit of full-fledged lower court analysis on the merits, and the Court's general practice is not to reach the merits of a dispute (even if it has the power to do so) when the courts below haven't. But that still doesn't quite explain why *Zivotofsky* is worthy of one of the Court's six- or seven-dozen precious slots for review in 2014–2015. After all, disputes over the validity of the statute are unlikely to recur very often, the D.C. Circuit opinion does not conflict with rulings from any other lower court, and there are no high financial stakes or life-death consequences of the ruling—the factors that most often account for a grant of review. On top of all that, the D.C. Circuit ruling was without a dissent, and appears to be carefully reasoned and likely (at least to many analysts) correct. Why grant, then?

I think the primary reason is that a federal appellate court has struck down a duly enacted congressional statute, and one way the Court shows its respect for Congress (even as it disrespects Congress in other ways) is to grant review in a high percentage of such cases, even when there is no likelihood of a lower court split and even when the ruling below is arguably quite solid. This may be especially true in separation of powers disputes. If the federal judiciary is going to side with the President against Congress, the least it can do is offer its "Supreme" forum to demonstrate it takes seriously Congress's interests and arguments and is not biased in favor of the President. The grant of review in this case may be as simple as that.

Comptroller v. Wynne: An Anomalous but Potentially Infectious Ruling

Comptroller v. Wynne comes to the Court not from a U.S. Court of Appeals Circuit, but from the Maryland state courts. They ruled that the Commerce Clause of the U.S. Constitution gives each taxpaying individual a constitutional right to reduce or eliminate the income tax he owes in his state of residence because of income taxes paid to other states on that same income. The Supreme Court granted review to take up this question a few weeks ago.

To understand why, let us begin by noting that the Supreme Court has already held that "a jurisdiction may tax all the income of its residents, even income earned outside the taxing jurisdiction." The Court reasoned that residents enjoy the privileges and benefits of living in their state of residence, and thus it is permissible to make them pay in that state even if the income was earned elsewhere. The Supreme Court has also held that a state can tax income of non-residents earned within that state. There is thus the possibility for income to be taxed multiple times, once by the state of the taxpayer's residence and again by the state(s) where the income was earned. The Supreme Court has intimated that this seeming unfairness is something states are free to redress by giving tax credits, but that the question is one of legislative grace rather than constitutional right.

In *Wynne*, the Maryland state courts (along with the taxpayers who were objecting to Maryland's tax) observed that the Supreme Court's consistent rulings upholding state tax regimes in this regard all involve challenges brought under the Due Process Clause of the Fourteenth Amendment, and that the Supreme Court has never spoken to whether the Commerce Clause of the Constitution permits multiple states to tax income multiple times in this way. Neither have the state supreme courts from states other than Maryland. For this reason, the ruling below in *Wynne* may not generate any clear conflict with other high appellate rulings. And yet the Supreme Court granted review. Again, the question is why. Part of the answer may be that the U.S. Solicitor General (SG)—invited by the Court to weigh in—urged the Justices to grant review. And why did the SG think review was warranted in spite of the absence of a clear split in lower court authority? Because the ruling below is most likely incorrect, because it introduces significant instability in at least one state's (Maryland's) tax regime, and because, if left unchecked, it has the potential to encourage a great deal of additional destabilizing litigation in other states. Once more, the absence of a clear lower court conflict does not make a case unworthy of review.

The Alabama Redistricting Disputes—Appeals Rather Than Petitions for Certiorari

The third case (or rather pair of cases) I will mention briefly arise out of the Alabama legislature's redrawing of election district lines throughout the state after the 2010 Census. The cases, *Alabama Legislative Black Caucus v. Alabama* and *Alabama Democratic Conference v. Alabama,* raise the question whether the State impermissibly considered race in the drawing of district lines by packing African American voters into districts so that these racial minorities would make up supermajorities in these voting districts. Such supermajorities would enable African American voters to elect candidates of their choice in those districts, but this also would be the case with mere simple majorities. A second (and possibly intentional) effect of the redistricting is that it would reduce the influence African American voters have in other districts. The lower federal court (a so-called three-judge district court panel that Congress created to hear redistricting cases) upheld Alabama's line-drawing, and the Supreme Court accepted review. The questions raised on the merits under the Constitution and the federal Voting Rights Act are quite complex and potentially important, but as with *Zivotofsky* and *Wynne,* the lower court rulings in the Alabama cases do not conflict with rulings from other lower courts. Why, then, was Supreme Court review indicated?

Here the answer is easier, but also more technical. These cases are among the kinds of disputes for which Congress has conferred so-called "appeals" jurisdiction of the Supreme Court, rather than the "certiorari" jurisdiction that accounts for the lion's share of the Court's docket. Unlike certiorari jurisdiction, which is entirely at the Court's discretion, appeals jurisdiction is mandatory. That is, persons who properly bring cases to the Court pursuant to an appeals route rather than via a petition for a writ of certiorari enjoy a "right" to have the Court to take their case and rule on the merits. Appeals cases today comprise a very small percentage of the Court's workload, but they used to be a much bigger component. When appeals are brought to the Court under one of the few remaining appellate access statutes that Congress has not repealed (and challenges to statewide apportionments decided by three-judge District Court panels are among the kinds of cases still to benefit from appeals jurisdiction), the Court must rule on the merits one way or another, and cannot simply deny review and express no view of whether the lower court properly applied the law. So the full briefing and oral argument ordered by the Court in the Alabama cases tells us little about how the Justices might feel on the merits, other than that the cases are difficult enough not to be susceptible to summary affirmance.

All three of these cases illustrate how complicated and multi-faceted the question of getting the Supreme Court to hear your dispute can be.

Why Did Supreme Court Punt on Same-Sex Cases?

By Tony Mauro
USA Today, October 8, 2014

When the Supreme Court of the United Kingdom decides it does not want to consider a case that was brought before it, it tells the parties and the public why.

The explanation is usually short and sweet, along the lines of "the application does not raise an arguable point of law which ought to be considered by the Supreme Court at this time." The justices who voted to turn down the case are named.

But when the U.S. Supreme Court on Monday decided not to take up several petitions dealing with one of the landmark issues of our time—same-sex marriage—no explanation was given. It never is, and the justices appear to like it that way.

Instead, the public was left to speculate on the reasons for this non-action action, which allowed lower court rulings in favor of same-sex marriage to take effect in 11 more states—a major development that should not be the result of a stealth-like process.

Were the conservative justices fearful that if the court did review the cases, they would lose—and same-sex marriage would win constitutional protection nationwide?

Alternatively, did the liberals worry that they would lose if the court took on the cases and ruled that states are not required to allow same-sex marriage?

Both scenarios turn on uncertainty about Justice Anthony Kennedy, the court's swing vote. The vote of four justices is needed to grant review of a case, but five to win. Kennedy has taken the lead on expanding gay rights, but as Justice Ruth Bader Ginsburg said in a Reuters interview in August, Kennedy has also said marriage is a state matter. Those two views, she said, "don't point in the same direction."

Ginsburg is the only justice of late who has seemed willing to shed light on the workings of the court. In a public appearance last month, she hinted at another reason why there was "no need for us to rush" on the issue of same-sex marriage.

The reason: so far, all of the appeals court rulings on the issue have gone the same way, striking down state bans on same-sex marriage. The Supreme Court traditionally waits on the sidelines until at least two courts in different parts of the country vote in opposite ways. Only then does it step in to decide the issue and make laws uniform across the nation.

But all of these scenarios are speculation. We may not know the real reason until a justice retires and opens his or her papers to the public, which could be years from now.

Supreme Court justices like to say they are the most open institution in government, because they explain in writing why they rule one way or the other. But when they decide not to decide, their silence is deafening.

Who's Getting the Work at the Supreme Court?

By Tony Mauro
The American Lawyer, October 24, 2014

At the U.S. Supreme Court, the dominance of veteran advocates and their law firms only continues to grow.

In the term that ended in June, the justices decided a meager 67 argued cases, less than half the caseload they handled in 1990. Three firms argued seven cases each, and two argued in six—meaning that just five firms fielded lawyers in half of the court's cases. "That is truly remarkable," says Harvard Law School professor Richard Lazarus of these numbers. Lazarus has written extensively about the development of the elite Supreme Court bar. In 2009, he went so far as to call it "docket capture" of the high court by a small group of lawyers who tend to file, and win, business cases.

The capture continues at a dizzying pace, in Supreme Court terms. Less than 30 years ago, the late Chief Justice William Rehnquist observed that "it is quite remarkable if a single lawyer argues more than one or two cases a year before us." Last term, a dozen private practitioners argued two or more cases, including several who argued four or more.

The firms that argued seven cases last term were Wilmer Cutler Pickering Hale and Dorr; Gibson, Dunn & Crutcher and Goldstein & Russell. Wilmer and Gibson Dunn—both Am Law 100 firms—boast former solicitors general in their ranks, Seth Waxman and Theodore Olson, respectively. Goldstein & Russell, with only four lawyers, is led by SCOTUSblog founder Tom Goldstein, who rewrote the book on how to snag Supreme Court work.

Former Solicitor General Paul Clement's Bancroft firm and Sidley Austin both had six arguments last term. Sidley's Carter Phillips has argued 78 cases in his career—more than any other lawyer currently in private practice. And former acting Solicitor General Neal Katyal at Hogan Lovells argued four Supreme Court cases last term.

"What this plainly underscores is that the 'superstar' model of Supreme Court advocacy marketing is prevailing," Lazarus says. "Better to be able to market yourself as having a high-profile superstar at top, rather than offer just a strong bench."

The superstars may bring in the business, but lately, that doesn't always mean that the superstar argues. At Jones Day, which prides itself on not having a single

Supreme Court superstar, practice leader Beth Heifetz cheerfully reported that the firm had "four arguments, four different lawyers, four wins" at the Supreme Court last term.

Sidley's Phillips used to routinely argue four times a term or more, but last term he argued only twice—giving Peter Keisler, Jeffrey Green and first-timer Jonathan Cohn a shot. Gibson Dunn's Olson has also cut back, arguing only once last term.

At Wilmer, Waxman argued four cases last term as usual, but he also handed the baton to Catherine Carroll, Mark Fleming and Danielle Spinelli. "It's been a project of mine to put other people in a position to argue at the court," he says.

Waxman agrees there has been "some degree of concentration" of the court's caseload in a handful of firms. "But it's not like a monopoly," he adds. "The marketplace for litigators is alive and well."

Gibson Dunn's Thomas Hungar credits the proliferation of law school Supreme Court clinics for minimizing any downside of docket domination by a few firms. The clinics can connect pro bono clients with top-notch advocates.

And despite the small number of big players, other firms keep trying to get into the exclusive game. Goodwin Procter, Sullivan & Cromwell and Baker Botts have all made recent forays into the Supreme Court, with mixed success so far. In part, what's behind such efforts is a "me-too" impulse, says Goldstein: "They want to match their peers—the firms that look like them, the ones they see when they look in the mirror."

A Supreme Court without Stare Decisis

By Orin Kerr
The Volokh Conspiracy, August 17, 2009

I sometimes come across arguments by lawyers or bloggers that the Supreme Court should not rely on the doctrine of stare decisis. (For nonlawyers, a rough definition of stare decisis is the practice of following prior court decisions unless there are very unusual circumstances.) The argument against stare decisis is a simple one: It's the Supreme Court's job to get it right, and the Justices can't get it right if they follow past decisions that may have gotten it wrong. As a result, the Supreme Court should always try to get it right, and it should only follow past cases to the extent the current Justices think the old decisions are correct. The goal should be loyalty to the Constitution, not loyalty to old cases by old courts.

This argument has some surface appeal, but I'm curious what a Supreme Court without stare decisis would look like. The problem is that most legal disputes are built on and framed by the precedents of dozens of previously decided disputes, and they only make sense in the context of those decisions. It seems to me that a world in which there was really no stare decisis at the Supreme Court, and every decision was reached de novo, with no deference to prior decisions, would be a serious mess. It would be sort of like a world without language: There would be no common ground to understand and frame legal disputes or to establish basic rules of the road.

Perhaps the best way to see this is with a simple example. Imagine a police officer pulls over a car for having a broken taillight. The driver looks very nervous, so the officer orders the suspect out of the car. The officer sees a bulge in the suspect's jacket that looks like a gun, so he frisks the man and finds a loaded pistol. A bit of research reveals that the driver is a felon, leading to charges for being a felon in possession of a weapon. The defendant files a motion to suppress, and the issue before the U.S. Supreme Court is whether the evidence should be suppressed.

How should the Justices rule? In a world without stare decisis, all nine of them need to start from scratch. They each need to answer the following questions, among others:

1) Does the Fourth Amendment confer a personal right?

2) If the answer to (1) is yes, does the Fourth Amendment apply outside the warrant context?

3) If the answer to (1) and (2) are yes, does the Fourth Amendment apply (either directly or through incorporation) to a state police officer?

4) If the answer to (1), (2), and (3) are yes, does the scenario described above reveal any searches or seizures? (And implicitly, what is a search? What is a seizure?)

5) If the answer to (1), (2), (3), and (4) are yes, what makes a search or seizure reasonable or unreasonable? Does a police officer have the power to pull over a car for a taillight violation? Does a police officer have the power to order a suspect out of the car? Does he have the power to frisk a suspect for weapons? Did any of these violate the Fourth Amendment?

6) What is the remedy for a violation of the Fourth Amendment, and how does it apply here? Is there a suppression remedy? Is there a fruit of the poisonous tree doctrine?

In a world with no stare decisis, each of the nine Justices would have to start from scratch in each case. Presumably there would need to be briefing and argument on all of these issues. Even if the Justices agreed as to a result, they would likely divide as to the rationale in every case. The emerging rule of law would often be unclear if not nonexistent.

Further, even if the Justices reached a majority rationale, it's unclear that this would matter. After all, the recognized legal significance of a majority rationale from the Supreme Court is itself a matter of stare decisis, which would have no weight. In the extreme version where there is no stare decisis at all, every Supreme Court case would be a shot to entirely reinvent everything about the law. Nor would the Justices have to comply with legal niceties we know of like the case or controversy requirement, standing, etc., unless they personally agreed with them and their application, as these doctrines are routinely followed today largely as a matter of (you guessed it) stare decisis.

You could imagine a much less extreme version of a world without stare decisis, to be sure. Perhaps the Supreme Court could only grant certiorari on very limited questions, explicitly keeping all else fixed. For example, in the Fourth Amendment case above, the Court could grant certiorari and decide only one of the very discrete questions listed above, leaving all the rest for another day. But if you really oppose stare decisis, I would think this is a terribly unsatisfactory answer: It's just stare decisis masquerading as cert jurisdiction. Stare decisis would apply de facto to every issue that the Supreme Court did not specifically agree to review, because the lower courts would still be bound by whatever the Supreme Court didn't agree to review.

Of course, this doesn't mean that stare decisis is invariably a good thing. Lots of people have different views about when and where the Supreme Court should rely on it, and my argument here isn't addressed to those judgments. My point is narrower. In my view, the debate should be on how much and how strongly the Supreme Court should rely on stare decisis, not whether it should be applied at all.

Supreme Court of the United States: Information about Opinions

Supreme Court of the United States

In General.

The opinions of the Supreme Court of the United States are published officially in a set of case books called the United States Reports. See 28 U.S.C. §411. At the beginning of October Term 2013, the U.S. Reports consisted of 554 bound volumes and soft-cover "preliminary prints" of an additional 5 volumes; a final 10 volumes' worth of opinions also existed in individual "slip opinion" form. Volumes are added to the set at the rate of three to five per Term; they are generally between 800 and 1,200 pages long. In addition to all of the opinions issued during a particular period, a volume may contain a roster of Justices and Court officers during that period; an allotment of Justices by Federal Circuit; announcements of Justices' investitures and retirements; memorial proceedings for deceased Justices; a cumulative table of cases reported; orders in cases decided in summary fashion; reprints of amendments to the Supreme Court's Rules and the various sets of Federal Rules of Procedure; a topical index; and a statistical table summarizing case activity for the past three Court Terms. The U.S. Reports is compiled and published for the Court by the Reporter of Decisions. See 28 U.S.C. §673(c). Page proofs prepared by the Court's Publications Unit are reproduced, printed, and bound by private firms under contract with the U.S. Government Printing Office (GPO). The Court's Publications Officer acts as liaison between the Court and the GPO.

Generations of Opinions.

The Supreme Court's opinions and related materials are disseminated to the public by means of four printed publications and two computerized services. Prior to the issuance of

(1) bound volumes of the U.S. Reports, the Court's official decisions appear in three temporary printed forms:

(2) bench opinions (which are transmitted electronically to subscribers over the Court's Project Hermes service);

(3) slip opinions (which are posted on this website); and

(4) preliminary prints.

1. Bench Opinions On days that opinions are announced by the Court from the bench, the text of each opinion is made available immediately to the public and the press in a printed form called a "bench opinion." The bench opinion pamphlet for each case consists of the majority or plurality opinion, any concurring or dissenting opinions written by the Justices, and a prefatory syllabus prepared by the Reporter's Office that summarizes the decision. Bench opinions are printed at the Court, generally in 5 ½" x 8 ½" self-cover pamphlets. They are made available to the public by the Court's Public Information Office. The text of each bench opinion is also disseminated electronically via Project Hermes, one of the Court's two opinion dissemination systems (this website is the other). Hermes subscribers include universities, news media and publishing companies. A number of these organizations provide on-line access to the bench opinions via the Internet within minutes after they are released by the Court. Hermes subscribers who redisseminate bench opinions to the general public are identified in ... "Where to Obtain Supreme Court Opinions." [http://www.supremecourt.gov/opinions/obtainopinions.aspx]

   Caution: In case of discrepancies between the print and electronic versions of a bench opinion, the print version controls. Moreover, bench opinions are replaced, generally within hours, by slip opinion pamphlets and, in case of discrepancies between the bench and slip opinions, the slip opinion controls.

2. Slip Opinions Several days after an opinion is announced by the Court, it is printed in a 6 "x 9 "self-cover pamphlet called a "slip opinion." Each slip opinion consists of the majority or plurality opinion, any concurring or dissenting opinions, and the syllabus. It may contain corrections not appearing in the bench opinion. Slip opinion page proofs are sent to a commercial printing company under contract with the GPO, and the company prints the slip opinions in accordance with the Court's specifications. The slip opinion pamphlets are distributed free of charge, while supplies last, by the Court's Public Information Office. They are also sold by the GPO. The text of each slip opinion is also disseminated electronically via posting on this website [http://www.supremecourt.gov/opinions/opinions.aspx.], usually within minutes after the opinion is announced. Slip opinions remain posted here until the opinions for an entire Term are published in the bound volumes of the U.S. Reports. The number of slip opinions published each Term has varied over the years from as few as 75 to as many as 170.

   Caution: In case of discrepancies between the print and electronic versions of a slip opinion, the print version controls. Moreover, individual slip opinions are cumulated and replaced within months by preliminary print pamphlets and, in case of discrepancies between the slip opinion and preliminary print version of a case, the preliminary print controls.

3. Preliminary Prints The preliminary prints of the U.S. Reports are the third generation of opinion publication and dissemination. These are brown, soft-cover "advance pamphlets" that contain, in addition to the opinions themselves, all of the announcements, tables, indexes, and other features that make up the U.S. Reports. The contents of two or three preliminary prints will eventually be combined into a single bound volume. Thus, the title of each preliminary print includes a part number, e.g., Preliminary Print, Volume 545, Part 1. Prior to publication, all of the materials that go into a preliminary print undergo an extensive editing and indexing process, and permanent page numbers are assigned that will carry over into the bound volume. Copies of the page proofs to be published in a preliminary print are sent to a commercial printing company under contract with the GPO, and that company prints the pamphlets in accordance with the Court's specifications. Official versions of preliminary prints are sold to the public by the GPO. The number of preliminary prints published for each Term varies from as few as 6 to as many as 12 separate issues, depending on the number of opinions issued during the Term. "Sliplists" identifying cases to appear in upcoming preliminary prints, as well as Counsel Listings for those cases, are posted on this website [http://www.supremecourt.gov/opinions/sliplists.aspx; http://www.supremecourt. gov/opinions/counsellist.aspx.].

   Caution: Individual preliminary prints are cumulated and replaced about a year later by bound volumes and, in case of discrepancies between the preliminary print and bound volume versions of a case, the bound volume controls.

4. Bound Volumes The fourth and final generation of opinion publication is the casebound set of law books entitled *United States Reports*. The opinions and other materials contained in the preliminary prints are republished in this series of books. Prior to publication, all of the opinions and other materials that make up each volume undergo a final editing and indexing process. The materials are then sent to a commercial printing company under contract with the GPO [Government Printing Office], and that company prints and binds the books in accordance with the Court's specifications. The official bound volumes are sold by the GPO. The number of bound volumes published each Term varies from as few as three to as many as five, depending on the number of opinions issued during the Term. Electronic versions of bound volumes issued for October Term 1991 and subsequent years are posted on this website [http://www.supremecourt.gov/opinions/ boundvolumes.aspx] after the printed bound volumes have been issued.

   Caution: In case of discrepancies between the print and electronic versions of these bound volume materials, the print versions control. In addition, GPO access includes, as a convenience to users, a database of unofficial versions of bound volume opinions issued between 1937 and 1975. This database was created by the Air Force and is made available as a finding aid only. Because neither GPO nor the Court has performed costly validation or authentication processes, the authenticity or completeness of the data cannot be verified. Only the bound volumes of the *United States Reports* contain the final, official text of the opinions of the Supreme Court.

Where to Obtain Opinions

Apart from the various print and electronic versions of the opinions and other materials published in the official U.S. Reports and sold by the GPO, a number of private companies sell unofficial versions of the opinions in print, microform, CD-ROM, and on-line formats. For information as to the availability of all official and unofficial sources of opinions, see the file entitled "Where to Obtain Supreme Court Opinions."

Caution: Only the bound volumes of the *United States Reports* contain the final, official text of the opinions of the Supreme Court of the United States. In case of discrepancies between the bound volume and any other version of a case—whether print or electronic, official or unofficial—the bound volume controls.

Writing Their Wrongs: Supreme Court Justices Regularly Seek to Change the Errors of Their Ways

By Mark Walsh
ABA Journal, August 1, 2014

Late in the recently completed Supreme Court term, Justice Antonin Scalia dissented in a little-noticed case about a federal bank fraud law.

In *Loughrin v. United States,* the Court held that the government did not have to prove that a defendant intended to defraud a financial institution to violate the statute. In the majority opinion, Justice Elena Kagan was making a point about financial transactions when she referred to a hypothetical "Jane," who "traded in her car for money to take a bike trip cross-country."

Justice Scalia, responding in his dissent to Justice Kagan's point, inadvertently changed the name to "Jill."

By the next day, the Supreme Court had revised the electronic slip opinion in the case, changing Scalia's references from Jill to Jane.

It was an inconsequential change, but one of a type that occurs far more frequently in Supreme Court opinions than most people realize, according to a new study.

"The court makes all sorts of revisions, ranging from the most mundane to the most intriguing, with the vast majority not surprisingly falling into the former category," writes Harvard Law School professor Richard J. Lazarus in "The (Non)Finality of Supreme Court Opinions," an upcoming article for the *Harvard Law Review.* "With regard to the latter, several distinct pathways have emerged for revising opinions with varying degrees of transparency."

Two more examples from this past court term help illustrate the kinds of after-the-fact changes made to the court's opinions.

In her May 5 dissent in *Town of Greece v. Galloway,* in which the court upheld a New York state hamlet's practice of opening its council meetings with prayer, Kagan discussed the message of religious tolerance that George Washington received in a 1790 visit to Newport, Rhode Island, which Kagan described as "the home of the first community of American Jews."

The court, after being apprised by scholars that Newport was not, in fact, the first such community, changed Kagan's dissent (presumably at her instigation or with her approval) to "home of one of the first communities of American Jews."

A few days earlier, in his dissent in *Environmental Protection Agency v. EME Homer City Generation,* Scalia had mischaracterized an EPA legal argument from an earlier Supreme Court case. Several law professors and other court observers noticed the mistake and took to the Web. Within days, the dissent was quietly amended, including a change in a subheading over one section from the colorful "Plus ça Change: EPA's Continuing Quest for Cost-Benefit Authority," to the bland "Our Precedent."

Lazarus says he had completed his 85-page article about a year ago, and it was being edited for publication in the *Harvard Law Review's* December 2014 edition when the *EME Homer City Generation* correction was made. "I realized I had to do more," he says. He released the study in draft form, which prompted a spate of media and scholarly attention.

Subject to Revision

Much of the article addresses the court's historical practices for revising its opinions, such as when Chief Justice Roger B. Taney added some 18 pages to his *Dred Scott* opinion months after it was announced in 1857.

But the rest largely deals with the period after 1970, when the court first started putting a notice on its bench opinions and slip opinions that they were "subject to formal revision before publication in the preliminary print of the *United States Reports."*

"Anyone can write to the reporter of decisions and notify [him or her] of a potential typographical or other formal error," Lazarus says. Evidently, they do.

The article identifies examples from recent years, such as slip opinions that: miscalculated the number of copyrighted works that had entered the public domain; misidentified a U.S. senator who'd made a particular comment; and misstated who was president in 1799.

That came in *American Insurance Association v. Garamendi,* a 2003 opinion in which Justice David H. Souter discussed the "long-standing practice" of making executive agreements to settle claims of American nationals against foreign governments. The first example, Souter originally wrote, was in 1799, when "the Washington administration" settled a maritime dispute with the Dutch government.

The problem is that John Adams was president in 1799. The opinion published in the *United States Reports* reflected the correction. However, demonstrating another point made by Lazarus, such changes are not always made uniformly among the various Web sources of Supreme Court opinions. A reporter's search for the *Garamendi* opinion found at least one source—Cornell University Law School's Legal Information Institute—that still posted the version with George Washington as president in 1799.

One of the most troublesome revelations is that some "justices have revised their opinions in significant, including highly substantive, ways prior to their final and official publication in the *U.S. Reports,"* Lazarus says in the article.

For example, in her concurrence in 2003's *Lawrence v. Texas,* in which the majority overruled *Bowers v. Hardwick* and struck down a Texas law criminalizing same-sex sodomy, Justice Sandra Day O'Connor characterized Justice Scalia's dissent in language that some law professors found significant, Lazarus says.

Justice O'Connor wrote that "the dissent apparently agrees that if [certain of the court's equal protection] cases have stare decisis effect, Texas' sodomy law would not pass scrutiny under the equal protection clause, regardless of the type of rational-basis review that we apply."

"The problem is that the 'final,' 'official' version of O'Connor's opinion no longer includes this sentence," Lazarus notes in the article. "It has been deleted in its entirety."

The professor surmises that Justice O'Connor may have removed the passage as an accommodation to Justice Scalia, or that it addressed language in a draft version of Scalia's dissent that was changed even before the first public release of slip opinions. (That is a frequent reason for post-announcement changes: A justice addresses points in a draft opinion that is later revised, but the justice does not fastidiously account for the colleague's revision in her own opinion.)

Need for Transparency

Lazarus says such substantive changes "without meaningful notice" can cause practical problems "when the version of the court's opinion upon which lower courts, other branches of government, and scholars and teachers rely can change—without notice—as many as five years after initial publication."

"I have no problem with the justices revising their opinions," Lazarus says. "But I think at the very least there needs to be transparency."

Lazarus offers a host of suggestions to increase that transparency. For example, the court could provide more guidance over what constitutes a "formal error" and set different procedures for different degrees of error. And the court should distinguish revisions based on whether the person proposing the change was a party, an amicus or someone within the court. Finally, the court should provide after-the-fact notice of any changes, something that isn't being done now.

The court's public information office offered no comment.

Josh Blackman, an assistant professor at South Texas College of Law in Houston and an observer of the Supreme Court, says he was shocked to read how significant some of the revisions to opinions have been.

"The article brought to life how common this is," he says. "Especially when it's not just Jane and Jill but significant changes in doctrine."

The legal technology community has come up with a solution that would add some transparency to opinion revisions.

David Zvenyach, a lawyer for the District of Columbia government, developed a relatively simple application that "scrapes" electronic slip opinions, looking for any changes. Next, Zvenyach developed an automatic Twitter feed that alerts subscribers to the changes. Soon after his open-source @SCOTUS_Servo feed launched in June, a tech-savvy follower added a function that shows changes in a side-by-side comparison between versions.

Zvenyach says the application is automated and is not dependent on his long-term participation.

Lazarus notes the justices have powerful reasons to get their opinions out quickly: to observe the court's tradition of deciding all argued cases by the end of each term, and to preserve their majorities.

"All of us would like to bury our mistakes," Lazarus says. "But we're not all on the Supreme Court."

The Justices, Their Papers, and the Claims of History

By Christopher Schmidt
ISCOTUS, December 15, 2014

Why do we care about what goes on behind closed doors at the Supreme Court? Do the justices have some sort of responsibility to ensure that the American people learn, at some point, the "inside" story of the Court? A recent article in the *New Yorker* ["The Great Paper Caper," December 1, 2014] by Jill Lepore on the theft of some of Justice Frankfurter's papers, along with a provocative response ["Frankfurter's Papers and History as Art," Dorf on Law blog, December 1, 2014] by Michael Dorf, raise yet again these perennial questions.

We can all agree that there is something of value in getting behind the scenes at the Supreme Court. Journalists and historians delve into the available records and resources—correspondence, unpublished opinions, conference notes, interviews with justices and clerks—to try to recreate what happened. As a result of these investigative forays, today we have extensive knowledge of what was happening within the Court as the justices deliberated over many of the Court's most significant decisions. Most recently, Joan Biskupic's book on Justice Sotomayor made news with her revelation that Justice Sotomayor had written a sharp dissent in an affirmative action case that was never published when some of the justices, apparently influenced by Sotomayor's dissent, switched sides.

But the question remains: what exactly is the value of these revelations? Historians and reporters don't typically concern themselves with this question. These are important events, and their job is to find out as much about them as possible. Thus we lament justices who restrict access to their papers or, worse, justices who destroy their papers. But the question becomes more difficult when we shift perspective from that of the historian or journalist to that of the Supreme Court justice. Do the justices have a special responsibility to preserve the records pertaining to their work? Should we have laws that require them to do so, as we do in other areas of government? Professor Dorf raises the legitimate point that in order to determine whether this responsibility really exists and how far it should go requires an assessment of the value of these behind-the-scenes stories.

I agree with Dorf that this issue is harder than we might assume. To simply claim that the justices have a responsibility to "history" feels intuitively gratifying, but it does not resolve the issue. Yet I think that Dorf provides too narrow an assessment of how we might measure the value of materials relating to the inner workings of the Court.

Dorf concludes that the value of increased knowledge of the internal workings of the Court "is more in the nature of a claim of art than it is about making democracy function or anything so practical." The papers of the justices, he writes, only rarely "contain documents that are relevant to some current controversy."

We don't need to know what Jackson said to Frankfurter or vice-versa to learn any useful lessons about the cases they decided or about interpersonal relations more broadly. Our interest (for those of us who have an interest in such matters) stems entirely from the fact that we find the matters inherently interesting . . . .

We can understand the broad picture of the work of the Supreme Court and its relation to other institutions without access to the Justices' papers. But for those who find history interesting, the minutiae of the decisionmaking process and even the behind-the-scenes gossip have inherent value. We can appreciate history in the way we appreciate art—for its own sake.

This goes too far, I believe. The supposed "lessons" of history to present-day dilemmas are invariably overstated, but there is value in knowledge about the ways in which the fundamental institutions of our society function. When it comes to the U.S. Supreme Court, its written opinions give us only a partial window into how it operates. Accounts of the Court's decisionmaking process provide additional insight. Details about how the Court actually functioned at some past point, about how the justices came to their most important decisions, is surely of some considerable value in a constitutional democracy. It deepens our understanding of what the Court did in the past, what it does today, and what it might do tomorrow.

Consider, for example, where our understanding of the Court would be without knowing that prior to the 1940s the norm within the Court was for the justices to suppress dissents in all but the most important of cases. The justices believed that in most cases the value of an individual dissent did not outweigh the value of presenting an image of a unified Court to the public. The fact that the high rates of consensus in the Court during much of its history was a product of a norm and not actual consensus tells us something vitally important about the Court and the issues it confronted. It changes our understanding of some of the unanimous opinions that came in this period, and it changes our understanding of those relatively rare dissenting opinions of the period. It also changes our understanding of the Court we have had since the 1940s, when dissenting opinions have become commonplace.

Or consider our quite thorough understanding of what happened behind the scenes in the *Brown* decision. Behind the united front of Chief Justice Warren's unanimous opinion were years of false starts, cajoling, and compromise. Although I would not look to the justices' deliberations to learn something about the problem of racial segregation in schools today, I do believe that this seminal moment reveals something about how a fundamentally conservative institution could, for a time, stand at the vanguard of one of the nation's most important social revolutions. Bruce Ackerman's most recent book [We the People, Volume 3: *The Civil Rights Revolution* (Belknap Press of Harvard University Press, 2014)] draws on the justices' papers to identify several moments when the Warren Court almost took some major doctrinal leap in the name of the civil rights revolution, only to pull back at the last minute for one reason or another. All of this surely has some value for those who today are considering whether the Supreme Court might advance their cause of choice.

None of this resolves the very difficult question of how far the justices' responsibility to history, legal or otherwise, goes when it comes to preserving and making accessible their papers. My goal here is simply to offer some thoughts as to how this issue should be approached. Dorf is surely right to argue that "history's" claim to the details of the justices' decisionmaking process cannot serve as a blanket call for transparency. But neither can this claim be reduced to the level of Supreme Court voyeurism. When historians and journalists recreate the inner workings of the Supreme Court, they are serving the legitimate claim of a democratic citizenry for knowledge about this critically important institution.

2
The Justices

Justices of the Supreme Court of the United States attending President Barack Obama's State of the Union Address at the Capitol, February 12, 2013. *Top, left to right:* Justice Sonia Sotomayor, Justice Stephen G. Breyer, Justice Ruth Bader Ginsburg, Justice Anthony M. Kennedy, and Chief Justice John G. Roberts, Jr.

Traditional Reserve, Contemporary Demystification

The Supreme Court is the apex of the American judicial system: the ultimate arbiter of law. There is no appealing a Supreme Court decision. The court is presided over by a chief justice and eight associate justices, all appointed to lifetime terms. And these nine jurists constitute an entire third of the American system of co-equal branches of government—the judicial branch. (The president and his cabinet constitute the executive branch; together, the two houses of Congress—the U.S. Senate and the House of Representatives—make up the legislative branch.)

Of these three branches, the court is probably the most paradoxical. The justices' lifetime appointments render them mostly immune—but not impervious—to public opinion; the cloistered nature of the institution ensures that much of the court's decision-making process is a mystery. Because of its small size, as Jeffrey Rosen has written, "quirks of personality and temperament can mean as much as ideology in shaping the law. . . . The backstage dramas . . . can be as important as what takes place in front of the spotlights" (*The Supreme Court* [2007], p. 6). Isolated though it may be, the institution also provides pivotal symbols of progressive social change: Thurgood Marshall, the first African American justice, was appointed in 1967; Sandra Day O'Connor, the first female justice, joined the court in 1981.

There has been a large element of veneration attached to the court. It is notable that one of President Franklin Roosevelt's rare political misfires occurred when he attempted to tamper with the court's workings. Roosevelt, who had been re-elected in 1936 by one of the greatest landslides in American history, had become increasingly distressed by the justices' rulings blunting his New Deal. Accordingly, in 1937 he proposed that the president be given the power to appoint up to five new justices for every justice over the age of 70 and a half. Even Franklin Roosevelt's vast power and prestige failed to protect him from mass outrage at his "court-packing" plan, which was withdrawn.

Nomination and Confirmation Politics

The Supreme Court, to an extent, was considered exempt from the usual partisan rough-and-tumble: the president picked his nominee (always, of course, a male), and the U.S. Senate confirmed the appointment. By the mid-twentieth century, this relatively nonpartisan process began to erode. In 1969 Justice Abe Fortas—tapped by President Lyndon Johnson to replace retiring Chief Justice Earl Warren—resigned from the court over allegations that he had improperly accepted fees from dubious sources. No other justice—before or since—departed the court under this sort of cloud. President Richard Nixon made two nominations to the court that were defeated by the Senate. In 1987 President Ronald Reagan's nominee, Robert Bork, engendered massive, divisive opposition that ultimately doomed his chances of join-ing the court; Reagan's follow-up choice, Douglas Ginsburg, was forced to withdraw after admitting to prior marijuana use. In 1991 the stormy confirmation hearings for President George H. W. Bush's nominee Clarence Thomas—who did, of course, take his seat on the court—riveted and polarized the nation. More recently, in 2005, President George W. Bush's pick for a court vacancy, Harriet Miers, who had been White House counsel, faced so much opposition and ridicule that her nomination was withdrawn before it could be subject to a Senate vote.

Chief Justice John Roberts, appointed by President George W. Bush, assumed the helm of the court in 2005, succeeding the late William Rehnquist. The court maintains a precarious ideological balance. Broadly speaking, there is the faction appointed by Democratic presidents: Stephen Breyer (Clinton), Ruth Bader Gins-burg (Clinton), Sonia Sotomayor (Obama), and Elena Kagan (Obama). There is the faction appointed by Republican presidents: Antonin Scalia (Reagan), Clarence Thomas (George H. W. Bush), John Roberts (George W. Bush), and Samuel Alito (George W. Bush). And there is Anthony Kennedy, who, although a Republican appointee (Reagan), is widely considered the court's pivotal swing vote. (These divi-sions, of course, are not entirely rigid, and there can be a certain ideological give-and-take.)

Tradition and Transparency

The Supreme Court functions mainly in private. Scholars, lawyers, and reporters who scrutinize the court are often referred to "court watchers," which implies a purely observational status. There is no Supreme Court equivalent to a presidential press conference or senators and congressmembers jostling for the microphone. And this lends itself to a sort of political tea-leaf reading: What is the significance of the fact that the current court lineup is devoid—for the first time in history—of Protestants? How will Justice Anthony Kennedy rule on a certain case? What is the true scope of the influence of the unassuming, affable Chief Justice John Roberts?

A large element of detective work is involved in observing the court and trying to decipher its inner workings. Jeffrey Toobin, writing in the *New Yorker* (February 21, 2014) made careful note of the justices' demeanors, noting, for example, that Stephen Breyer, "in his twentieth year on the court, is still having the time of his life. He laughs at all the jokes, especially his own." These observations—as interesting as they may be—can also take on a real importance that transcends simple curiosity. "It is wise," Toobin points out, "to listen closely" to what Chief Justice Roberts and Justice Samuel Alito are advocating, since "they are rarely on the losing side."

Another of the paradoxes of the court is that it hides in plain sight. That most private part of its institutional functioning, oral arguments, are now archived online. The court allows visitors—as do Congress and the White House—although the court imposes much greater restrictions on visitors. There are no cameras permit-ted, for example. The justices are cloistered, but they are also active jurists, with widely disseminated judicial philosophies; they lecture and speak at universities and law schools. And a major shift began with the 1979 publication of the hugely successful *The Brethren: Inside the Supreme Court.* Co-written by famed Watergate reporter Bob Woodward and Scott Armstrong, *The Brethren* pierced the veil of the court's genteel secrecy to reveal—not surprisingly— rivalries, factions, and back-biting. Since the floodgates were opened, it seems, there has been no end to the demystification of this most august body—yielding some startling results. In 2013, for example, composer Derrick Wang announced plans for *Scalia/Ginsburg,* a comic opera structured around the judicial opinions of these two friends, colleagues, and political opposites.

The Justices in Their Own Words

In a development unthinkable for most of the Supreme Court's long history, there is now a surprising amount of personal information available about the justices. Antonin Scalia and Stephen Breyer have written widely on legal matters (Breyer's *Making Our Democracy Work: A Judge's View,* was published in 2010). The justices have not just shared their opinions and experience of the law but offered up a re-vealing, intimate window in their personal lives. Anthony Kennedy has admitted that there is an element of loneliness to the job; Justice Samuel Alito referenced his Italian-immigrant father during his confirmation hearings. Many of the court's members have penned real, flesh-and-blood memoirs. Former Justice Sandra Day O'Connor—who in 1981 made history when she became the first woman appointed to the court—has written not only *Out of Order: Stories from the History of the Supreme Court* (2013) but also *Lazy B: Growing Up on a Cattle Ranch in the American Southwest* (2002), an evocative reminiscence of her upbringing along the Arizona–New Mexico border: "high desert country—dry, windswept, clear, often cloudless." Clarence Thomas—surely one of the most controversial appointees to the court—wrote *My Grandfather's Son* (2007), a chronicle of his harsh upbringing in a South where Jim Crow was still very much alive. The bow-tied, ninety-something retired Justice John Paul Stevens wrote *Five Chiefs: A Supreme Court Memoir* (2011)—in which, disregarding expected protocol, he referred to his fellow justices by their first names.

One of the court's newest members, Sonia Sotomayor, wrote *My Beloved World* (2013), a frank discussion of her hardscrabble life in the Bronx, living with diabetes, and the struggles of a Latina breaking into a legal system long resistant to any sort of inclusivity. In her memoir Sotomayor was unafraid to wax rhapsodic about her elevation to the court: the polar opposite of the traditionally stuffy, Olympian jus-tice: "The moment when, in accordance with tradition, I . . . placed my hand on the Bible to take the oath of office for the Supreme Court, I felt as if an electric current were coursing through me, and my whole life . . . could be read in the faces of those most dear to me who filled that beautiful room. I looked out to see my mother with tears streaming down her cheeks and felt a surge of admiration for this remarkable woman who had instilled in me the values that came naturally to her—compassion, hard work, and courage to face the unknown."

The current court's justices have also expanded the scope of their public appearances. Richard Wolf, writing in *USA Today* (December 26, 2014), pinpointed the particulars of these public forums. Antonin Scalia, Clarence Thomas, and Samuel Alito, the "most conservative justices, tend to favor religious schools and organizations." Anthony Kennedy, Sonia Sotomayor, and Elena Kagan (a former Harvard Law School dean, like, as Wolf reports, "to address students." "Sotomayor," he continues, "makes a point of posing for photographs with those who ask her questions. Kennedy occasionally teaches law school classes. . . . Chief Justice John Roberts and Justice Stephen Breyer often focus on history."

Ultimately, of course, the court consists of nine flesh-and-blood people. Elena Kagan, the court's newest member, discussed the travails of being the junior justice in a *People* magazine profile (November 21, 2014)—a venue unthinkable in the recent past: "I take notes as the Junior Justice . . . and answer the door when there's a knock. Literally, if there's a knock on the door and I don't hear it, there will not be a single other person who will move. They'll all just stare at me." (Kagan made similar comments at forum with Dean Martha Minow at Harvard Law School on September 3, 2014, as reported by Colleen Walsh on September 4 at the *Harvard Gazette* website.)

Old age, illness, and personal circumstances will no doubt alter the court's composition in the years to come. There will certainly be vacancies on the Supreme Court, and the sitting president will need to fill those vacancies. Whatever the various outcomes, the court will have the power and opportunity to greatly—and controversially—shape the national agenda.

—Richard Klin

Bibliography

Atkinson, David N. *Leaving the Bench: Supreme Court Justices at the End.* Lawrence: University Press of Kansas, 1999.

Feldman, Noah. *Scorpions: The Battles and Triumphs of FDR's Great Supreme Court Justices.* New York: Twelve, 2010.

O'Connor, Sandra Day. *Out of Order: Stories from the History of the Supreme Court.* New York: Random House, 2013.

Rosen, Jeffrey, *The Supreme Court: The Personalities and Rivalries That Defined America.* New York: Times Books, 2007.

Stevens, John Paul. *Five Chiefs: A Supreme Court Memoir.* New York: Little, Brown, 2011.

Toobin, Jeffrey. *The Nine: Inside the Secret World of the Supreme Court.* New York: Random House, 2007.

Tribe, Laurence H. *God Save This Honorable Court: How the Choice of Supreme Court Justices Shapes Our History.* New York: Random House, 1985.

Woodward, Bob, and Scott Armstrong. *The Brethren: Inside the Supreme Court.* 1979; reprint, New York: Simon & Schuster, 2005.

John Roberts, Chief Conservative Strategist

By Paul M. Barrett
Bloomberg Businessweek, April 10, 2014

For those who follow the Supreme Court, psychoanalyzing Chief Justice John Roberts is irresistible. His mild manner and measured tone baffle observers who expect bombast from conservative jurists. He refrains from Antonin Scalia's rhetorical theatrics and Clarence Thomas's enthusiasm for overturning precedent. He most notably shied away from a potentially explosive political confrontation in June 2012, casting the decisive vote to uphold the Affordable Care Act. That earned Roberts a barrage of invective from conservatives. In a pair of cases a year later, he whipsawed liberals who'd fantasized about a rift on the court's right by curbing voting rights and affirmative action. His latest majority opinion, in a 5–4 decision announced on April 2 that ended decades-old restrictions on campaign contributions, provides fresh fodder for scrutiny. It also hints at the plans of a chief justice who, at 59, could remain in his powerful post for 20 years or longer.

In the April 2 decision, Roberts argued that Watergate-era limits on how much money individuals can spread around each election year, intended to thwart corruption, interfered with free speech. "Money in politics may at times seem repugnant to some," he wrote, "but so, too, does much of what the First Amendment vigorously protects. If the First Amendment protects flag burning, funeral protests, and Nazi parades—despite the profound offense such spectacles cause—it surely protects political campaign speech despite popular opposition." With that concise declaration, Roberts diminished the federal government's power and increased wealthy individuals' influence over elections. Within hours of the ruling, fundraisers were on the phones hitting up previously maxed-out donors for more cash.

A Department of Justice lawyer during the Reagan administration and a judge on the federal appeals court in Washington, Roberts ascended to the chief justice's chair by accident. President George W. Bush chose him in mid-2005 to replace the retiring Sandra Day O'Connor. When then–Chief Justice William Rehnquist died two months later, Bush switched an already-vetted Roberts to the Rehnquist slot. Roberts delivered a self-assured performance at his Senate confirmation hearings and took office in September 2005.

The chief justice goes out of his way to project a conciliatory image. "I do think the rule of law is threatened by a steady term-by-term focus on 5–4 decisions," he told Jeffrey Rosen, a law professor at George Washington University, in a July 2006 interview published in the *Atlantic*. The court was ripe for a refocus "on functioning as an institution," Roberts added, "because if it doesn't, it's going to lose its credibility." Six years later, Rosen reflected on the interview. "Roberts saw the promotion of consensus in service of the court's long-term interests as the greatest test of a successful chief justice," he wrote in the *New Republic*.

Roberts has not passed this test. With a handful of exceptions, the 5–4 split in ideologically significant cases remains persistent and profound. His stewardship over the last nine terms suggests he is less focused on consensus building than on leading an incremental, tactically savvy shift to the right.

The chief justice confused a lot of people in 2012 when he was the only conservative on the court to join the four liberal justices in voting to uphold Obamacare. In his syndicated column, Pat Buchanan accused him of employing "tortured reasoning" in the service of being "seen among the cognitive elite" (apparently an insult in Buchanan's mind). The *National Review* charged that Roberts had "done violence" to the U.S. Constitution. In contrast, Linda Greenhouse, a former *New York Times* Supreme Court correspondent and a leading voice of the liberal cognitive elite, praised Roberts for demonstrating "evolution" as a jurist. Greenhouse, who now teaches at Yale Law School, described in positive terms Roberts's refusal to ally himself with what she called "the breathtaking radicalism of the other four conservative justices."

It turned out that both sides read too much into Roberts's performance in the case. He exercised canny statesmanship to avoid a clash over Obama's signature legislation—the sort of showdown that could have stirred a backlash against the court. Roberts accomplished this with subtle lawyering. He said Congress lacked authority under the Constitution's Commerce Clause to impose the law's insurance mandate but then rescued the law by declaring it passed muster as a form of taxation. Roberts's quirky definition of the mandate as a tax likely won't have lasting jurisprudential impact. His narrow reading of the Commerce Clause, on the other hand, could well resurface in other cases as a potent tool to undercut regulatory statutes. What many saw as a conservative defeat thus in the long run might be the opposite.

In 2013, Roberts returned to a more straightforward position as leader of the conservative wing in rulings limiting the reach of voting-rights protections and affirmative action in higher education. Now it was conservatives who praised his rigor and liberals who shook their heads. Greenhouse declared that "the real John Roberts" had revealed himself. She described his majority opinion in the voting-rights case as demonstrating a "sweeping disregard of history, precedent, and constitutional text . . . startling for its naked activism." A less fraught way of describing the same decision is that the conservative justices compelled Congress to revisit the half-century-old Voting Rights Act and justify continued federal oversight of historically segregationist Southern states.

This month's campaign-finance ruling marks another step in Roberts's calibrated campaign to assert conservative priorities via the court. Building on the 2010 ruling in *Citizens United,* which struck down limits on independent campaign spending by corporations and unions, his opinion finds that the only legitimate basis for con-straining campaign cash is to prevent outright greenbacks-in-the-briefcase bribery. Yet Roberts chose not to follow this line of reasoning to its logical conclusion: He declined a call by Justice Thomas in a concurring opinion to throw out the entirety of existing campaign-finance law. That task, the politically astute chief justice im-plied, can await another day.

Roberts's approach sometimes annoys the most combustible of the conserva-tives, Justice Scalia. When the chief justice adopted a similarly incrementalist strat-egy in a 2007 campaign-finance case, Scalia derided the approach as "faux judicial restraint," or even "judicial obfuscation."

Step by step, the chief justice makes his mark. In cases yet to be decided this term, his guiding hand will likely be evident in disputes over religious invocations before legislative sessions, state constitutional amendments to ban affirmative ac-tion, and medical clinic "buffer zones" to deter anti-abortion demonstrators from pressuring women not to seek the procedure. Obamacare is back on the docket, too, in a narrower religious-liberty challenge to the requirement that employers provid-ing health insurance make contraception coverage available. By early July it's likely that conservatives once again will be counting their victories, as they will be for some time to come, unless a Democratic president has the opportunity to make ap-pointments that deny Chief Justice Roberts his majority.

The Devastating, Sneaky Genius of John Roberts' Opinions

By Emily Bazelon
Slate, April 2, 2014

I am ever in awe of Chief Justice John Roberts. He has an unparalleled talent for making the sweeping seem small and the sharp seem mild. His rhetoric is all about sounding reasonable and earnest, even if (especially if) the outcomes of his rulings are anything but. He's a champion of the long game. He's Scalia's stylistic opposite, the no-bombast justice. Isn't it lucky for conservatives to have them both?

Roberts is at his minimizing best in his opinion today striking down a key portion of the post-Watergate campaign-finance laws. Congress may still "regulate campaign contributions to protect against corruption or the appearance of corruption," he declares, and then whittles the definition of corruption down to a little nub that has nothing to do with how donors actually buy influence. And then Roberts tells Congress it can still achieve the ends of fairer and cleaner elections, it just has to alter the means it chose for getting there. Never mind that this Congress will do no such thing, just as it has failed to take up Roberts' invitation last June to pass a new version of the Voting Rights Act. And also never mind that Congress had lots of evidence to support the means it already chose. Within the four corners of his opinion, it's Roberts who gets to sound patient and wise.

In 1971, and then as amended in 2002, Congress set aggregate limits on campaign donations. For the current election cycle, individuals could give a total of $5,200 per candidate for each two-year congressional election cycle (plus more for PACs and parties), up to $48,600 total. Congress put this aggregate limit in place to close a loophole. Without it, lawmakers thought, wealthy donors would figure out how to circumvent the $5,200 per-candidate limits and write big checks. Their million-dollar donations, say, would supposedly be divvied up among many candidates, but actually funneled back to just one, or to the political parties. The idea was to prevent donors from buying great gobs of influence with either direct contributions or soft money.

Rick Hasen lays it out ["Die Another Day," Slate, April 2, 2014]. Roberts justifies his decision to kill the aggregate limit by refusing to see ingratiation and access as corruption, which he defines down to mean only bribery. Congress can still regulate campaign donations to protect against quid pro quo corruption or the appearance of corruption—actual tit for tat. But what's really going on here, as Justice Stephen Breyer points out in his dissent (more on it here ["Justice Roberts Hearts Billionaires," Slate, April 2, 2014] from Dahlia Lithwick) is Roberts taking a few seemingly unimportant lines from *Citizens United*, the 2010 decision that opened the door to unlimited campaign donations by corporations and unions, and turning them into unquestionable support for his new slimmed-down definition of corruption. A "generic favoritism or influence theory . . . is at odds with standard First Amendment analyses," the court said in Citizens United.

But that was a description, not the holding in the case. Nowhere did the court make clear in *Citizens United* that it was overruling the broader concept of corruption in the 2003 case *McConnell v. Federal Election Commission*. In that key decision, the court (with a different majority than today's, naturally) upheld the soft-money restrictions in the McCain-Feingold campaign law of 2002 precisely because it understood corruption to encompass "privileged access to and pernicious influence upon elected representatives." It's basically impossible to recognize the realistic understanding of influence-peddling in *McConnell* with the narrow definition the court has now adopted. And that's why Breyer writes his sad line: "Taken together with *Citizens United* . . . today's decision eviscerates our Nation's campaign finance laws, leaving a remnant incapable of dealing with the grave problems of democratic legitimacy that those laws were intended to resolve."

Back in 2003, the court worried about soft money. Not any more. Breyer and Roberts fight over how many big checks will pour through now that the aggregate limits are gone. Roberts says it's either illegal or "divorced from reality" for major donors to figure out how to get around the $5,200 per-candidate, per-cycle limits. Breyer walks through three plausible scenarios for doing exactly that. He shows how one donor could give $1.2 million in two years to one political party, or $2 or $3 million to one candidate. Sure, there's some fancy footwork involved. But not that fancy. Breyer looked for cases brought by the Federal Election Commission to prevent donors from getting around one regulation that is key to Roberts' argument—the one that blocks contributions to a political action committee to support a candidate to which a donor has already contributed, if he has "knowledge that a substantial portion" of his contribution will be used for that candidate. Going back to 2000, Breyer found exactly one case in which the FEC was able to prove the donor had this knowledge. And those were donations to PACs supporting Kansas Senate candidate Sam Brownback by members of his own family.

Every time the rules of campaign finance loosen, money finds new ways to get to the giver's intended recipient. Surely that will be the case this time, too. As Breyer says, "in the real world, the methods of achieving circumvention are more subtle and more complex." Roberts waves away these concerns by telling Congress to just tighten up if it sees new problems emerging. Restrict transfers among candidates and political committees. Make it harder to earmark donations. Rely on the benefits of disclosure. It will be Congress's fault, not the court's, if politics tilt further toward the rich.

Of course Congress will never do any such fixes. And even if Congress did get its act together, Roberts reserves for himself the last word. "We do not mean to opine on the validity of any particular proposal," he says after reeling off his supposed congressional antidotes. It's another mild and reasonable sounding bit of rhetoric with plenty of bite.

How Not to Misunderstand Scalia

By Cass R. Sunstein
Bloomberg.com, July 1, 2013

Supreme Court Justice Antonin Scalia may be the most polarizing figure in all of American law. Conservatives tend to see him as an icon who is faithful to the Constitution, unfailingly clearheaded and outraged when the occasion calls for it. Liberals tend to see him as an ogre who is on the wrong side of history, unbecomingly strident and hypocritical to boot.

Last week, liberals asked a pointed question: How can Scalia have the temerity to express constitutional doubts about affirmative-action programs on Monday and to vote to invalidate the Voting Rights Act on Tuesday—and then piously argue on Wednesday that the Supreme Court should defer to Congress and uphold the Defense of Marriage Act?

It's a legitimate question, and whether or not it has a good answer, Scalia remains poorly understood by his admirers and his critics alike. Perhaps his central goal has been to promote the rule of law, which (as he contended in an important essay in 1989) is "a law of rules." He seeks to increase predictability and to reduce the risks associated with judicial discretion. He favors general rules, not case-by-case judgments.

In his view, such rules simplify life for ordinary people and the legal system as a whole. They also reduce the danger that political preferences will end up dominating judicial decisions.

Because of his commitment to predictability and democratic self-government, Scalia insists that laws must be interpreted in accordance with their ordinary public meaning—the meaning that their words had in the nation or community that enacted them.

Ambiguous Words

Of course, Scalia is aware that words can be ambiguous; in such cases, he is willing to defer to the interpretation of the executive branch (whether the president is a Democrat or a Republican). What he insists on is that the ordinary meaning governs if judges can identify it.

That commitment isn't connected with any political ideology; it can lead to liberal results. For example, Scalia recently wrote an important voting-rights opinion (over vigorous dissents from Justices Clarence Thomas and Samuel Alito), ruling that the language of the National Voter Registration Act bans Arizona from requiring voters to provide documentary evidence of U.S. citizenship.

As an "originalist," Scalia believes that provisions of the Constitution mean what they meant at the time that they were ratified. He thinks that originalism increases predictability and ensures the sovereignty of We the People. The meaning of constitutional provisions is a question of history, not morality.

With respect to the Defense of Marriage Act, originalism (as Scalia understands it) leads to a clear conclusion: Congress may refuse to recognize same-sex marriages. In his words, "the Constitution neither requires nor forbids our society to approve of same-sex marriage, much as it neither requires nor forbids us to approve of no-fault divorce, polygamy, or the consumption of alcohol."

Is this position incompatible with his conclusion that affirmative-action programs violate the Equal Protection Clause? Maybe not. In his view, the constitutional requirement of "equal protection," understood in accordance with its original public meaning, forbids any and all forms of racial discrimination.

Chief Justice John Roberts wrote the court's Voting Rights Act opinion, but Scalia probably believes something like this: If the 15th Amendment is to be interpreted in accordance with its original meaning, Congress's power to enforce that amendment "by appropriate legislation" doesn't allow lawmakers to continue to use an outdated preclearance formula that covers states on the basis of practices that were eradicated long ago.

Originalism Objections

None of these points means that Scalia is correct in his general approach or in his particular conclusions. There are formidable objections to originalism, which is hard to square with some widely accepted constitutional practices (including the prohibition on racial discrimination by the federal government and on sex discrimination in general).

Affirmative action may well be consistent with the original understanding of the 14th Amendment. It remains puzzling that Scalia has yet to discuss the historical materials, which create serious problems for his insistence on colorblindness.

By all accounts, Scalia is a wonderful colleague, but some of his opinions test the boundaries of civility. One of the most vivid writers in the court's history, he knows how to deliver a punch. Sometimes he seems to think that people who don't see things his way aren't merely in error but are also foolish, unacceptably political, even lawless.

Those who disagree with Scalia are entitled to object to his votes and his tone. At the same time, they should understand that his broadest commitment is to the rule of law. They should honor that commitment, and they should respect his efforts to develop an approach to interpretation that is compatible with it.

What Is Clarence Thomas Thinking?

By Garrett Epps
The Atlantic, February 26, 2014

On Monday, as usual, Justice Clarence Thomas asked no questions at the important though relatively narrow oral argument in *Utility Air Regulation Group v. Environmental Protection Agency.* As usual, however, Thomas remained active behind the bench—at times reclining in his chair, at times whispering to seatmate Stephen Breyer, and at least once sending a page out of the courtroom to fetch a volume for reference. On Tuesday, onlookers in the chamber heard his voice, as he read the Court's unanimous decision in *Walden v. Fiore,* a personal jurisdiction case.

New Yorker staff writer, CNN Contributor, and legal gadfly Jeffrey Toobin over the weekend published an online column ["Clarence Thomas's Disgraceful Silence," *New Yorker,* February 21, 2014] noting the eighth anniversary of Thomas's prolonged silence on the bench. Toobin proclaims Thomas "a disgrace" who "is simply not doing his job." Toobin writes that, during oral argument,

> Thomas only reclines; his leather chair is pitched so that he can stare at the ceiling, which he does at length. He strokes his chin. His eyelids look heavy. Every schoolteacher knows this look. It's called "not paying attention."

As noted above, that part of the indictment isn't so. Sitting only a few feet from Thomas day after day, I often wonder what he is thinking, what books he is consulting, and what he is whispering to Breyer. But I usually think that the Justice is at home.

He's there, he just doesn't choose to say anything.

For his own part, Thomas doesn't seem to feel that there's any reason to speak up. "Maybe it's the Southerner in me," he has mused. "Maybe it's the introvert in me, I don't know. I think that when somebody's talking, somebody ought to listen."

But while I am not sure I would label his silence a "disgrace," as Toobin did, it is a lost opportunity for all of us. Thomas is a complex figure. I think his legal ideas profoundly wrong. Over the years he has expressed deep resentment over the battle over his confirmation—resentment that his admirers may find understandable but that to me seems excessive. ("Whoop-de-damn-do," Thomas reports himself as saying when confirmed. But winning a Supreme Court Justiceship, even in ugly circumstances, is an honor. A slight show of gratitude might have been becoming.)

Like every justice, Thomas has a number of areas where he can offer special understanding. He's the only justice who has studied for the priesthood and the only one who has worked in state government. Most relevant to the clean air case, he's the only one who has served as head of an important executive agency (in his case, the Equal Employment Opportunity Commission).

And when he has spoken out, the results have on occasion been extraordinary. Consider the 2003 case of *Virginia v. Black.* Several convicted defendants challenged a Virginia statute that made it a felony to burn a cross where others could see it "with the intent of intimidating any person or group." Not long before, in *R.A.V. v. City of St. Paul,* the Court had struck down a city ordinance making it a crime to use any symbol in public with the knowledge that it "arouses anger, alarm or resentment in others on the basis of race, color, creed, religion or gender." Even though the Virginia law was narrower, many observers were confident the majority would also strike the Virginia law as an invalid ban on "symbolic expression."

Thomas, the only African American on the court, was born into poverty in a segregated community, and he knows a few things that most of his gently raised colleagues do not. He calmly interrupted: "[A]ren't you understating the—the effects of—of the burning cross? . . . Now, it's my understanding that we had almost 100 years of lynching and activity in the South. The Knights of Camellia and—and the Ku Klux Klan, and this was a reign of terror and the cross was a symbol of that reign of terror. Was—isn't that significantly greater than intimidation or a threat?"

Even heard 12 years later in audio, those words dramatically change both the tone and content of the argument. Suddenly the question was not how the case fit into existing First Amendment precedent but whether the history of the burning cross was in some way different, worse. The Court's haughty disdain for "political correctness" was displaced by Thomas's powerful suggestion that the cross was "a symbol of that reign of terror."

Sure enough, the Court finally held that a statute proscribing cross-burning was different from the statute it voided in *R.A.V.* By a margin of 6–3, it said that a state could outlaw the fiery cross. Thomas wrote separately to argue that the Court's opinion construed this power too narrowly: "In every culture, certain things acquire meaning well beyond what outsiders can comprehend," he wrote. "That goes for both the sacred and the profane." The result seemed to flow directly out of Thomas's decision, as an insider, to share the meaning of racial terror with his colleagues and the public.

Toobin rates the influence of Thomas's opinions highly—more highly than I do. If I were looking for grounds to criticize Thomas, in fact, it would be that his opinions aren't influential, and that they show an often shocking disregard of a judge's duty to precedent. His opinions are sometimes powerful—see his agonized dissent in *Grutter v. Bollinger,* the 2003 affirmative action case—and sometimes, well, silly—see his faux-historical dissent in *Brown v Entertainment Merchants Association.*

Those who value those opinions should realize that the voice they represent might sway the Court more often—and might educate some of the fellow citizens from whom Thomas seems to feel alienated—if the Justice shared it in the Court chamber as well as on the page.

We can disagree about whether Thomas's performance makes him a good Justice or a bad one. But as his employers, we all can expect from him the best that he can give. A President appointed him, a Senate majority confirmed him, and he now plays a central role in our democracy. It seems both infuriating and sad that he would choose to play it less fully than he might.

His silence may perhaps not fairly be called a disgrace; but each day it persists represents a lost chance to serve his country and his Court.

Ruth Bader Ginsburg's Retirement Dissent

By Amy Davidson
The New Yorker, September 24, 2014

"I had, I think, 12 minutes, or something like that, of argument," Justice Ruth Bader Ginsburg tells Jessica Weisberg, in an interview with *Elle,* remembering her first appearance as a lawyer before the Supreme Court, in 1973. "I was very nervous. It was an afternoon argument. I didn't dare eat lunch. There were many butterflies in my stomach. I had a very well-prepared opening sentence I had memorized. Looking at them, I thought, I'm talking to the most important court in the land, and they have to listen to me and that's my captive audience."

"And then you relaxed?" Weisberg asks.

"I felt a sense of empowerment because I knew so much more about the case, the issue, than they did," Ginsburg says.

She wasn't anyone's instrument, or at anyone's mercy; she was the one in control. Ginsburg had a sense of her own authority, even if the judges she was speaking before didn't yet. In the 1973 case, she was presenting the A.C.L.U.'s amicus-curiae brief in a case brought by a woman soldier. As Jeffrey Toobin wrote in a profile of Ginsburg ["Heavyweight," *New Yorker,* March 11, 2013], when Ginsburg again stood before the Court, in 1976, this time as the lead lawyer, "Chief Justice Warren E. Burger stumbled when introducing her. 'Mrs. Bader? Mrs. Ginsburg?' he said. . . . Later in the same case, Justice Potter Stewart made a similar mistake, calling her 'Mrs. Bader.'" She was forty-three then.

How much time does Justice Ginsburg have now? There is an argument, an increasingly tired one, that if she is not careful, she will die when a Republican is in office—and then who knows who will take her spot on the bench. The plea is that, to avoid this possibility, she should resign—indeed, she should have resigned the minute that Obama was reelected. If the Democrats lose control of the Senate in November, there will be expressions of despair: Doesn't she know that she could die at any minute? Why isn't it her priority to make sure the Court house is tidy before she leaves? Ginsburg's dissent, to Weisberg, is a strong one:

> Who do you think President Obama could appoint at this very day, given the boundaries that we have? If I resign any time this year, he could not successfully appoint anyone I would like to see in the court. [The Senate Republicans] took off the filibuster for lower federal court appointments, but it remains for this court. So anybody who thinks that if I step down, Obama could appoint someone like me, they're misguided.

She knows how good she is and she is not afraid to judge others. (When Weisberg asks why the Court, while moving forward on gay rights, has swung in such a conservative direction on women's rights, Ginsburg says, "To be frank, it's one person who made the difference: Justice [Anthony] Kennedy.") Given her profession, that's as much as saying that she's not afraid. And she is quite right: if she had resigned when the party-line worriers would have liked her to, one wouldn't have her magnificent dissent in the Hobby Lobby case, or her matchless voice. That 1973 case was about whether the husbands of soldiers had to prove that they were economically dependent before getting benefits, while wives got them automatically. The Court's jurisprudence on gender is something that Ginsburg has been building since then. And not only on gender: she, not John Roberts, deserves the credit for saving the Affordable Care Act. The Court is, no doubt, an extremely partisan institution. But that doesn't mean that its members are just pegs to be traded. The Court is also an institution where seniority matters. There is no Ginsburg whom Ginsburg is holding back.

Do Democrats want to make sure that a President of their party is in office when Ginsburg leaves the Court? Then win the next election; battle it out, rather than fretting and sighing about how an older woman doesn't know when it's time to go. (Ginsburg is urged to be selfless a lot more loudly than is Stephen Breyer, who, at seventy-six, is only five years younger, and less of a presence.) If all this talk reflects sublimated doubt about the candidate that the Democrats look likely to field in 2016, then be open about that, and deal with it. Or make sure that the same constraints that—as Ginsburg quite correctly points out— the Republicans, even as a minority party in the Senate, place on Obama, are put on any Republican in the White House. As Dahlia Lithwick put it ["Ruth Bader Ginsburg Is Irreplaceable," Slate, March 19, 2014] in a thorough dismantling of the Ginsburg-should-go nonsense, "It's perverse in the extreme to seek to bench Ginsburg the fighter, simply because Senate Democrats are unwilling or unable to fight for the next Ginsburg." (Lithwick adds, "I have seen not a lick of evidence that Ginsburg is failing. . . . If anything, Ginsburg has been stronger in recent years than ever.")

But, the counter-argument goes, Obama could appoint a fifty-year-old Democrat—maybe not, to borrow Ginsburg's phrase, "anyone I would like to see in the court," but also not a Republican, and that would be enough. (That thinking helps explain why the President tried to name Michael Boggs to the federal bench, despite his anti-choice, anti-same-sex-marriage votes in the Georgia legislature; earlier this week, Democrats effectively killed his nomination.) Justices can be unpredictable: John Paul Stevens, admired by liberals, was appointed by Gerald Ford (and was on the Court until he was ninety). But this is clearly not a good moment to get anyone with ambitious positions—anyone interesting—through the Senate. Why seek it out? An exchange that requires the certain sacrifice of Ginsburg for the uncertainty of whomever Obama could get through is not even sensible in a coldly pragmatic way.

There is another reason why Ginsburg should be on the Court for this particular stretch of its history. In the *Elle* interview, Ginsburg speaks about the period after

Sandra Day O'Connor, the only other woman on the Court at the time, retired (to take care of her dying husband). "When Sandra left, I was all alone," she says.

> I'm rather small, so when I go with all these men in this tiny room, now Kagan is on my left, and Sotomayor is on my right. So we look like we're really part of the court and we're here to stay. Also, both of them are very active in oral arguments. They're not shrinking violets. It's very good for the schoolchildren who parade in and out of the court to see.

Justices Sonia Sotomayor and Elena Kagan—women, respectively, from the Bronx and Manhattan—are the ideological successors to Ginsburg, who grew up in Brooklyn. (One looks forward to the day when there are women on the Court from each of the city's five boroughs.) As Ginsburg says, they are not shrinking violets, and they know what they want to do. But there is still plenty to learn on the way from being a strong younger Justice to being a great, precedent-defining one. Working side by side with Ginsburg can be part of that process. In that way, her presence on the Court is a bet on its long-term future, too. (From Toobin's Profile: "Kagan uses the same trainer as Ginsburg, and when the younger Justice struggles with fifteen-pound curls the trainer says, 'C'mon! Justice Ginsburg can do that easily!'" There are many ways to be a mentor.)

So how long? "As long as I can do the job full steam," she tells Weisberg. (It's a phrase she's used before.) "I think I'll recognize when the time comes that I can't any longer. But now I can. I wasn't slowed down at all last year in my production of opinions." She also says that she fully expects some of her dissents, in the long run, to be "recognized as the position of the court." In that respect, she compares herself to Justices Brandeis and Holmes. And why not? She also mentions another name: "A student at NYU started something with NOTORIOUS R.B.G., and then somebody at Stanford did another T-shirt." As R.B.G. says that, the transcript notes, "She grins."

Active Liberty Lives!

By Adam Winkler
Slate, July 8, 2014

When a justice is in the minority on the Supreme Court, as Justice Stephen Breyer has long been, there aren't many opportunities to write truly landmark opinions. Those are the spoils of the majority, or at least of Anthony Kennedy. Yet Breyer found himself writing for a surprising majority this term in *NLRB v. Noel Canning*, which held unconstitutional recess appointments made by the president when the Senate was still in pro forma session. While media accounts of the decision understandably emphasized how it was a loss for the president, Breyer's opinion is about a far more important and enduring question than the lawfulness of these handful of recess appointments: How should courts interpret the Constitution? As has always been the case, the answer to this deeper question will shape judicial rulings across the spectrum of constitutional law issues, from gay rights and states' rights to God and guns.

In his opinion, Breyer offers the most forceful defense of what's often termed "living constitutionalism" to appear in a majority Supreme Court opinion in a generation. Rejecting Antonin Scalia's 18th-century approach of originalism—in which all that matters is what the framers thought—Breyer in *Noel Canning* stakes a bold claim for interpreting the Constitution "in light of its text, purposes, and our whole experience." His is a progressive vision of the Constitution, one articulated previously in his books, like *Active Liberty*, and in various concurring and dissenting opinions he has authored over the years. But now, in the wake of *Canning* it is also the opinion of the court. As a result, it will influence how future courts—state and federal, trial and appellate—will apply the Constitution to answer tomorrow's controversies.

It may seem like a niggling academic problem. But it has real-world consequences. That's one of the reasons Justice Antonin Scalia—who agreed with Breyer that these recess appointments were unconstitutional—nevertheless disagreed with the court's opinion so vigorously. While it may be a sign of how far the Roberts court has shifted that Scalia is forced to file his blustery dissents in the form of angry concurrences, the substance of Scalia's complaint is unchanged: The court "casts aside the plain, original meaning of the constitutional text." Breyer responds by saying that Scalia's originalism asks the wrong question. "The question is not: Did the Founders at the time think about" the exact issue before the court? "The question is: Did the Founders intend to restrict the scope" of the Constitution only to the "forms . . . then prevalent," or did they intend the Constitution "to apply, where appropriate, to somewhat changed circumstances"? Fidelity to the Constitution, he suggests, means using its timeless principles to address new and unforeseen situations. You know, like figuring out how to preserve privacy in an age of smartphones—as the court did this term in *Riley v. California*, another case decided without relying on originalism.

For Breyer, the recess appointments power dramatically illustrates the advantages of his approach. Originalism, Scalia argues, requires reading the recess appointment power narrowly to apply only to formal breaks between sessions. Those were the types of recesses referred to in the dictionaries of the period, so that's what the founders expected. Yet due to institutional changes in the Senate (more midsession breaks, shorter breaks between sessions), such a narrow view of what counts as a recess would render the whole Recess Appointments Clause, as Scalia admits, "an anachronism." It wouldn't have any contemporary relevance. Breyer calls out Scalia, who "would basically read it out of the Constitution." "He performs this act of judicial excising in the name of liberty," Breyer stings. Not content to stop there he adds: "We fail to see how excising the Recess Appointments Clause preserves freedom."

Contrary to some of the critics of active liberty or its grandfather, evolving constitutionalism, reading the Constitution broadly in service of its "reason and spirit" isn't a license for justices to simply impose their own values on society. Breyer grounds his understanding of the core purposes of the Recess Appointment Clause in data and evidence. To determine whether midsession breaks qualify as recesses, the former law professor surveys every single recess appointment since the founding. He wades through Senate reports and a century of presidential legal opinions. He factors in the historic practices of the comptroller general. He analyzes the recess power at key moments in history, when its scope and meaning were publicly contested. His judgment is shaped by empirical data on the average length of Senate confirmations and on the duration of recesses in which appointments have been made. He adds two appendices, one on every congressional recess and another reporting the results of a "random sample of recess appointments" under recent presidents.

Breyer's approach to constitutional interpretation doesn't ignore the framers; the views of Madison, Jefferson, Washington, and Marshall are all taken carefully into account. Yet he also seeks to discover how the recess appointment power has functioned and been understood since the founding—by the various attorneys general, by the Senate, and by presidents making appointments. "There is a lot of history here," Breyer reminds us. Constitutional law, he suggests, should be informed by data as much as by dictionaries.

No theory of constitutional interpretation is "perfect"—if by that one means denying a judge any meaningful discretion over how to rule. Breyer's leaves a number of open questions. How broadly or narrowly should constitutional principles be defined? When historic practices conflict, which take precedence? What if relevant data is unavailable? Still, *Noel Canning* is significant for the fact that, after 20 years on the intellectual ropes, a principles-based approach to constitutional interpretation has been so prominently endorsed by the court.

Scalia himself admits that even originalism permits of some judicial discretion. His theory, he insists, just has to be better than the alternative, invoking the analogy of two campers being chased by a bear. One asks the other, "How are we going to outrun the bear?" The other responds, "I don't have to outrun the bear, I just have to outrun you!" After *Noel Canning,* it looks like Breyer's active liberty is giving originalism a good race.

Six years ago, Scalia wrote the majority opinion in *District of Columbia v. Heller,* the landmark Second Amendment case that established an individual right to use handguns in the home. Scalia's heavy reliance on founding-era history in that case led some to call *Heller* Scalia's crowning achievement. Originalism, however, now has some competition. *Noel Canning* embraces a progressive vision of the Constitution. And that may be Breyer's greatest legacy.

How Sonia Sotomayor Became the Supreme Court's Preeminent Defender of Civil Liberties

By Scott Lemieux
The Week, December 26, 2014

A decision handed down by the Supreme Court earlier in December may have disturbing implications for Fourth Amendment rights. But *Heien v. North Carolina* is notable for another reason: it marks the emergence of Sonia Sotomayor, President Obama's first Supreme Court nominee, as the strongest voice for civil liberties on the court.

There are many who may be surprised by the clout she has amassed in just a few short years. It's worth remembering the remarkable condescension—in some cases tinted with sexism and racism — that greeted her nomination.

Sotomayor's formal credentials were essentially identical to President George W. Bush's second nominee, Samuel Alito: Princeton undergraduate degree, Ivy League law degree, prosecutor, long and distinguished career on the federal judiciary. But while nobody questioned whether Alito was qualified (as opposed to ideologically suitable) for the bench, many conservative pundits asserted that Sotomayor lacked the the basic qualifications for the job. Some even compared Sotomayor to Harriet Miers, the failed Bush nominee who was very similar to Sotomayor except for her lack of elite educational credentials, judicial experience, or basic knowledge of constitutional law. (Tellingly, they do share one thing in common: their sex.)

Nor did these criticisms come solely from the right. Like many others, I'm saddened by the recent mass resignations at *The New Republic*. But I can't forget that it published a disgraceful hit job on Sotomayor by its legal affairs editor Jeffrey Rosen. The article's anonymous smears, which attacked her temperament and intelligence, were short on substantiation and long on the sexist stereotypes that have been used to characterize women on the bench for years.

As Joan Biskupic demonstrates in *Breaking In,* her fine new book about Sotomayor, after a somewhat tentative beginning Sotomayor has become a very important liberal voice on the court. Her draft opinions in the *Fisher* affirmative action case, for example, may well have prevented the court from ruling virtually all affirmative action in higher education unconstitutional. She ultimately withdrew the opinions, after Justice Kennedy narrowed his opinions in an apparent response to Sotomayor.

The recent Fourth Amendment ruling, while not as important, is another case in point.

In *Heien,* the court ruled that a police search of a car that ultimately found cocaine was "reasonable" under the Fourth Amendment, although the single broken brake light the police used as a pretext to stop the car was legal under North Carolina law. Sotomayor was the only dissenter. Two of the liberal justices who voted with the majority—Justices Ginsburg and Kagan—emphasized the unusual facts of the case: the North Carolina courts had not definitively ruled that driving with only one broken brake light was legal until after the arrest.

But as Sotomayor noted in her dissent, the ruling has consequences that extend beyond this case. The vague standard created by the majority—that a search based on a misunderstanding of the law is permissible under the Fourth Amendment as long as the police officer's misinterpretation of the law was "reasonable"—has the potential to create a substantial amount of mischief. Lower courts are likely to use the standard to give the police more leeway to conduct searches based on legal errors, a problem that is exacerbated by the fact that the Supreme Court did not provide adequate guidance to the lower courts.

In addition to her dissent, as Slate's Dahlia Lithwick observes ["The Supreme Court Ignores the Lessons of Ferguson," Slate, December 16, 2014], at oral argument Sotomayor was the only justice to raise the disturbing, broader issues lurking in the background of the case. A Hispanic man had his car pulled over and extensively searched after being followed for the utterly banal behavior of having a 10-and-2 hand position on his steering wheel and "looking straight ahead." Even if the police did find a legitimate, albeit trivial, violation of the law to justify pulling the suspect over, the search raises very serious Fourth Amendment problems. The court has refused to take these issues seriously, and it can be expected that Sotomayor, the court's first Latina justice, will continue to urge her colleagues to do so.

Nor is this the first time that Sotomayor has made a major contribution to the court's civil liberties jurisprudence. In a solo concurrence in a case involving GPS tracking, Sotomayor emphasized that the court's assumption that individuals almost never have an expectation of privacy with respect to data shared with third parties has become an anachronism in an age in which people routinely save large amounts of personal information on their phones. She also underscored the extent to which government surveillance "chills associational and expressive freedoms." Her concurrence has already proven to be highly and deservedly influential.

Combined with her pathbreaking writing on racial equality, Justice Sotomayor's civil liberties jurisprudence has proven her detractors very wrong. We can only hope that more of her views will be expressed in majority opinions, rather than in lone dissents and concurrences.

Court Sense

By Colleen Walsh
Harvard Gazette, September 4, 2014

It's understood that with the role of U.S. Supreme Court justice comes tremendous responsibility. For Associate Justice Elena Kagan, part of her job as the most junior member of that body involves answering the door.

When the nine justices enter their private conference room to decide a case, sometimes one forgets something, such as a critical case file, or reading glasses, or coffee cup. When clerks arrive with the missing item, "They will knock on the outer door, and then I have to hop up and open the inner door," said Kagan. "Truly, if I don't do it, nobody will. If I don't do it, they'll just all stare at me: 'Elena, that was a knock on the door.'"

In an entertaining talk in HLS's Wasserstein Hall with Dean Martha Minow on Wednesday, Kagan displayed her trademark wit and wisdom, honed during her years as a Harvard Law School (HLS) student, professor, and dean, her work with the Clinton administration, and her stint as solicitor general. She also pulled back the curtain a little on the nation's highest court.

Kagan delved into topics that ranged from her most difficult court decision (a case about violent video games) to which justice gets the most laughs during oral arguments (a close call between Antonin Scalia and Stephen Breyer) to her reputation for writing readable decisions (she loves making complicated legal arguments clear) to her thoughts on amending the U.S. Constitution (she doesn't believe it's the role of a Supreme Court justice).

Since joining the court in 2010, Kagan has made regular visits to her alma mater to talk with students. This week she also took up her former role as teacher, heading an HLS reading group that examined a series of decisions from the court's last term.

Reflecting on her previous job, Kagan said that being solicitor general "is almost the closest thing to being a Supreme Court justice," adding that in some ways the job is even better preparation for the high court than being a lower court judge. Before she was confirmed, some critics had complained that her lack of judicial service made her less qualified for the role.

As the lawyer tasked with arguing cases before the Supreme Court on behalf of the U.S. government, "what the solicitor general does is basically think about the Supreme Court all day long," said Kagan. That thinking ranges from supervising brief-writing for all of the cases in which the government takes part to thinking about which cases the court is likeliest to hear to deciding how best to argue the cases before the justices.

"By doing the solicitor general's job, I really got a kind of crash course in the Supreme Court and how it operates and what the justices were thinking about."

Being literally on the other side of the bench now is much easier, said Kagan, acknowledging that she and her colleagues don't give the lawyer presenting a case at oral argument "much time to collect your thoughts and to express yourself. . . . You stand at the podium, and you get a sentence out, two sentences if you are lucky, and then the questions start . . . you are just bombarded."

The judges have lots of questions, and with only about an hour or so with each attorney, the pace is always rapid-fire. Often, said Kagan, the questions are just a means for the justices to talk to each other, "a way to communicate with your colleagues" about the case.

"We're not really actually all that interested sometimes in what you have to say; we're a little bit more interested in talking with each other. And there are reasons for that," she said, adding that the first time the justices convene about a case as a group is at oral argument.

There's another reason Kagan asks lots of questions. As the most junior member of the bench, Kagan comments last when the court meets in conference to discuss and decide a case. The pecking order means "I don't really get to say anything at conference until everybody had indicated an intention about how they're going to vote," she said. "So to the extent that I have something that I think is a slightly different take on a case, or something that I want my colleagues to hear before they say how they are going to vote, argument is the time for me to do that. And I think we're all aware of that, that argument is a time when one can put ideas into your colleagues' heads . . . before they go back to their chambers and they mull things over for a couple of days."

Kagan said she tries to remember what it was like on the firing line as solicitor general and "to at least be polite" when asking questions.

Kagan said she prepares for oral argument by reading the briefs carefully and discussing the cases with her clerks in detail, including what kinds of questions it would be helpful to ask. Asked about the collegiality on the court and how she deals with disagreements, Kagan said she takes a page from her friend and hunting partner Scalia, who told her, "If you take the disagreement personally, you are in the wrong line of business."

"People are all operating in good faith, and trying to do the right thing, and taking their jobs extremely seriously, and sometimes you are going to reach different outcomes," Kagan said.

"I think it's an incredible group of people — smart, engaged, interesting, personable, really decent people," she added. "And I enjoy being with them. Sometimes the folks who I disagree with are really among my favorites to spend time with."

A blog that keeps track of the biggest laugh lines during oral argument put Scalia and Breyer ahead of the pack. Kagan said the blogger also wrote that he thought she was "underperforming what he knew to be my true potential."

Chief Justice John Roberts is "very, very witty and very, very fast. Other people occasionally surprise you. Justice [Ruth Bader] Ginsburg loves it when she makes people laugh," said Kagan.

Her opinions, which Minow said have gained a reputation "for being distinctively readable," are the products of hard work. Kagan said her goal is to make her writing approachable by everyone, from the legal experts to "the ordinary people who are interested in what we do."

"To try to explain what's at issue or why it matters in a way that people can understand takes more than one draft," she said. "Mostly I just work at it, and work at it the more."

The judges agree more often than they disagree, said Kagan, something the public doesn't always appreciate. But when they do disagree there is often "a lot of back and forth and a lot of attempts to persuade, and that's tremendously fun and exciting to be part of." Kagan tries to model herself on her predecessor, John Paul Stevens, whose chair she now sits in. Even after decades on the court, he approached every day, she said, eager and ready to learn.

Kagan urged her listeners to be open to new things, and "take more risks than you think you should," adding that, "Law students are too risk-averse." Many students pressed her on difficult topics, including her most conflicted moment on the court.

Kagan said that while she doesn't suffer from "back-and-forth angst" with most cases, a First Amendment case involving violent video games and children's access to them was particularly challenging. "That was one where I thought that all of First Amendment doctrine pushed one way, and all of common sense pushed another way, and that was very difficult for me. But I ended up going the way I thought the First Amendment doctrine pushed."

She admitted that if she were a parent, she wouldn't want her child watching such games, and that keeping children from buying these games "without a parent" present struck her as "eminently sensible." Still, she said, she couldn't "square that result with essential First Amendment rules that the court has."

Amending the Constitution "is not my job," said Kagan in response to another question. "I feel very strongly about that actually." She said that her job is simply to "interpret, as best I can, apply as best I can, the Constitution that we have."

"Why are justices at the Supreme Court any better positioned to say what the Constitution means than anyone else in this room?" wondered one student.

"I am going to say that I know more than most people in this room, at least I hope I do," Kagan said with a laugh, adding on a more serious note, "It's a lot of chance that the nine of us are there rather than nine other people. All you can do is try your best to do the best job you can."

Breyer and Scalia Debate the Role of Established Practice in Constitutional Interpretation

By Christopher Schmidt
ISCOTUS, June 26, 2014

Although Justices Breyer and Scalia ended up on the same side in today's landmark decision on the President's recess appointment power [*National Labor Relations Board v. Noel Canning*], they offered starkly opposing views on the question of whether the past practice of the executive can resolve this constitutional question.

In his Opinion of the Court, Justice Breyer emphasizes early in the opinion that "in interpreting the [Recess Appointments] Clause, we put significant weight upon historical practice." For support for this, he offers lengthy quotations from *McCulloch v. Maryland* (1819) and from an 1819 letter written from James Madison to Spencer Roane in which he writes that it "was foreseen at the birth of the Constitution, that difficulties and differences of opinion might occasionally arise in expounding terms & phrases necessarily used in such a charter . . . and that it might require a regular course of practice to liquidate & settle the meaning of some of them." From these and other sources, Justice Breyer concludes: "[T]his Court has treated practice as an important interpretive factor even when the nature or longevity of that practice is subject to dispute, and even when that practice began after the founding era." With regard to the question before the Court, he writes: "We have not previously interpreted the [Recess Appointments] Clause, and, when doing so for the first time in more than 200 years, we must hesitate to upset the compromises and working arrangements that the elected branches of Government themselves have reached."

Justice Scalia accepts that basic premise that established practice can inform the Court's interpretation of ambiguous constitutional provisions. But he insists upon a higher threshold for what actually constitutes established practice. He writes: "Of course, where a governmental practice has been *open, widespread, and unchallenged since the early days of the Republic*, the practice should guide our interpretation of an ambiguous constitutional provision" (emphasis added). The recess appointment practice challenged in this case does not meet this incredibly demanding threshold, however. "Plainly, then, a self aggrandizing practice adopted by one branch well after the founding, often challenged, and never before blessed by this Court—in other words, the sort of practice on which the majority relies in this case—does not relieve us of our duty to interpret the Constitution in light of its text, structure, and original understanding."

Justice Scalia accuses Justice Breyer of "cast[ing] aside the plain, original meaning of the constitutional text in deference to late-arising historical practices that are ambiguous at best." Finding historical practice fails to resolve the constitutional question, he turns to his preferred grounds of constitutional interpretation of "text, structure, and original understanding." The two Justices end up in the same place on this particular constitutional dispute, although they chart quite different paths getting there.

Time to Fix—or Scrap—the Confirmation Hearings

By Andrew Cohen
Vanity Fair, July 16, 2009

Having now sat through the biggest part of my third Supreme Court confirmation hearing, I feel I have earned the right to say this: they have become an utter sham, a travesty upon truth and enlightenment and insight and knowledge, and they ought to be completely re-engineered into the meaningful exercise they can be when done right. Either that or they ought to be scrapped altogether and we should return to the good old days, when these sorts of things were hashed out in a matter of hours behind closed doors.

Members of the Senate Judiciary Committee, indeed all members of the Senate, ought to rise up against the White House (any White House, not just this one) and say: no more. We will not confirm your Supreme Court nominees—we won't even vote on them—if they continue to come before us and speak for days without saying anything at all. It's a waste of everyone's time and money, an affront to the co-equal legislative branch, and a disservice to the American people. And it's getting worse, not better.

Never mind views on abortion and gun rights, there is no legitimate excuse for a Supreme Court nominee not to be able or willing to explain to the American people whether she or he believes the Court ought to accept more cases each term or whether cameras in the Court is a good idea in the 21st century. There is no reason for a nominee to immediately toggle into rote analysis of existing case law every time she or he is asked to explain a position on legal doctrine or philosophy. It's insulting, and disingenuous, and we have a right to expect more. Judge Sonia Sotomayor is no more or less guilty of these sins than were her immediate predecessors, Samuel Alito, John Roberts, Stephen Breyer, and Ruth Bader Ginsburg. It's not a Republican thing or a Democratic thing. G.O.P. Senators this week were as legitimately frustrated with Sotomayor's evasiveness as were Democratic lawmakers in 2006, when it was Alito who was ducking and dodging and weaving through his answers. It's a bipartisan problem and it ought to be resolved in a bipartisan fashion.

Except that nothing gets resolved in a bipartisan fashion anymore. The White House (any White House, not just this one) will say: we won the election and we get to choose who we want on the bench. That sort of attitude has helped choke the pipeline that populates the federal judiciary, so much so that litigants can't get cases heard because there simply aren't enough sitting judges. For every Supreme Court nominee like Sotomayor who gets rushed to the beginning of the line, there are 10 lower court judges who wallow in limbo.

Congress is complicit, too, in its own humiliation. It's helped create and foster the meaninglessness of confirmation hearings. We are now nearly 25 years past the vicious Bork hearing; nearly 20 years past the distasteful Clarence Thomas affair. Less than a handful of Senators are still on the Committee from those dark days. It's time to move on. But we won't move on so long as Senators try to play "gotcha" on silly issues—like an out-of-court comment in a speech—while accepting non-answer answers on substantive issues. The focus upon insignificant things only highlights the absence of a meaningful dialogue about core legal issues (or even peripheral ones, like how many cases the Court should hear each year).

I'm fed up. And you should be, too. Judge Sotomayor is a good judge and will be an acceptable Justice—she's certainly no worse than some of the other people who have come before her. But that doesn't mean we all ought to congratulate each other on a job well done.

Yale, Harvard, Yale, Harvard, Yale, Harvard, Harvard, Harvard, Columbia: The Thing That Scares Me Most about the Supreme Court

By Dahlia Lithwick
The New Republic, November 13, 2014

Under Chief Justice John Roberts, the Supreme Court has emerged as one of the most ideologically aggressive in decades, and its rightward trajectory is usually attributed to this simple fact: a majority of the justices are very conservative. Today's Court contains, according to one study, four of the five most conservative justices to sit on the bench since FDR; Anthony Kennedy, the putative swing vote, is in the top ten.

But having covered the Court for 15 years, I've come to believe that what we're seeing goes beyond ideology. Because ideology alone would not propel the justices to effect such massive shifts upon the constitutional landscape, inventing rights for corporations while gutting protections for women, minorities, and workers. No, the real problem, I think, is that the Court as a whole has gotten too smart for our own good.

The current justices are intellectually qualified in ways we have never seen. Compared with the political operators, philanderers, and alcoholics of bygone eras, they are almost completely devoid of bad habits or scandalous secrets. This is, of course, not a bad thing in itself. But the Court has become worryingly cloistered, even for a famously cloistered institution. Every justice is unavoidably subjected to "public deference" when they ascend to the bench, as I heard Sonia Sotomayor describe it at a conference last June. Now, on top of that, today's justices filter out anything that might challenge their perspectives. Antonin Scalia won't read newspapers that conflict with his views and claims to often get very little from amicus briefs. John Roberts has said that he doesn't believe that most law-review articles—where legal scholars advance new thinking on contemporary problems—are relevant to the justices' work. Ruth Bader Ginsburg, Scalia's opera-going buddy, increasingly seems to revel in, rather than downplay, her status as a liberal icon. Kennedy spends recesses guest-teaching law school courses in Salzburg.

Before the Affordable Care Act cases were heard in 2012, aspiring spectators lined up for days (mostly in vain, because seats are so limited). Meanwhile, this Court goes to considerable lengths to keep itself at oracular remove. The texts of many of the justices' speeches are not publicized. Cameras and recording devices remain barred from oral arguments, and protesters may not even approach the spotless white plaza outside. But the most symbolically potent move came in 2010, when the justices closed off the giant bronze doors at the front of the building, above which the words EQUAL JUSTICE UNDER LAW are engraved. Today, the public must enter the building from the side, beneath the marble staircase, through dark, narrow entrances feeding into metal detectors. It is a fitting setup for a Court that seems to want neither to be seen nor to really see us.

Paradoxically, the Court that has gutted minority voting rights in Shelby County and limited women's access to birth control in Hobby Lobby has never looked more like the country whose disputes it adjudicates. It includes three women, an African American, the first Hispanic, two Italian Americans, six Catholics, and three Jews. On the federal bench, President Obama has appointed more women, minorities, and openly gay judges than any president in history.

But while we have gained diversity of background, we haven't gained diversity of experience. A study released in February revealed that 71 percent of Obama's nominees had practiced primarily for corporate or business clients. The Supreme Court is even more homogeneous, because the modern confirmation gauntlet only lets one kind of person through. Post–Robert Bork, a nominee must not have too obvious an ideological agenda, as some judges and almost all elected officials do. Post–Harriet Miers, a prospective justice must possess not just a stellar résumé but also a track record of judicial rulings and legal writings from which future decisions can be confidently deduced.

The result has been what Professor Akhil Reed Amar of Yale Law School calls the "Judicialization of the Judiciary," a selection process that discourages political or advocacy experience and reduces the path to the Supreme Court to a funnel: elite schools beget elite judicial clerkships beget elite federal judgeships. Rinse, repeat. All nine sitting justices attended either Yale or Harvard law schools. (Ginsburg started her studies in Cambridge but graduated from Columbia.) Eight once sat on a federal appellate court; five have done stints as full-time law school professors. There is not a single justice "from the heartland," as Clarence Thomas has complained. There are no war veterans (like John Paul Stevens), former Cabinet officials (like Robert Jackson), or capital defense attorneys. The Supreme Court that decided *Brown v. Board of Education* had five members who had served in elected office. The Roberts Court has none. What we have instead are nine perfect judicial thoroughbreds who have spent their entire adulthoods on the same lofty, narrow trajectory.

A Supreme Court built this way is going to have blind spots. But right-wing legal and political groups—who are much better at the confirmation game than their equivalents on the left—have added a final criterion that ensures the Court leans strongly in their favor. They have succeeded in setting the definition of the consummate judge: a humble, objective, nearly mechanical umpire who merely calls "balls and strikes," in Roberts's insincere but politically deft phrasing. This lets conservatives sell nominees who are far more conservative than liberal nominees are liberal.

A Democratic-appointed justice makes the short list by having her heart in the right place, but will be disqualified for heeding it too much.

And so we have a Supreme Court that, for all its credentials, produces some truly confounding opinions. One sub-genre of these is typified by the split decision in *Citizens United*, which runs to 183 pages of intricate legal arguments. (The *Brown v. Board* ruling took only ten pages to declare, in a clarion voice, that "separate but equal" hurts schoolchildren.) Kennedy's majority opinion is a beautiful work of abstract reasoning, but it seems to suggest that only something akin to blatant bribery fosters corruption or the appearance of it. On the ground, where actual campaigns occur, that simply is not true. Then there are cases like *McCullen v. Coakley*, which challenged a Massachusetts law imposing buffer zones around abortion clinics. The measure, enacted years after two fatal clinic shootings, was designed as protection from violence and verbal abuse. But the buffer zones also applied to pro-life "sidewalk counselors," who challenged the law on free-speech grounds. However much women might be affected by doing away with the safeguard, the doctrine was clear: The Court struck down the Massachusetts law, nine-zero.

Perhaps the strongest and scariest signal that this Court has no use for real life came late last spring, when Sotomayor broke from the Court's current operating procedure during an important case about affirmative action in Michigan. Sotomayor, a onetime prosecutor and a graduate of Princeton and Yale Law School, is as thoroughbred as they come. But when the majority opinion invalidating the program devolved into a highly abstracted discussion about voter preferences, the first Latina justice attempted to puncture the force field of hyper-legalism. From the bench, she read aloud from a passionate dissent that described in deeply personal terms "the slights, the snickers" that remind her that racism remains very alive. Roberts, in response, called her out for elevating "policy preferences" over rigorous doctrine.

Thurgood Marshall used to talk about race, too. But his colleagues listened. Sandra Day O'Connor famously explained in an essay that his stories about the Jim Crow South changed how she and several of her colleagues approached the law. "Justice Marshall imparted not only his legal acumen, but also his life experiences," O'Connor wrote, "constantly pushing and prodding us to respond not only to the persuasiveness of legal argument but also to the power of moral truth." They don't talk about "life experience" at the Roberts Court, much less "moral truth." Personal narrative of any sort has been downgraded to sloppy sentimentality, rather than something that might enrich the justices' thinking.

In the coming months and years, this group of Ivy-trained Washington insiders will have to decide whether Texas voters who don't have driver's licenses and are required to take three buses across town to pay $30 for a voter ID have effectively been disenfranchised. They will determine whether women who need to travel 300 miles to procure an abortion (women who may lack cars, or paid time off, or money to spend on hotels) face an "undue burden." But some of the same justices who will bar empathy from those considerations forget that they do evince empathy when they side with those beleaguered "sidewalk counselors," or multimillionaire campaign donors, or the owner of a mega-chain of craft stores who believes his religious freedoms have been impinged. All of us import our values and experiences into our decision-making. The double-whammy at the current Court is that the justices are no longer allowed to acknowledge it, and that the pool of those with whom they unavoidably identify is so dangerously small and privileged.

When the next court vacancy occurs, there will be lists of brilliant, Yale- and Harvard-trained jurists to choose from. But there will also be many accomplished lawyers toiling in elected office and legal-aid clinics and state-school faculties. Progressives need to identify those prospects and to push them forward. The alternative is ceding the court to ever-more dazzling minds, while seeing less of our own realities in its jurisprudence.

How Judges Think: A Conversation with Judge Richard Posner

By Jonathan Masur
The Record Online, Spring 2008

Over the past four decades, Judge Richard A. Posner, a judge of the Seventh Circuit Court of Appeals and longtime member of the Law School faculty, has built a reputation as one of the nation's foremost polymaths. He has authored influential and provocative works that span a vast swath of law and life, ranging from antitrust regulation to human sexuality, to national security, to political philosophy, and to climate change and catastrophe, to name just a few.

In his latest book, *How Judges Think,* Judge Posner turns his formidable analytical lens on an especially well-suited target: his own profession. Drawing upon law and economics (the field he helped to found), behavioral psychology, and political theory, Posner presents a more comprehensive portrait of the judicial mind than has ever before been attempted. In so doing, he offers a biting critique of the many misconceptions about judging that have been held by scholars, the public, and even the judges themselves. What follows is a conversation between Judge Posner and Jonathan Masur, Assistant Professor of Law and one of Judge Posner's former clerks.

JM: Your description of judges is striking for the lack of resemblance it bears to the standard portrayals of the judicial figure. According to your model, how do judges behave, and how has public—or even scholarly—perception of their work come to be so skewed?

RP: American judges operate in a setting of extreme uncertainty, which forces them to exercise an uncomfortably large amount of discretion, casting them often in the role of de facto legislators. They are reluctant to admit that they are (as I call them in the book) "occasional legislators," and have been skillful in concealing the fact from the public, being abetted in this regard by the legal profession, which has an interest in depicting the law as a domain of sophisticated reasoning rather than, to a considerable extent, of politics, intuition, and emotion. The secrecy of judicial deliberations is an example of the tactics used by the judiciary to conceal the extent to which such deliberations resemble those of ordinary people attempting to resolve disputes in circumstances of uncertainty. The concealment feeds a mystique of professionalism that strengthens the judiciary in its competition for power with the executive and legislative branches of government, the branches that judges like to call "political" in asserted contradistinction to the judicial branch.

JM: There is an easy caricature of your position that ignores the word "occasional" and paints judges as unbound, feckless politicians. This view of judging gained quite a bit of popular currency after the Supreme Court's decision in *Bush v. Gore,* one that struck most observers as patently ideological. You don't entirely reject this model of judging, but neither do you embrace it. Where do you think it has gone wrong, or in what way is its focus too narrow?

RP: I don't think it's wrong, but it's incomplete insofar as it focuses entirely on the political motivations of judges. Those motivations are important, though it is simplistic to equate them with loyalty to a political party, but they are not the only important elements of a judge's motivational structure. *Bush v. Gore* actually illustrates the point. The decision is not conservative from the standpoint of political ideology; it is liberal. The most plausible explanation for the outcome is that judges, including Supreme Court justices, want their colleagues and successors to be like-minded to them, and so they want as President someone who can be expected to appoint such judges when vacancies occur.

JM: Judges, as you describe them, approach cases very much as a layperson might: influenced by politics, intuition, and emotion, wanting to be surrounded by like-minded colleagues, and (as you say in the book) with an eye towards consequences and common sense. Isn't this somewhat surprising? Wouldn't we expect the judicial profession, by its very nature, to attract only certain types of people— people with particularly great reverence for the determinacy of language or the power of reasoning by logical syllogism, for instance?

RP: That's an excellent question, one I should have devoted more attention to. The answer I think is that confronted with having to decide an actual case, the judge discovers (consciously or not) that semantic and logical analysis simply will not yield a "reasonable" answer, where what is reasonable depends on ideology, common sense, human emotions, and other factors that are not part of formal legal analysis.

JM: A portion of your book is devoted to discussing the failings of modern lawyers, who believe that law is a purely legalistic system and so provide judges with none of the purpose-driven or policy arguments that judges would find useful. Why do you think it is that lawyers have failed to adapt to pragmatic judging despite operating within such a competitive marketplace? Shouldn't lawyers have learned long ago that their typical arguments regarding precedent and language are of extremely limited value?

RP: I don't have a good answer. Your point about competition is a challenge to the answer I suggest in the book, which is that legal education has refused to be realistic about judges. Lawyers eventually learn that judges are more realistic than formalistic, but they have not been equipped by their education to articulate and substantiate pragmatic arguments in a form convincing to judges. Of course there are exceptions, and judges will make pragmatic judgments even if given little help by the lawyers. But their judgments would be sounder if they got more help from the lawyers.

JM: How is it that law schools have come to play such a substantial role in fostering this level of ineptitude within the profession? American legal education (and even much modern legal scholarship) focuses predominantly on the study of appellate decisions. Why haven't law schools done a more capable job of informing their students as to what really drives those decisions?

RP: The law schools naturally focus on imparting the vocabulary and rhetoric of legal rules and standards, without which one cannot function as a lawyer. And increasingly, with the rise of law and economics (economic analysis of law), the law schools provide students with sophisticated policy analysis of those rules and standards. What they do not much do is take the next step and impart a realistic understanding of the judicial process and of how, in light of such an understanding, to present cases most effectively to judges and juries.

JM: The principal goal of your book is to describe what judges are actually doing, as opposed to prescribing what you believe they should do. And yet many, if not most, sitting judges—including some of the country's most prominent jurists—would disagree (at least publicly) with your claims. Do these judges simply not understand their own work? Or have they found a reason to perpetuate a public perception that does not reflect reality?

RP: I think there is a degree of self-deception. A judge is more comfortable in thinking that his decisions are compelled by "the law"—something external to his own preferences—than by his personal ideology, intuitions, or suite of emotions. But there is also a natural tendency to try to reassure the public that judicial discretion is minimal, in order to defend the legitimacy of the judiciary. The tendency is paradoxically most pronounced at the Supreme Court level, the paradox being that it is the most political court. Precisely because it is a political court, its members feel the greatest need to deny that it is that. The aim is to enhance judicial power relative to that of other branches of government. I am not, however, meaning to suggest that it is wrong for the judges to be concerned about their power relative to those branches. The judiciary is a vital branch of government and needs to protect itself against inroads, though I am sympathetic to arguments that the judiciary, and in particular the Supreme Court, flexes its muscles too strongly.

3
Politics and the Court

© Bill Clark/CQ Roll Call/Getty Images

Sen. John Barrasso (R-WY), does an interview with CNN in front of the Supreme Court building shortly before the politically fraught ruling on the Affordable Care Act, June 28, 2012.

The Supreme Court and the Political Landscape

It is the stuff of standard television drama: A suspect is taken in by the police and read their Miranda rights—a procedure so codified that most of the viewing audience can recite right along with the police officer: "You have the right to remain silent. Anything you say can, and will, be used against you . . . " Miranda rights have been so absorbed into the general cultural fabric that its origins have been basically forgotten. Miranda rights stem from the questionable confession of accused criminal Ernesto Miranda, who was finally exonerated in a seminal 1966 Supreme Court ruling in a case known as *Miranda v. Arizona*.

The Court's Influence

The Supreme Court has become such a part of the American political landscape that it is easy to overlook the Court's vast influence, past and present. The Court is dwarfed in size and scope by the executive branch (the president) and the legislative branch (the Congress). After all, as Alexander Hamilton observed, the executive branch holds the sword; the legislative holds the purse. For generations and generations of schoolchildren, American history has been the study of pivotal battles, famous speeches, and presidential administrations. The Supreme Court—the judicial branch—is usually treated as an afterthought.

But the Supreme Court has always had a monumental influence on both sword and purse. In the 1830s the French aristocrat Alexis de Tocqueville arrived in the United States and some years later wrote *Democracy in America*, his perceptive study of the American political system. Even in this early era of American democracy, de Tocqueville observed that the Court's "power extends to all cases arising under laws and treaties made by the national authorities . . . and, in general, to all points that affect the law of nations. . . . Its sole object is to enforce the execution of the laws of the Union."

The Court's decisions—for good and ill—have had a monumental impact on the course of American history. The infamous *Dred Scott v. Sandford* ruling (1857) declared that black men, whether slave or free, could never become full citizens. Chief Justice Roger Taney, while conceding the point that the Declaration of Independence contained the words "all men are created equal," nonetheless asserted "that the enslaved African race were not intended to be included." To Taney, this seemed obvious. To abolitionists, anti-slavery forces, and politicians such as Abraham Lincoln himself, it represented a challenge too great to ignore. *Plessy v. Ferguson* (1896), another low point in the Court's history, enshrined the concept of "separate but equal" and did a great deal to legitimize segregation and racism, effectively rolling back many of the gains in racial equality since the end of the Civil War in 1865.

And in so many instances, of course, the effect was just the opposite. In perhaps the most renowned ruling in the Court's history, *Brown v. Board of Education* (1954) established a new, simple precedent: Segregation was illegal. The Supreme Court had made a unanimous, emphatic ruling that became a catalyst for the modern civil rights movement. This was the beginning of the era known as the Warren Court—a Supreme Court headed by Chief Justice Earl Warren that tackled societal ills and redressed inequities to an unprecedented extent. It was a controversial chapter of judicial history that to this day has its vehement defenders and detractors.

The Court and Controversy

The Supreme Court has ruled on just about every hot-button issue of the day—with rulings that have an immediate, personal effect: *Loving v. Virginia,* for example, was a pivotal ruling that overturned racist state laws banning interracial marriage. (And yes, interracial marriage was still illegal in some parts of the country up to 1967.) Since the days of the Warren era, the Court has become a politically charged entity and now is a looming issue in every presidential campaign. 1973's *Roe v. Wade* greatly expanded abortion rights and has set off a continuous legal and political battle that, in the last forty years, has only gained in intensity, its anniversary celebrated by supporters and mourned by opponents.

The Supreme Court was pulled front and center to arbitrate on a high-profile case of enormous consequence: the election of the president of the United States. In the 2000 presidential election between Vice President Al Gore and Governor George W. Bush of Texas, the results hinged on the disputed, make-or-break results from the state of Florida. Forty-seven election-related lawsuits were filed in Florida, and for more than a month the nation had no president-elect. Eventually, the Court's 5–4 ruling in *Bush v. Gore* yielded the presidency of George W. Bush—and, like *Roe v. Wade,* lasting controversy.

The Court continues to occupy a pivotal, public role in national policymaking. In 2013 the cause of gay rights—specifically the right of same-sex couples to legally wed—received a pivotal boost when the Court struck down, by a 5–4 vote, a key element to the Defense of Marriage Act (DOMA), which prevented same-sex marriage. DOMA, the Court ruled, was unconstitutional because it violated the right to liberty and equal protection for gay couples.

Likewise, the ongoing debate over the Affordable Care Act—widely known as Obamacare—has played out in the Supreme Court. After the act became law, 26 states and a contingent of organizations sued—unsuccessfully—to eliminate the provisions of the Affordable Care Act. The battle and the litigation continued, as it does with other issues that fall under the Court's jurisdiction: the rights and legal status of immigrants; free-speech and privacy issues on Facebook and social media; campaign-finance regulations, and the racial composition of voting districts. And, according to a 2014 story in the *Economist,* the Court grappled with who, precisely, has the power to whiten teeth: "Just over a decade ago the North Carolina Board of Dental Examiners noticed that many people were getting their teeth whitened at spas or kiosks in shopping centers. The procedure typically involves placing dispos- able strips impregnated with a whitening agent . . . the strips are deemed safe by the Food and Drug Administration and regulated as cosmetics. Salons charge as little as a tenth as much for this service as a dentist would do." The North Carolina board tried to shut these endeavors down, "accusing them of practicing dentistry without a license and driving them out of business." There is something undeniably amusing about this case. But there is also a serious overlay: The Supreme Court— perhaps more than any other branch of government—has a broad-ranging influence intimately involved with day-to-day life.

Judicial Impartiality and Political Pressure

Just how impartial is the Supreme Court? It is an endless, open question that spawns yet more debate. The Justices, steeped in the tradition of judicial impartial- ity and appointed to life terms, should, theoretically, be immune from political pres- sure. There is also—crucially—the bedrock "concept of stare decisis, or adherence to the decisions made in prior cases," as Suzanna Sherry has written, which "limits the range of the Court's discretion. Absent extraordinary circumstances, the Su- preme Court will follow precedent—the cases it has previously decided. Even jus- tices who might disagree with a precedent (including those who dissented when the case was originally decided) will almost always feel bound to apply it to later cases. As decisions on a particular issue accumulate, the Court might clarify or modify its doctrines, but the earlier precedents will mark the starting point. . . . Stare decisis ensures that doctrinal changes are likely to be gradual rather than abrupt and that well-entrenched decisions are unlikely to be overturned. This gradual evolution of doctrine, in turn, fosters stability and predictability, both of which are necessary in a nation committed to the rule of law."

But no matter how impartial the justices, they are, after all, still flesh-and-blood human beings under their black robes. "Politics," Nan Aron has written ("The Su- preme Court: Just Politics by Other Means?," Huffington Post, June 26, 2012), "is inherently part of the judicial system. Supreme Court justices don't come from some mystical Planet Purity, having lived lives devoid of politics or the taint of ideol- ogy. We don't recruit judges from monasteries."

The current Roberts Court—led by Chief Justice John Roberts—often divides along the lines of Democratic and Republican appointees. And yet the Court's swing voter—the Justice least tethered to one particular judicial philosophy—is Anthony Kennedy, a Republican appointee. Chief Justice Earl Warren and Justice William Brennan—both legendary liberals who had a profound influence on the Court's legacy—were appointed by Dwight Eisenhower, a Republican. Harry Blackmun, a Justice appointed by Republican Richard Nixon, became a reliably liberal member of the Court and provided the ideological impetus for *Roe v. Wade.* Byron White, the only Justice nominated by John Kennedy, became a conservative force on the Court, dissenting from many of the Court's liberal opinions and developing more of a kinship not with the progressive Warren Court, but the more conservative Court of Chief Justice William Rehnquist. Although there has been data collected on the voting patterns on the various Justices throughout history—including the formulation of Martin-Quinn scores, which chart and codify the ideological leanings of the Supreme Court—it is not, by any stretch, an exact science.

The Court was historically viewed as an impartial entity, altogether separate from the political rough-and-tumble. This view has undergone an enormous transformation—to the chagrin of many, including Chief Justice John Roberts. "We are not Democrats and Republicans in how we go about it," Roberts claimed in a 2014 talk at the University of Nebraska College of Law. "We're not subject to the popular will." The Chief Justice has framed his own judicial approach in baseball terms: as an umpire calling balls and strikes.

The contradiction of the Supreme Court is that it is a steadying, august body, but also very changeable: a vacancy, a new president, can dramatically shift the ideological balance. There is an inherent element of volatility to the Court.

Predicting the future of the Supreme Court is a near-impossibility. What is certain, though, is that the Court will continue to dominate the headlines, will continue to generate controversy, and will play a front-and-center role in the lives of the American public.

—Richard Klin

Bibliography

Banks, Christopher P., and John C. Green., eds. *Superintending Democracy: The Courts and the Political Process.* Akron, OH: University of Akron Press, 2001.

Bickel, Alexander M. *The Last Dangerous Branch: The Supreme Court at the Bar of Politics.* 2d ed. New Haven: Yale University Press, 1986.

Chemerinsky, Erwin. *The Case against the Supreme Court.* New York: Viking, 2014.

Coyle, Marcia. *The Roberts Court: The Struggle for the Constitution.* New York: Simon & Schuster, 2013.

Hansford, Thomas G., and James F, Spriggs II. *The Politics of Precedent on the U.S. Supreme Court.* Princeton, NJ: Princeton University Press, 2006.

Kahn, Ronald, and Ken I. Kersch, eds. *The Supreme Court and American Political Development.* Lawrence: University Press of Kansas, 2006.

Keck, Thomas M. *The Most Activist Supreme Court in History: The Road to Modern Judicial Conservatism.* Chicago: University of Chicago Press, 2004.

McKenna, Marian C. *Franklin Roosevelt and the Great Constitutional War: The Court-Packing Crisis of 1937.* New York: Fordham University Press, 2002.

Miller, Mark. *Exploring Judicial Politics.* New York: Oxford University Press, 2009.

Peabody, Bruce, ed. *The Politics of Judicial Independence: Courts, Politics, and the Public.* Baltimore: Johns Hopkins University Press, 2011.

Powe, Lucas A. Jr. *The Warren Court and American Politics.* Cambridge, MA: Belknap Press of Harvard University Press, 2000.

Rosen, Jeffrey. *The Most Democratic Branch: How the Courts Serve America.* New York: Oxford University Press, 2006.

Tribe, Laurence H., and Joshua Matz. *Uncertain Justice: The Roberts Court and the Constitution.* New York: H. Holt, 2014.

Whittington, Keith E. *Political Foundations of Judicial Supremacy: The Presidency, the Supreme Court, and Constitutional Leadership in U.S. History.* Princeton, NJ: Princeton University Press, 2007.

Zelden, Charles L. *The Supreme Court and Elections: Into the Thicket.* Washington, DC: CQ Press, 2010.

Can the Supreme Court Be Rescued from Politics?

By Scott Lemieux
The Week, May 15, 2014

During his Supreme Court confirmation hearings in 2005, John Roberts famously claimed that a justice's job is "to call balls and strikes and not to pitch or bat." Similarly, in 2009, Sonia Sotomayor pledged her "fidelity to the law," perpetuating the notion that the law is some objective standard that can be applied uniformly to cases that come before the nation's highest court.

But recent evidence shows that the notion of an apolitical Supreme Court has only become more antiquated.

Adam Liptak, the invaluable Supreme Court reporter for the *The New York Times,* recently wrote about a study conducted by the legal scholars Lee Epstein, Christopher Parker, and Jeffrey Segal. The study showed that Supreme Court justices betrayed "in-group" bias in their First Amendment jurisprudence—that is, they were more likely to uphold the First Amendment claims of defendants whose speech they liked.

The findings of the study are consistent with what Segal and Harold Spaeth have called the "attitudinal model" of judging. This model holds that Supreme Court votes are explained by what judges consider desirable policy. Samuel Alito votes the way he does because of his conservative politics, and likewise Ruth Bader Ginsburg votes the way she does to achieve liberal ends. Contrary to the balls-and-strikes analogy, every case by definition is one in which reasonable people can disagree about what the law requires, which means we're particularly likely to see voting based primarily on political preferences.

To be sure, like all social science models, the attitudinal model is an oversimplification. Supreme Court voting is too complex to be explained by any single factor. As Epstein's own research has proven, Supreme Court justices do not just vote their sincere preferences, but also for strategic reasons—both to assemble majority coalitions on the court and because Supreme Court decisions generally need compliance by other political actors to be carried out. There are also cases, believe it or not, when a justice's notion of good law trumps his or her political preferences.

The court's decision narrowly upholding the Affordable Care Act—but striking down the ACA's mechanism for funding Medicaid—is a case in point. A majority of the justices applied conceptions of national power that, for better or worse, they've applied in cases that considered both conservative and liberal policies. These judicial preferences are not "apolitical"—there are reasons why liberals tend to favor expansive federal power and conservatives are less likely to—but they're not identical to the votes of legislators.

Antonin Scalia and Anthony Kennedy, on the other hand, appeared to vote opportunistically, holding that the ACA was unconstitutional despite having upheld expansive assertions of federal power by the administration of George W. Bush. The votes of Stephen Breyer and Elena Kagan to strike down the Medicaid funding mechanism were most likely strategic. And, finally, it's hard to explain Roberts' idiosyncratic vote to hold the ACA unconstitutional under the commerce power, but constitutional under the tax power, unless it was his genuine view about what the law required.

Supreme Court voting, in other words, is influenced by a complex mix of variables, and what is "law" and what is "politics" cannot be defined with mathematical precision.

If the attitudinal model is an oversimplification, however, it still contains a great deal of truth. The fact that First Amendment jurisprudence is significantly colored by the identity of the speaker and the content of the speech is a case in point.

The frequently political nature of Supreme Court votes is particularly important because of another phenomenon recently discussed by Liptak: partisan polarization. Just as for much of the 20th century American political parties were loose aggregations, Supreme Court justices did not have ideological views that fell neatly along party lines. Both Woodrow Wilson and FDR appointed staunch liberals and racist Southern segregationists to the Supreme Court. Several of the most liberal judges of the second half of the 20th century—William Brennan, Earl Warren, and John Paul Stevens—were Republican nominees, while JFK nominee Byron White dissented in *Miranda v. Arizona* (which established Miranda rights) and *Roe v. Wade* (which upheld the right to an abortion).

Now, Democratic and Republican appointments are very ideologically predictable. The four most liberal justices on the court are Democratic nominees, and the five most conservative justices are Republican nominees. Moreover, it is nearly certain that any nominee selected by a Republican president would be more consistently conservative than the court's current swing vote, Kennedy.

The result going forward is likely to be what the political scientist Mark Graber calls a"constitutional yo-yo," in which the Supreme Court lurches between periods of consistently conservative and liberal outcomes rather than producing decisions that tend to fall within the center of public opinion (as has been the historical norm).

There is, however, an important proviso. Partisan polarization in American politics has not been symmetrical—the Republican Party has moved much more to the right than the Democratic Party has to the left. This asymmetrical polarization is also visible on the Supreme Court. The First Amendment study shows liberal justices having a modest tendency to favor liberal speakers, while conservative justices have a huge tendency to favor conservative ones. (Scalia, Clarence Thomas, and

Roberts are more than 40 percent more likely to favor conservative speakers, while for Ginsburg and Stevens the figure is under 20 percent, and with Breyer the favoritism shown to liberal speakers is tiny.)

This asymmetrical polarization is not visible just in First Amendment cases, either. The court's four most conservative members are among the four most conservative justices to have served on the Supreme Court since World War II, with the court's most liberal current member (Ginsburg) well to the right of Warren Court-era liberals like William Brennan and Thurgood Marshall.

All of this means that future Supreme Court choices have the potential to have a huge impact on the country. It's not clear, however, that both parties have an equal understanding of this: While the Bush administration saw the confirmation of unapologetically conservative justices like Roberts and Alito, the Obama administration has worked to nominate those—Sotomayor and Kagan—who are considered fairly moderate on the liberal spectrum.

Politicizing the Supreme Court

By Eric Hamilton
Stanford Law Review, August 30, 2012

To state the obvious, Americans do not trust the federal government, and that in-cludes the Supreme Court. Americans believe politics played "too great a role" in the recent health care cases by a greater than two-to-one margin.[1] Only thirty-seven percent of Americans express more than some confidence in the Supreme Court.[2] Academics continue to debate how much politics actually influences the Court, but Americans are excessively skeptical. They do not know that almost half of the cases this Term were decided unanimously, and the Justices' voting pattern split by the political party of the president to whom they owe their appointment in fewer than seven percent of cases.[3] Why the mistrust? When the Court is front-page, above-the-fold news after the rare landmark decision or during infrequent U.S. Senate confirmation proceedings, political rhetoric from the President and Congress drowns out the Court. Public perceptions of the Court are shaped by politicians' arguments "for" or "against" the ruling or the nominee, which usually fall along partisan lines and sometimes are based on misleading premises that ignore the Court's special, nonpolitical responsibilities.

The Framers of the Constitution designed a uniquely independent Supreme Court that would safeguard the Constitution. They feared that the political branch-es might be able to overwhelm the Court by turning the public against the Court and that the Constitution's strict boundaries on congressional power would give way. As evidenced in the health care cases, politicians across the ideological spec-trum have played into some of the Framers' fears for the Constitution by politicizing the decision and erasing the distinction between the Court's holding and the policy merits of the heath care law. Paradoxically, many of the elected officials who proudly campaign under the battle cry of "saving our Constitution" endanger the Court and the Constitution with their bombast. Politicization of the Supreme Court causes the American public to lose faith in the Court, and when public confidence in the Court is low, the political branches are well positioned to disrupt the constitutional balance of power between the judiciary and the political branches.

The Framers' Supreme Court

It would have been unsurprising had the Constitutional Convention granted Con-gress the power to take a vote to change Supreme Court decisions. In fact, the antifederalists' chief argument against the judiciary was that it was too powerful

From 65 Stan. L. Rev. Online 35 © 2012 Eric Hamilton.

without a congressional revisionary power on Court opinions.[4] Many of the early state constitutions that were enacted between the Revolution and the ratification of the U.S. Constitution permitted the state executive and legislature to remove, override, or influence judges. Rhode Island judges were called before the legislature to testify when they invalidated legislative acts.[5] The New Hampshire legislature vacated judicial proceedings, modified judgments, authorized appeals, and decided the merits of some disputes.[6]

Instead, the Framers created a Supreme Court that was independent from the political branches and insulated from public opinion. The Supreme Court would be the intermediary between the people and the legislature to ensure that Congress obeyed the Constitution. Congress could not be trusted to police itself for compliance with the Constitution's limited legislative powers. Courts would be "the bulwarks of a limited Constitution against legislative encroachments."[7]

Still, the Framers believed Congress would overshadow the Supreme Court. The Framers were so concerned about helping the Court repel attacks by the legislature that they considered boosting its power and inserting it into political issues. James Madison's draft of the Constitution included an additional check against congressional power, the Council of Revision.[8] Instead of the presidential veto, the Council would have placed several Supreme Court Justices on a council with the President or asked the President and the Supreme Court to separately approve legislation before it became law.[9] Justices would have the power to oppose legislation on nonlegal policy grounds. The Council is nowhere to be found in the Convention's final product, but delegates' arguments from the Council debates reveal a suspicion of Congress, fear for the Court's ability to defend itself, and concern for the Court's public reputation. Madison believed that even with the Council, Congress would be an "overmatch" for the Supreme Court and President and cited the experience of spurned state supreme courts.

> Experience in all the States had evinced a powerful tendency in the Legislature to absorb all power into its vortex. This was the real source of danger to the American Constitutions; & suggested the necessity of giving every defensive authority to the other departments that was consistent with republican principles.[10]

Delegates ultimately decided that politicizing the Court would undercut its legitimacy. Luther Martin, a delegate who later became Maryland's longest-serving attorney general, offered the most prescient comment on the subject: "It is necessary that the Supreme Judiciary should have the confidence of the people. This will soon be lost, if they are employed in the task of remonstrating [against] popular measures of the Legislature."[11] "It was making the Expositors of the Laws, the Legislators which ought never to be done," added Elbridge Gerry, a Massachusetts delegate.[12]

"Saving the Constitution from the Court"

The Framers correctly connected loss of public confidence in the Court with judicial policymaking. Of course, the Constitution does not force judges to "remonstrate" against legislation, but experience proves Martin to be correct. Too often that becomes the public perception when Congress and the President politicize the Supreme Court. Chief Justice Roberts started and ended his health care opinion with the basics—the important distinction between whether the Affordable Care Act is good policy from whether it is a constitutional law. Within two hours, President Obama and Mitt Romney, both Harvard Law School graduates, looked into television cameras and told Americans the opposite. "Today, the Supreme Court also upheld the principle that people who can afford health insurance should take the responsibility to buy health insurance," said Obama.[13] Romney criticized the majority for deciding not to "repeal Obamacare." "What the Court did not do on its last day in session, I will do on my first day if elected President," said Romney.[14]

Congress and the President have belittled the Court. President Obama told the public at the 2010 State of the Union address that "the Supreme Court reversed a century of law" with its *Citizens United* decision and suggested that the Court opposed honest elections. The ensuing image was even more damaging. With 48 million Americans watching, the camera panned to a cadre of expressionless Supreme Court Justices sitting in the front row while lawmakers sitting next to them rose to their feet and applauded.[15] Presidents Obama and Bush and members of Congress have derided the Court for its "unelected" nature, with President Obama publicly wondering before the health care decision whether "an unelected group of people would somehow overturn a duly constituted and passed law."[16]

Judges lack clear defenses. Judges would risk their credibility if they shouted back at the President, appeared on the Sunday morning talk shows, or held a press conference after a decision. Unlike speeches from members of Congress and the President, Supreme Court proceedings are difficult to follow without legal training. The media coverage of the Supreme Court can be incomplete or inaccurate. FOX News and CNN famously misunderstood Chief Justice Roberts' oral opinion and misreported that the individual mandate had been invalidated. The publicly available audio recordings of oral arguments contribute little to public understanding of the Court. Even before the decision, the Republican Party doctored audio clips of Solicitor General Don Verrilli coughing and pausing during oral argument to suggest in an ad suggesting that the health care law was indefensible.[17]

Politicization of the Court is dangerous because it primes the public for a power grab by the political branches. If the Court loses authority to check political power and make unpopular decisions, it cannot enforce the Constitution with the same effectiveness. Without enforcement of the Constitution, Congress is free to invade constitutional rights and exceed its lawful powers.

The Supreme Court came frighteningly close to losing some of its independence when the Court made politically significant decisions striking down parts of the New Deal, and President Franklin D. Roosevelt responded with the Court-packing plan. His arguments alleged misconduct by the Court.

The Courts, however, have cast doubts on the ability of the elected Congress to protect us against catastrophe by meeting squarely our modern social and economic conditions. . . . The Court has been acting not as a judicial body, but as a policymaking body. . . . We have, therefore, reached the point as a nation where we must take action to save the Constitution from the Court and the Court from itself. We must find a way to take an appeal from the Supreme Court to the Constitution itself.[18]

Roosevelt's words from seventy-five years ago could be repeated today by Court opponents. In his recent presidential primary campaign, Newt Gingrich promised to employ the tactics of early state constitutions by ignoring disagreeable Court decisions and ordering Justices to testify to congressional committees.[19]Proposals to invade the Court's independence ignore the Framers' fears for enforcement of the Constitution without the Supreme Court. Madison believed if the legislature and executive united behind a law and convinced the public that it was in their interest, the people could not properly judge its constitutionality, even if it was patently unconstitutional. The "passions" of the people on the particular issues would prevail over well-reasoned constitutional judgment.[20]

***

The health care law's closely watched journey through the three branches of government concluded in the Supreme Court, a rare opportunity in the sun for the Court. What would have been a shining moment for the Constitution in a vacuum was instead validation of the Framers' apprehensions. Our Constitution is the longest-lasting in the world because of Americans' enduring reverence for it. But when elected officials exploit Americans' patriotism to score political points, they jeopardize the Framers' carefully constructed balance of power. Instead, honest public discourse on the Constitution and the Court is the surest security for our government.

Notes

1. Lydia Saad, "Americans Issue Split Decision on Healthcare Ruling," Gallup (June 29, 2012), http://www.gallup.com/poll/155447/Americans-Issue-Split-Decision-Healthcare-Ruling.aspx; Frank Newport et al., "Gallup Editors: Americans' Views on the Healthcare Law," Gallup (June 22, 2012), http://www.gallup.com/poll/155300/Gallup-Editors-Americans-Views-Healthcare-Law.aspx.

2. Jeffrey M. Jones, "Confidence in U.S. Public Schools at New Low," Gallup (June 20, 2012), http://www.gallup.com/poll/155258/confidence-public-schools-new-low.aspx.

3. "Stat Pack for October Term 2011," SCOTUSblog 5, 14 (June 30, 2012), http://dailywrit.com/blog/uploads/2012/06/SCOTUSblog_Stat_Pack_OT11_final.pdf.

4. See "Brutus No. 15" (Robert Yates) (Morton Borden ed., 1965), available at http://www.constitution.org/afp/brutus15.htm.

5. Daniel A. Farber and Suzanna Sherry, *A History of the American Constitution* 67 (2d ed. 2005).

6. Edward S. Corwin, "The Progress of Constitutional Theory Between the Declaration of Independence and the Meeting of the Philadelphia Convention," in *The Confederation and the Constitution: The Critical Issues* 18 (Gordon S. Wood ed., 1973).

7. See *The Federalist* No. 78, at 437 (Alexander Hamilton) (Clinton Rossiter ed., 1961).

8. James Madison, Tuesday May 29 in Convention, in 1 *The Records of the Federal Convention of 1787*, at 21 (Max Farrand ed., 1937).

9. It is difficult to visualize the effects of the Council of Revision if it had been included in the Constitution. Imagine that when Congress approved the Affordable Care Act, it was never taken to the White House for presentment. Rather, if the Council included the two most senior Supreme Court Justices, then President Obama, Chief Justice Roberts, and Justice Scalia might have met in the Capitol at a regular Council meeting and announced in a postmeeting press conference that the Council had rejected it. Assume Chief Justice Roberts believed the law was bad policy. Justice Scalia might say the bill was unconstitutional and a bad bill, President Obama would say it was constitutional and a good bill, and Chief Justice Roberts might say it was constitutional but a bad bill. Had the Framers split the revisionary power between the Court and the President, perhaps the Court would have announced before President Obama's signing ceremony that it had rejected the bill by a vote of five to four, with Chief Justice Roberts casting the decisive vote against the bill on policy grounds despite majority support for the bill's constitutionality.

10. James Madison, Saturday July 21 in Convention, in 2 *The Records of the Federal Convention of 1787*, at 74 (Max Farrand ed., 1937).

11. Id. at 77.

12. Id. at 75.

13. "Remarks on the United States Supreme Court Ruling on the Patient Protection and Affordable Care Act," 2012 Daily Comp. Pres. Doc. 521 (June 28, 2012), available at http://www.gpo.gov/fdsys/pkg/DCPD-201200521/pdf/DCPD-201200521.pdf.

14. Mitt Romney, "Remarks on the Supreme Court's Decision on President Obama's Healthcare Law" (June 28, 2012), available at http://www.mittromney.com/news/press/2012/06/mitt-romney-i-will-repeal-obamacare-0.

15. "Address before a Joint Session of the Congress on the State of the Union," 2010 Daily Comp. Pres. Doc. 55, at 8 (Jan. 27, 2010), available at http://www.gpo.gov/fdsys/pkg/DCPD-201000055/pdf/DCPD-201000055.pdf; "Obama Criticizes Supreme Court in State of the Union Address," YouTube (Jan. 28, 2010), http://www.youtube.com/watch?v=BiDiHX50zT4.

16. "The President's News Conference with President Felipe de Jesus Calderon Hinojosa of Mexico and Prime Minister Stephen Harper of Canada," 2012 Daily Comp. Pres. Doc. 241, at 7 (April 2, 2012), available at http://www.gpo.gov/fdsys/pkg/DCPD-201200241/pdf/DCPD-201200241.pdf.

17. Julie Hirschfeld Davis and Greg Stohr, "Republicans Tampered with Court Audio in Obama Attack Ad," Bloomberg (Mar. 30, 2012), http://www.bloomberg.com/news/2012-03-29/republicans-tampered-with-court-audio-in-obama-attack-ad.html; see Republican Nat'l Comm., "ObamaCare: It's a Tough Sell," YouTube (Mar. 28, 2012), http://www.youtube.com/watch?v=MXhLtb-NKY0.

18. President Franklin D. Roosevelt, "Fireside Chat on Reorganization of the Judiciary" (Mar. 9, 1937), available at http://xroads.virginia.edu/~ma02/volpe/newdeal/court_fireside_text.html.

19. See Alexander Bolton, "Gingrich: Congress Can Send Capitol Police to Arrest Rogue Judges," *The Hill* (Dec. 18, 2011 12:06 PM), http://thehill.com/blogs/ballot-box/gop-presidential-primary/200149-gingrich-congress-can-send-capitol-police-marshals-to-arrest-judges; David G. Savage, "Newt Gingrich Says He'd Defy Supreme Court Rulings He Opposed," *L.A. Times* (Dec. 17, 2011 1:52 PM), http://www.latimes.com/news/politics/la-pn-gingrich-judges-20111217,0,1295899.story.

20. See *The Federalist* Nos. 48, 49 (James Madison) (Clinton Rossiter ed., 1961).

By Any Means Necessary

By Linda Greenhouse
The New York Times, August 20, 2014

The Affordable Care Act—Obamacare—has endured so many near-death experiences that digging into the details of still another effort to demolish it is admittedly not an inviting prospect. (My own reaction, I confess, to hearing some months back about the latest legal challenge—this one aimed at the supposed effect of a single word in the 900-page statute—was something along the lines of "wake me when it's over.")

But stay with me, because this latest round, catapulted onto the Supreme Court's docket earlier this month by the same forces that brought us the failed Commerce Clause attack two years ago, opens a window on raw judicial politics so extreme that the saga so far would be funny if the potential consequences weren't so serious.

To be clear, I'm not suggesting that there is anything wrong with turning to the courts to achieve what politics won't deliver; we all know that litigation is politics by other means. (Think school desegregation. Think reproductive rights. Think, perhaps, same-sex marriage.) Nor is the creativity and determination of the Affordable Care Act's opponents any great revelation—not after they came within a hairsbreadth of getting the law's individual mandate thrown out on a constitutional theory that would have been laughed out of court not too many years ago.

Boy, are they ever determined. Flash back to December 2010, when the Commerce Clause challenges to the new law were beginning to fill the legal pipeline en route to the Supreme Court. At a conference held at the American Enterprise Institute, a conservative research organization in Washington, Michael S. Greve, an A.E.I. scholar and chairman of the Competitive Enterprise Institute, had this to say in reference to the Affordable Care Act:

> "This bastard has to be killed as a matter of political hygiene. I do not care how this is done, whether it's dismembered, whether we drive a stake through its heart, whether we tar and feather it and drive it out of town, whether we strangle it. I don't care who does it, whether it's some court some place, or the United States Congress. Any which way, any dollar spent on that goal is worth spending, any brief filed toward that end is worth filing, any speech or panel contribution toward that end is of service to the United States."

Mr. Greve went on to urge a litigating strategy that looked beyond the mandate to "concentrate on bits and pieces of this law."

And that's exactly what his Competitive Enterprise Institute proceeded to do. It is financing a set of lawsuits with a seemingly modest ambition: seeking not a constitutional ruling but a mere statutory interpretation. The suits put forward an interpretation of the statutory language that would deny tax credits to people who buy insurance on the exchanges set up by the federal government in the 36 states that have refused to establish their own exchanges. If the Supreme Court buys that statutory argument, a core goal of the Affordable Care Act—facilitating the purchase of insurance by people of modest income—would be undermined to the point of collapse. Modest indeed. . . .

It was at the American Enterprise Institute conference that the statutory argument first came to light, in a PowerPoint presentation by a lawyer from Greenville, S.C., Thomas M. Christina, who specializes in employee benefits. He said he had essentially stumbled on the reference in Section 36B of the act that refers to the availability of tax credits to offset the cost of insurance plans "enrolled in through an exchange established by the state." His conclusion was that the tax credits—the federal subsidy that makes the system work—were not available in what he called the "non-capitulating states," those that refused to set up exchanges and, as another section of the law permitted them to do, left the job to the federal Department of Health and Human Services. . . .

As to the merits, six federal appellate judges have evaluated the statutory argument, and four have rejected it. One judge, Harry T. Edwards of the United States Court of Appeals for the District of Columbia Circuit, called the case "specious," a "not-so-veiled attempt to gut" the law in defiance of "the will of Congress."

The problem is that Judge Edwards's totally persuasive opinion was written in dissent. The majority opinion, concluding that the Internal Revenue Service is without statutory authority to issue tax credits for insurance purchased on the federally established exchanges where more than five million people have bought their health insurance, was written by Judge Thomas B. Griffith and joined by Judge A. Raymond Randolph.

Judge Griffith is a thoughtful judge who spent five years as the Senate's legal counsel; sadly, whatever he learned in that job about the legislative process was not on display in this opinion, *Halbig v. Burwell*. (Of course there are ambiguities and inconsistencies in a 900-page bill that never went to a conference committee for a final stitching together of its many provisions.) Judge Randolph is one of the most outspoken and agenda-driven conservatives on the entire federal bench. In a speech to the far-right Heritage Foundation in 2010, for example, he denounced the Supreme Court for having granted habeas corpus rights to the Guantánamo detainees and compared the justices to Tom and Daisy Buchanan in "The Great Gatsby," "careless people who smashed things up" and "let other people clean up the mess they made."

He then proceeded in a series of opinions on the appeals court to shrink the detainees' habeas right to the vanishing point that it eventually reached.

The decision joined by the two judges trained a laser focus on a single section, indeed on a single word, in the massive statute: the reference to "an exchange established by the state." The opinion not only ignored the broader context, in which Congress clearly intended to make insurance affordable so that as many healthy people as possible would join an economically viable pool, but also rejected the government's argument that language in other sections of the law supported the view that Congress didn't mean to treat the state and federal exchanges differently.

Section 1321(c) provides that if a state fails to establish an exchange, the secretary of Health and Human Services shall "establish and operate such Exchange within the state and the Secretary shall take such actions as are necessary to implement such other requirements." The words "such Exchange," the government argues, mean that the federal government stands in the state's shoes when it complies with this instruction; for these purposes, the federal government is the state.

That interpretation "makes sense," all three members of a three-judge panel of the United States Court of Appeals for the Fourth Circuit, in Richmond, Va., concluded in *King v. Burwell,* a decision that, by an amazing coincidence of timing, was issued the same day, July 22, as the contrary D.C. Circuit opinion. Those three judges, Roger L. Gregory, Stephanie D. Thacker and Andre M. Davis, examined the statute as a whole, in light of its purpose, and at the end of the day found the federal-state issue to be ambiguous. That's all they needed to find for the government to win the case.

The Supreme Court has a clear rule on what courts should do about agency regulations adopted in the face of statutory ambiguity: as long as the agency's action is based on a permissible interpretation of the statute, courts must defer to the agency. The situation is so common that the 30-year-old decision establishing the deference rule, *Chevron v. Natural Resources Defense Council* is one of the most frequently cited of all Supreme Court decisions.

To avoid the *Chevron* rule, the D.C. Circuit majority had to find that the statute was clear in ruling out tax credits on the federal exchanges. The majority even shed a few crocodile tears: "We reach this conclusion, frankly, with reluctance." The conclusion is simply wrong.

In fact, one judge on the Fourth Circuit panel, Andre M. Davis, wrote a separate concurring opinion to say that the statute was completely clear in the other direction. The plaintiffs' argument, he said, was based on "a tortured, nonsensical construction of a federal statute whose manifest purpose, as revealed by the wholeness and coherence of its text and structure, could not be more clear."

With the two contrary decisions having come down on the same day, the judicial politics surrounding the fate of the Affordable Care Act immediately got rich. The Obama administration quickly announced its intention to seek rehearing by the entire 11-member D.C. Circuit; it filed its rehearing petition on August 1. Michael A. Carvin, the lawyer for the law's opponents (he argued the two cases) might have made the same request to the Fourth Circuit. But he did the opposite: he appealed to the Supreme Court, taking only two weeks to file his petition instead of the allotted 90 days. The race was on.

What, exactly, is the race? Clearly, the law's opponents have their best chance—indeed, probably their only chance—in the Supreme Court. They not only lost in the Fourth Circuit, but they are likely to lose in the D.C. Circuit as well if that court, its membership recently bolstered by four Obama appointees, grants rehearing. And conversely, the administration has a clearer path to victory before the entire appeals court than it does in the Supreme Court. So the opponents' challenge is to persuade the justices to take the case as quickly as possible. And the best way to do that is to keep the D.C. Circuit panel's opinion on the books.

Why? Because the one reliable marker of a case the justices deem worthy of their attention is a conflict in the federal circuits on an important legal issue. But a decision by the D.C. Circuit's judges to grant rehearing automatically wipes the panel opinion off the books, even before the rehearing itself takes place. With the panel opinion vacated, there would be no conflict—only a single ruling, a government win in the Fourth Circuit, not (if neutral principles govern, as of course they may not) a particularly attractive case for Supreme Court review.

So the opponents' effort is trained on persuading the D.C. Circuit not to grant rehearing or—if that effort fails—to delegitimize a grant of rehearing in the eyes of friendly Supreme Court justices. The conservative blogosphere has been buzzing with messages to the appeals court, bank shots intended to be read by the justices, or at least their law clerks. Carrie Severino, a former clerk to Justice Clarence Thomas who blogs for *National Review,* wrote earlier this month that "clearly this type of case is exactly what the President had in mind when he made his court-packing blitz last year." Would the new judges be "willing to take the fall for the president in this case," she wondered: "Now those judges will have to decide whether they want their first high-profile act on the court to be one that is baldly political: overturning a meticulously reasoned decision that overturned the IRS's attempt to rewrite the Affordable Care Act. It would make the new judges look like presidential pawns who are attempting to save his bacon, lowering them to the level of the disgraced and politicized IRS itself."

The Volokh Conspiracy blog on *The Washington Post* carried a somewhat more politely worded imprecation to the D.C. Circuit by Jonathan H. Adler, a law professor at Case Western Reserve University and an architect of the statutory strategy. So did the *Wall Street Journal*'s op ed page. All these and others appeared within a day of one another. It's safe to say that never has so much (virtual) ink been spilled in public over the question of whether a federal appeals court should grant a rehearing petition. And for this politically driven crowd to claim the moral high ground in preemptively accusing others of playing politics borders on fantasy.

As I said at the beginning of this column, it would be funny if it wasn't so serious.

Americans Divided on How the Supreme Court Should Interpret the Constitution

By Jocelyn Kiley
Pew Research Center, July 31, 2014

Democrats and Republicans remain deeply divided about how the U.S. Supreme Court should interpret the Constitution, according to a new analysis by the Pew Research Center. And there are many differences across demographic groups—especially when it comes to religious affiliation.

About half of the public (49%) say the decisions of the Supreme Court should be based on its understanding of what the Constitution "means in current times," while roughly as many (46%) say decisions should be based on what the Constitution "meant as it was originally written."

But Republicans—by more than two-to-one (69% to 29%)—say the justices should base their rulings on the Constitution's original meaning rather than on what it means in current times. Democratic opinion goes the other way: 70% say the court should base its rulings on an understanding of the Constitution's meaning in current times (26% say rulings should be based on the document's original meaning). (See Figure 1)

These differing views of how the court should interpret the Constitution may account for some of the partisan differences in opinions of the court itself seen in the Pew Research Center's latest survey.

And these opposing views on constitutional interpretation are even starker along ideological lines. Fully 92% of those who are consistently conservative on a 10-question scale of political values, along with 72% of those who are mostly conservative on this scale, say interpretation should be based on original intent. By contrast, 83% of those with consistently liberal political values, and 70% of those who are mostly liberal, say the justices' rulings should be based on the Constitution's meaning in current times (the items used in the 10-item scale [Appendix A: The Ideological Consistency Scale] can be found [at www.people-press.org/2014/06/12/appendix-a-the-ideological-consistency-scale/] in Pew Research's report on Political Polarization in the American Public).

To some extent, the ideological split in the public's views mirror the ideological divide of the court itself. The originalist position is most closely associated with Justice Scalia, one of the court's conservative justices. Justice Scalia has often publicly stated his view that interpretation should be based on the document as originally written. Though there are differences among the conservative justices on this question, the view that the current meaning should be taken into account in constitutional interpretation is more closely associated with the positions of the court's liberal justices.

Among the public, there are also sizeable differences in views of constitutional interpretation, not just by ideology but also by education, race, age and religion.

For example, while 62% of those with post-graduate degrees say constitutional interpretation should be based on the document's meaning in current times, those who have not graduated from college are more divided on the question (46% current meaning, 49% as originally written). And while about six-in-ten African Americans and Hispanics (61% each) say the court should base its interpretation of the Constitution on the document's meaning in current times, only 44% of whites say so. (See Table 1)

Table 1.

Most Post-Graduates Say Rulings Should be Based on Current Meaning

% who say the Supreme Court should base rulings on what the Constitution...

	Means in current times	Meant as originally written
	%	%
Total	49	46
Men	47	49
Women	52	43
White	44	51
Black	61	33
Hispanic	61	34
18-29	59	38
30-49	50	44
50-64	48	48
65+	39	56
Post grad degree	62	34
College degree	56	40
Some College	49	46
HS or less	44	51
White evang Protestant	23	73
White mainline Protestant	48	44
Black Protestant	57	37
Catholic	54	42
Unaffiliated	63	34

Survey conducted February 12-26, 2014. Don't know responses not shown.

PEW RESEARCH CENTER

But some of the starkest divides are along religious lines. Nearly three-quarters of white evangelical Protestants (73%) say the justices should base their rulings on the original meaning of the Constitution. By contrast, just 44% of white mainline Protestants, 42% of Catholics and 37% of Black Protestants share this view. By nearly two-to-one (63% to 34%), more of those who are unaffiliated with a religious tradition say justices should rule based on the Constitution's meaning in current times. And—in contrast to other demographic differences—religious differences on this question remain significant even when partisanship and ideology are taken into account.

Figure 1.

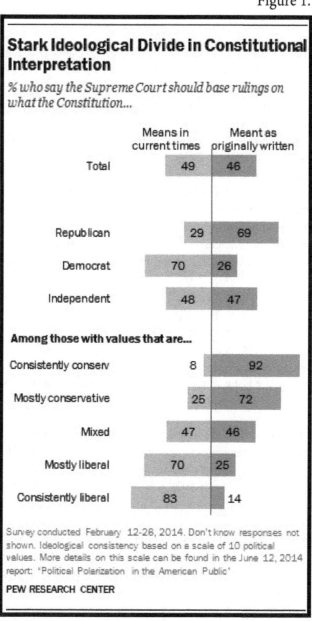

Stark Ideological Divide in Constitutional Interpretation

% who say the Supreme Court should base rulings on what the Constitution...

	Means in current times	Meant as originally written
Total	49	46
Republican	29	69
Democrat	70	26
Independent	48	47

Among those with values that are...

	Means in current times	Meant as originally written
Consistently conserv	8	92
Mostly conservative	25	72
Mixed	47	46
Mostly liberal	70	25
Consistently liberal	83	14

Survey conducted February 12-26, 2014. Don't know responses not shown. Ideological consistency based on a scale of 10 political values. More details on this scale can be found in the June 12, 2014 report: "Political Polarization in the American Public"

PEW RESEARCH CENTER

Fault Lines Re-emerge in Supreme Court at End of Term

By Joan Biskupic
Reuters, July 1, 2014

WASHINGTON, June 30 (Reuters) - Sometimes there is no middle ground. Through much of the U.S. Supreme Court's term, the nine justices found common if narrow ground to bridge their differences. Many of their high-profile decisions avoided the polarization that defines Washington today. That all changed on Monday, the last day of the nine-month term, with the re-emergence of a familiar 5–4 fault line in a dispute over a U.S. law requiring employers to provide insurance for contraceptives.

For 30 minutes Justice Samuel Alito, a conservative who wrote the majority opinion, and liberal Justice Ruth Bader Ginsburg, who wrote the lead dissent, voiced their competing views of the meaning for America of the decision permitting some corporate employers to object on religious grounds to certain kinds of birth control.

In recent weeks the justices had resolved an array of disputes, including over abortion protests and presidential appointment power, police searches of cellphones and environmental regulation, as well as rules for class-action lawsuits.

In all of those, the nine managed to find shared terrain, even some unanimity. In the cases over abortion protests and presidential "recess" appointments, the justices ruled 9–0 on the bottom line, even as four justices broke away each time to protest the majority's legal reasoning.

But religion is different. The justices divide bitterly over it. Monday's case was further clouded by the issue of reproductive rights and the assertion by the family-owned companies in the dispute that some contraceptive drugs and devices are akin to abortion.

In the case of *Burwell v. Hobby Lobby Stores,* the companies challenged the Obamacare insurance requirement for employee birth control. They objected to four methods, including the so-called morning-after pill. They said they should qualify for an exemption under a 1993 religious freedom law. The Obama administration countered that for-profit corporations, even closely held ones, are not covered by the 1993 law.

In his opinion for the court's five conservatives, Alito said there was a federal interest in ensuring that people who run their businesses for profit not compromise their religious beliefs. "A corporation is simply a form of organization used by human beings to achieve desired ends," he said. He asserted the decision would have limited effect.

Alito said Congress did not want to exclude people who operate for-profit businesses from the law's protections. Ginsburg countered that such a view effectively allows religious owners to impose their views on employees who might not share their belief.

"Startling Breadth"

In her dissent representing the four liberals, Ginsburg called the ruling one of "startling breadth." A women's rights advocate in the 1970s, she recalled how the court had long declared contraceptive coverage crucial to women's participation in the economic life of the country.

The last announced opinion of the term, Monday's case was arguably the most high-profile. It forced the justices to confront difficult issues against the backdrop of the enduringly controversial 2010 signature healthcare law of Democratic President Barack Obama.

The term featured none of the blockbuster decisions of the past two years when the court upheld the Obamacare law and set the pace for same-sex marriage and voting rights. All told, this term's cases failed to capture public attention the same way. The rulings gave each side—left and right—something to call a triumph.

The justices also ruled narrowly, and even unanimously, in some major business cases, including one brought by Halliburton testing how easily shareholders can band together in class-action lawsuits for damages.

When the court separately ruled that the streaming video service Aereo Inc had violated copyright law, the majority stressed the decision was limited and did not cover other technologies such as cloud computing.

In politically gridlocked Washington, the justices, particularly Chief Justice John Roberts, could be feeling institutional pressure to come together rather than pull apart, Harvard law professor Richard Fallon said.

"We have this enormous gap in politics today, between liberals and conservatives," Fallon said. "The chief justice may be naturally concerned that people not look at the Supreme Court and see it divided in this same way."

But the justices found themselves more apart than together on Monday. Sitting alongside each other on the long mahogany bench, Alito and Ginsburg barely looked at each other while reading from their opinions.

Rare Unanimity in Supreme Court Term, with Plenty of Fireworks

By Nina Totenberg
National Public Radio, July 7, 2014

The nation greets the coming of July each year with fireworks on the National Mall and, days earlier, explosive decisions at the U.S. Supreme Court.

While the Mall fireworks dissipate within moments, the court's decisions will have repercussions for decades. Indeed, no sooner was the ink dry on this term's contraception decision than the court's three female justices accused their male colleagues of reneging.

"Those who are bound by our decisions usually believe they can take us at our word," wrote Justice Sonia Sotomayor for herself and Justices Ruth Bader Ginsburg and Elena Kagan. "Not so today."

The last-minute imbroglio capped a term marked by both unanimity and division. Although high-profile decisions on contraception, campaign finance rules, public prayer and union power all were decided by 5-to-4 conservative majorities, the court achieved a rare degree of unanimity in its decision-making overall.

"There is something really remarkable that happened this year at the Supreme Court," says former Obama administration acting Solicitor General Neal Katyal. "In roughly two-thirds of the cases, they agreed unanimously with one another, and you have to go back to the year 1940 to find that happening."

That unanimity, however, is illusory, often just a technical agreement on the bottom line of a case—who won and who lost.

"Specious Unanimity"

As strange as it may seem, who won or lost is not all that important in Supreme Court cases, because it is the legal principle laid down by the majority that must be followed by the lower courts.

And so it was this term that Justice Antonin Scalia seemed to perfect a new judicial format: the enraged concurrence. He wrote three such concurrences, declaring in one, "I prefer not to take part in the assembling of an apparent but specious unanimity."

That case is illustrative. At issue was a 35-foot buffer zone to protect patients and staff from protesters at clinics that provide abortions in Massachusetts. All nine justices agreed the buffer zone was too big because it unduly restricted the free speech rights of the protesters. But there the agreement ended. And the difference is a big deal. Five justices said there can be buffer zones of some smaller size; four said no, there should not be any buffer zone ever under the Constitution.

Genuinely in Agreement

The theme of what one wag called "faux-nanimity" repeated itself again and again. "It represents a success in herding cats, but there is deep division underneath," observes Harvard Law School professor Laurence Tribe.

The one big, genuinely unanimous ruling was Chief Justice John Roberts' opinion for all nine justices declaring that police may not search a person's cellphone without a warrant, even at the time of an arrest.

"They all have cellphones, so they really understood this," says Clinton administration acting Solicitor General Walter Dellinger. "This is one area where they could be said to have empathy."

Some court observers have called the decision a "yuppie" spin on the Fourth Amendment's ban on unreasonable searches, noting that many of the justices, from both the conservative and liberal camps, are more tolerant of warrantless street searches for drugs.

"I think the class dimension of this is pretty obvious," says Georgetown Law professor Louis Michael Seidman.

Whether or not that critique has merit, the court's genuine unanimity on cellphones and less-genuine unanimity in other major cases masked clear disagreement in some of the most controversial cases of the term.

Clearly at Odds

In the area of separation of church and state, the court seemed to abandon the idea that public endorsement of a particular religion is banned by the constitution's separation of church and state. Instead, by a 5–4 vote, the court upheld sectarian prayers at town meetings.

The majority said it was enough that there was no coercion involved for members of the public who were attending; they could simply leave the room if they found the prayer offensive, the court said.

By the same 5–4 vote, the court's conservatives—all Republican appointees—prevailed over the court's liberals—all Democratic appointees—on campaign finance regulations, union power and mandated contraceptive coverage for corporations under the Affordable Care Act. In each of these decisions, the conservative majority reversed decades of previous rulings, or came close.

"Precedent is getting a very hard knock all over the place," says Harvard Law professor Charles Fried, who served as solicitor general in the Reagan administration.

In the campaign finance case, the conservative majority reversed 40 years of established Supreme Court precedent, striking down the $123,000 cap on how much individuals can donate to political parties in each election. The decision, coupled with the court's 2010 ruling that struck down a longstanding ban on corporate and union spending in candidate elections, further opened the floodgates of cash pouring into campaigns.

It also redefined corruption. For the first time, the court said Congress can only seek to curb quid pro quo corruption, something like an outright bribe. No longer is influence-peddling deemed corruption.

In the union power case, the court stopped short of overruling a 1977 decision that allows public employee unions to collect so-called fair-share fees from non-union members in order to pay for negotiating a contract that nonunion members benefit from, too. But the five-justice majority invited those opposed to these fees to bring another suit to challenge what it called the court's "questionable" 1977 precedent.

And in the case of contraceptive coverage under Obamacare, the conservative majority for the first time ruled that a for-profit corporation can refuse to comply with a general government mandate because doing so would violate the corporation's asserted religious beliefs.

In each of these cases, the conservative majority based its ruling on the First Amendment right of free speech or free exercise of religion. And some scholars on both the right and left see that as something of a new twist on an old story.

Today, legal historians speak disparagingly of the so-called Lochner era from the 1880s to the mid-1930s. During that time, the Supreme Court, in the name of property rights, consistently struck down legislation barring onerous working conditions or seeking to increase the bargaining power of employees in dealings with employers.

Almost all of the precedents from the Lochner era are now gone, viewed as wrongly decided. But some scholars suggest those decisions are being reborn in a new guise: the First Amendment.

"It's the new Lochner," laments Yale Law School's Akhil Amar, who comes from the moderate left of the legal spectrum. "The First Amendment is increasingly becoming everyone's first resort for all kinds of claims that historically were not thought of as First Amendment claims."

By that, Amar means voiding a century of campaign finance understandings, 80 years of precedent on government mandates for profit-making corporations, and nearly overruling 40 years of precedent on fair-share union fees.

Political Split, Step by Step

From the moderate right of the legal spectrum, Harvard's Fried remarks, "On campaign finance, a cynic could ask the famous question, cui bono? Who profits from this?"

The answer, he says, is clear: the Republican Party, its conservative backers and special interest groups. But is that the result of a conservative legal ideology that narrowly dominates the Supreme Court, or is it a partisan agenda?

"I would need to be a psychoanalyst, and I am not, to say whether the ideological commitment is a superstructure on the cui bono or the cui bono is just a coincidence," Fried says.

Still, in the contraception and union power cases, and in some others this term, many liberals and moderates breathed something of a sigh of relief on the theory that it could have been worse. "By the end of the term, the court had stepped back from the precipice in virtually all of these cases," contends Martin Lederman of Georgetown Law School. "It had not overruled any of its major precedents."

At the same time, many conservatives gnashed their teeth over the high court's failure to go all the way. "It's very frustrating that they take this baby-step approach rather than just be done with the business and overrule the bad precedent," says Erik Jaffe, a conservative who practices regularly before the court.

But, he says, smaller steps avoid "unintended consequences" and are probably smarter. As an example of a decision that went too far too fast, he cites *Roe v. Wade*, which essentially legalized abortion in one fell swoop. And as a contrary example, he cites gay rights decisions, which have headed in a one-way direction for almost two decades, giving the country and the body politic "time to catch up" along the way.

"At the end of the day, they're hard questions," opines Jaffe. "Leaping in and giving a final answer on it is only going to create more conflict when the political process really needs to work it through."

It's not entirely clear whether the conservative majority took smaller steps this term out of caution or because there was no fifth vote for a more radical course. The truth is probably a bit of both.

The court is deeply split, and for the first time in its history, its ideological alignment reflects partisan splits, too. The decisions made today are for the most part the product of choices made by past presidents with their appointments.

And as professor Lederman observes, the "ultimate fate" of union fair-share fees, campaign finance, affirmative action, abortion restrictions and many other controversial issues depends on "which justices are appointed to the court over the course of the next generation, which of course depends on who wins presidential elections."

Split Definitive

By Lawrence Baum and Neal Devins
Slate, November 11, 2011

All eyes are on the Supreme Court this week as it considers what to do with the landmark lawsuits challenging President Obama's health care legislation. While the question that intrigues court watchers is whether the nine justices will transcend their reputations as liberals or conservatives, it is a little-noticed irony that, for the first time in more than a century, the ideological positions of the justices on today's Supreme Court can be identified purely by party affiliation. What that means is that, for the first time in our political lifetimes, each of the four Democratic appointees has a strong tendency to favor liberal outcomes, while the five Republicans typically take conservative positions.

The days of liberal Republicans and conservative Democrats are behind us, and the days of judicial moderates from either party may soon seem a relic of the past. What does that mean for the future of the Affordable Care Act, and for the court itself?

This change has been brewing for some time, but with the August 2010 confirmation of Elena Kagan to succeed liberal Republican John Paul Stevens, the deal was sealed. In its 2010–11 term, the Court divided along partisan lines to a striking degree. An unusually high proportion of cases (18 out of 75) were decided by 5–4 votes on at least some portion of the outcome (or 5–3, with Justice Elena Kagan recused because of her work as solicitor general). In 12 of those cases, including many of last term's most important rulings, the court's Republicans were all arrayed on one side, its Democrats on the other. These cases involved regulation of campaign funding, the right to sue for violations of rights by a prosecutor's office, and state powers to enforce restrictions on immigration.

Far more telling, George W. Bush's and Barack Obama's appointees are particularly likely both to agree with each other and disagree with the other pair. According to data compiled by the SCOTUS Blog, Obama nominees Kagan and Sonia Sotomayor voted together 94 percent of the time last term; Bush nominees Samuel Alito and Chief Justice John Roberts were aligned 96 percent of the time. By contrast, these two pairs disagreed with each other more than 30 percent of the time overall (an extremely high percentage considering that more than 60 percent of the decisions were either unanimous or 8–1).

Justice Anthony Kennedy, a Ronald Reagan appointee, is generally thought of as the "swing" justice on the court, one who stands between the four justices to the left of him and the four to his right. That depiction of Kennedy is basically accurate. Last term, Kennedy was in the majority in all but two of the Court's 5–4 decisions. But that doesn't mean Kennedy stood equidistant from the Court's liberals and conservative blocs. His rates of agreement on the Court's judgment in the 2010 term ranged from 83 percent to 90 percent with the other four Republicans; his rates of agreement with the Democrats ranged from 66 percent to 74 percent.

At one level, none of this seems very surprising. We have become accustomed to a political world that features strong polarization between the parties. Congress is sharply and bitterly divided along partisan lines, and President Obama has achieved little success in winning Republican votes for his major initiatives. Why should the Supreme Court be any different? But that obscures the fact that, at least until last year, the Supreme Court was different. The court has often featured close divisions between ideological factions, but those divisions have usually crossed party lines rather than following them. Going back at least as far as the late 19th century, there has never been another year on the court like the 2010 term, when there was a contingent of Republican conservatives on one side and a contingent of Democratic liberals on the other side.

Indeed, what's striking is how far the court has departed from this sort of partisan polarization. The "Four Horsemen" who regularly voted to strike down New Deal legislation in the 1930s included a Democrat—Woodrow Wilson appointee James McReynolds—and the three justices who most regularly opposed those men included two Republican appointees—Harlan Fiske Stone and Benjamin Cardozo. In the famously "liberal" Warren Court of the 1950s and 1960s, which adopted a wide array of new rules expanding legal protections for civil liberties, two of the leaders in that effort were selected by President Eisenhower—William Brennan and Chief Justice Earl Warren himself. For their part, the justices who questioned much of the court's civil liberties revolution at that time included FDR appointee Felix Frankfurter and, later, Kennedy appointee Byron White.

As the court gradually moved to the right beginning in the 1970s, White abetted much of that effort while Republican appointees such as John Paul Stevens, David Souter, and (in the later portion of his career) Harry Blackmun stood in the liberal opposition, while other Republicans such as Sandra Day O'Connor and Lewis Powell took relatively moderate positions.

What, then, brought about the partisan court of the 2010 term? The simple answer is changes in the selection process of justices. From the 1940s until the election of Ronald Reagan, the political parties were anything but polarized. Conservative Southern Democrats and liberal Rockefeller Republicans were important counterweights within both parties. Indeed, George Wallace justified his third-party bid for president in 1968 by saying that "there's not a dime's worth of difference between the Democrat and Republican parties."

Supreme Court appointments reflect these larger trends. Before party polarization took hold, ideology was not the controlling factor in court appointments. Presidents gave attention to other considerations, such as rewarding political allies, appealing to voters, and avoiding confirmation battles in the Senate. For those reasons, Democratic presidents have often selected justices who turned out to be conservative, and a good many Republican appointees turned out to be liberal.

President Harry Truman's choices of relatively conservative nominees reflected his interest in rewarding political associates rather than choosing reliable liberals. And President Eisenhower's choices of Warren and Brennan resulted largely from political (but not ideological) considerations. Warren helped Eisenhower secure the 1952 Republican presidential nomination; Brennan was appointed to the court's so-called Catholic seat because Eisenhower wanted to appoint a Democrat to demonstrate his ability to transcend political partisanship. Kennedy appointed White, his deputy attorney general and a longtime supporter (dating back to White's writing the intelligence report on the sinking of a boat piloted by Kennedy during World War II). Richard Nixon, although criticizing Warren court criminal justice rulings, discounted ideology in his efforts to appoint a Southerner to the court. Gerald Ford's appointment of John Paul Stevens was directly linked to Watergate and Ford's need to rise above politics.

This pattern continued even as the larger political system was becoming more polarized. Strongly conservative Ronald Reagan chose relatively moderate Sandra Day O'Connor because there was only a small pool of credible Republican women from whom to choose. More striking, Reagan Attorney General Edwin Meese thought the pool of conservative Republicans so weak that he set about to devise strategies to deepen that pool for future presidents.

Today, appointment strategies have changed. As politics has become even more polarized, presidents have given greater emphasis to the goal of choosing ideologically reliable justices. More than anything, Republican presidents are now under great pressure to appoint true blue conservatives. From 1969 to 1991, even though Republicans appointed 12 justices (and Democrats none), the court frequently backed liberal outcomes. By 2001, when George W. Bush became president, the rallying call of conservative Republicans was "No More Souters." Indeed, when Bush initially chose Harriet Miers for what became Alito's seat, vehement criticism from conservatives who doubted her ideological reliability figured into Miers' decision to quickly withdraw, underlining changes in the political atmosphere.

For their part, Bill Clinton and Barack Obama have contributed to the court's partisan divides by nominating four liberals to the court. And while some Democratic partisans lament that these justices are nothing like earlier liberals such as William Brennan or Thurgood Marshall, it is nonetheless true that today's Democratic nominees are distinctly to the left of all their Republican colleagues.

All this could change. But it's unlikely unless and until partisan polarization declines. Future appointments, like the most recent ones, will emphasize ideological reliability over anything else. And because presidents will look for nominees whose ideological views are deeply rooted, the justices who are selected will be less likely to move toward moderation after they join the court.

The court's strong polarization does not necessarily mean that the justices will divide strictly along partisan lines when they address the constitutional challenge to the healthcare law. Even on politically controversial issues, the court frequently departs from such partisan divisions. But because the court is now composed solely of Democratic liberals and Republican conservatives, decisions that follow partisan lines have become far more likely. If this situation continues, as we think it will, the most powerful effects may be on how Americans think about the Supreme Court as an institution.

4
Major Decisions

© Coast-to-Coast/iStock

Demonstrators for and against *Roe v. Wade* gather in front of the Supreme Court building on the fortieth anniversary of that momentous decision, January 25, 2013. A protective scrim is in place while work is being done on the building façade.

The Supreme Court's Major Decisions in Historical Perspective

<hr>

The Supreme Court's power of "judicial review" most often commands our attention when it affects some momentous and contentious political issue. In 2014 alone it made a number of such decisions. It told the president that he could not use his so-called "recess appointment power" unless Congress said it was, in fact, in recess (*NLRB v. Noel Canning*). It ruled that laws banning individuals from approaching another person near abortion clinics in order to counsel or convince them not to get an abortion violate the freedom of speech (*McCullen v. Coakley*). And it rejected a claim that opening a town's legislative sessions with prayer violates the First Amendment's no establishment of religion clause (*Greece v. Galloway*). If any or all of these go down as major decisions of the Supreme Court, they will join other recent cases such as *United States v. Windsor* (2013), *NFIB v. Sebelius* (2012), and *Citizens United v. FEC* (2010) in defining this decade in the court's history.

When speaking of the Supreme Court's "major" decisions, we mean those cases that have exerted, and may continue to exert, a profound influence on our political, economic, and social relations, and on our understanding of ourselves as a self-governing people committed to liberty, equality, and justice under law. But rare is the case whose mere outcome exerts such influence. When discussing a judicial decision we attend primarily to the opinion explaining why the outcome was necessary. The reason of the case is what commands our attention—such reasoning as generally expounds some provision of the federal Constitution. Topping most lists of major decisions is the 1803 case *Marbury v. Madison*, which has been understood as the cornerstone of judicial power in the United States and the reason why we allow our courts of law to halt and reverse executive actions, void state and congressional statutes, and sit in judgment on how a city government begins its yearly business.

Origins of Judicial Power

The story is a familiar one: Chief Justice John Marshall took a losing hand and turned it into a winning one through a careful, if not creative, bit of judicial jujitsu. Justice in the *Marbury* case demanded that Mr. Marbury be given his commission as justice of the peace, which the outgoing Adams administration had signed and sealed but which the Jefferson administration had refused to deliver. Marshall knew that Jefferson's secretary of state, James Madison, would also refuse any judicial order to deliver the commission, doing untold damage to the Court's prestige and authority. So he decided instead to sacrifice justice for William Marbury to the institutional needs of the Supreme Court and the greater good of the nation. He accomplished this by finding a conflict between a minor provision of the Judiciary Act of

1789 and Article III of the Constitution and then declaring the offending provision unconstitutional and legally void. In doing so, the great Chief Justice laid down the precedent for judicial review in a way that could not be resisted by the more powerful political branches, because it did not ask anything of them.

This account of the origin of judicial review and the idea that the courts are the ultimate, if not exclusive, arbiters of the Constitution began with judicial biographers and scholars of constitutional law at the beginning of the twentieth century and soon became the orthodox view of the matter. More recent scholarship, however, has called this account into question, noting that *Marbury* was rarely discussed in the nineteenth century and was not cited as the basis of judicial review until the late 1950s. But however questionable its accuracy, the legend of *Marbury* remains strong, and as long as that legend is printed in the textbooks, spoken in the halls of academia, and honored in the courts, the case will continue to be ranked in the constitutional canon with the dignity and status of firstborn among the Court's major decisions.

Far more important in their day were a number of the Marshall Court's other decisions, chief among which is *McCulloch v. Maryland* (1819). By upholding the supremacy of national law against state attempts to counter and undermine it—in this case by taxing the Bank of the United States—the Court helped assure the continued reality of the "more perfect Union" envisioned in the Constitution. Decisions like *McCulloch* were indispensable bulwarks against the forces of disunion during the early decades of the republic.

The Legacy of *Dred Scott v. Sandford*

If the goal of Chief Justice Roger Taney's opinion in *Dred Scott v. Sandford* (1857) was similarly to resist the forces of disunion, by resolving contentious political questions surrounding the institution of slavery, the result of that infamous decision was just the opposite. This decision touched a national nerve to a degree unrivaled before or since. Reaction to it swelled the ranks of the new Republican Party, divided Northern and Southern Democrats (assuring Lincoln's election in 1860), and pushed the nation further down the road to civil war. No other case has marked American history as profoundly.

The case arose when a slave named Dred Scott sued for his freedom after being taken by his master to live first in the free Wisconsin Territory and then in the free State of Illinois. Taney explains the Court's denial of Dred Scott's appeal with two holdings. First, blacks could not be considered as citizens of the United States because they were never meant to be included either in the "We the People" of the Constitution's Preamble or in the "all men are created equal" of the Declaration of Independence, and therefore they had no standing to sue in the federal courts. Second, Congress had no right to prohibit slavery in the territories, a holding that declared the storied Missouri Compromise of 1820 to have been unconstitutional. In response, Abraham Lincoln argued that both of these holdings were plainly wrong and that it was the duty of the people—the true guardians of the Constitution—to oppose them and seek their reversal.

Equal Protection and Due Process

While slavery ended with the Thirteenth Amendment and the newly freed slaves had been promised full and equal citizenship by the Fourteenth, the hopes these entailed were soon disappointed, in part by the Supreme Court's decisions in *The Civil Rights Cases* (1883) and *Plessy v. Ferguson* (1896). In the first of these, the Court struck down those portions of the Civil Rights Act of 1875 that forbade discrimination in privately owned public accommodations, stating that the Fourteenth Amendment authorizes Congress only to regulate the actions of state governments, not of the individuals within those states. In the second, the Court rejected the claim that Louisiana's segregated railroad cars ran contrary to the Fourteenth Amendment's promise of "equal protection of the laws," stating that "separate" was not the same as "unequal."

During this same period, an idea began to percolate that the Fourteenth Amendment's command that "[n]o state shall deprive any person of life, liberty, or property without due process of law" gave new power to federal courts to nullify state laws that interfere with individual rights. Called "substantive due process" by its detractors (because of the apparent contradiction between "substance" and "process"), this doctrine focused, in the early years, on the economic rights of contract and property. The high-water mark of this development was *Lochner v. New York* (1905), in which a New York law limiting the numbers of hours that bakers can work was struck down as violating the liberty to contract out one's labor as one sees fit.

The Commerce Power

Joining "liberty of contract" in thwarting legislative attempts to control the economy were cases that tightly drew the boundaries of Congress's commerce power. In a number of these cases the Court halted legislative attempts to regulate certain business practices, including those involving wages, hours, and child labor. When it began striking down signature pieces of New Deal legislation in the 1930s, President Franklin D. Roosevelt pushed back, and by his fourth term, he had replaced enough of the justices to bring about a radical change in the Court's approach to these matters. For some time thereafter, the courts would simply defer to Congress on the general boundaries of its powers (see *Wicker v. Filburn*, 1942), and by 1955 (*Williamson v. Lee Optical*) it was clear that Lochnerian liberty of contract was defunct.

The Modern Court

Well into the twentieth century, Jim Crow laws found shelter under the Plessy decision's "separate but equal" rule, but the Court finally discarded it in the celebrated case of *Brown v. Board of Education* (1954). In the wake of this case, Chief Justice Earl Warren led the Court in a renewed expansion of judicial power. The tip of the spear was *Cooper v. Aaron* (1858), in which the Court held that the oath to uphold the Constitution that all public officials take was, in effect, an oath to heed the dictates of the Supreme Court. The clear implication was that the Constitution is just exactly what the Supreme Court says it is, the contrary views of Lincoln and FDR notwithstanding.

The dizzying number of major decisions since then is far too great to list them all here. The Warren Court focused not only on racial equality but also on new applications of substantive due process, replacing the old concern for "economic liberty" with a new solicitude for "personal liberty." This approach gave new salience to the Bill of Rights as most of its protections became "incorporated" against the states. In a somewhat more confused manner, the "right to privacy" (which does not appear in the Constitution) also entered into our constitutional law. And from these developments stem the rulings on things like abortion (*Roe v. Wade,* 1973), flag-burning (*Texas v. Johnson,* 1989), prayer in public schools (*Engel v. Vitale,* 1962), and the need for police to obtain warrants before entering someone's home uninvited (*Mapp v. Ohio,* 1961).

The relation of these cases to the recent cases discussed in the opening paragraph should be apparent. Many of the same types of questions that arose during the Warren years continue to preoccupy the Court today. Sometimes it extends and builds on those precedents; sometimes it limits them. Sometimes it pulls them back a little, as it did in *U.S. v. Lopez* (1995) when it rediscovered judicially enforceable limits to Congress's commerce power. On the central question of judicial power, however, it has not wavered. The Supreme Court continues to believe it is the sole authoritative interpreter of the Constitution, and it is quick to respond to any challenges to its authority (see *Boerne v. Flores,* 1997). So it is in practice, and so it shall remain as long as virtually everyone else agrees.

—Anthony D. Bartl

Bibliography

Clinton, Robert Lowry. Marbury v. Madison *and Judicial Review.* Lawrence: University of Kansas Press, 1989.

Corwin, Edward S. *John Marshall and the Constitution.* New Haven, CT: Yale University Press, 1919.

Franck, Matthew J. *Against the Imperial Judiciary: The Supreme Court vs. the Sovereignty of the People.* Lawrence: University of Kansas Press, 1996.

Greenburg, Ethan. Dred Scott *and the Dangers of a Political Court.* Lanham, MD: Lexington Books, 2010.

Kramer, Larry. *The People Themselves: Popular Constitutionalism and Judicial Review.* New York: Oxford University Press, 2005.

McCloskey, Robert G., and Sanford Levinson. *The American Supreme Court.* 5th ed. Chicago: University of Chicago Press, 2010.

Schwartz, Bernard. *A History of the Supreme Court.* New York: Oxford University Press, 1993.

Wilson, Bradford P., and Ken Masugi, eds. *The Supreme Court and American Constitutionalism.* Lanham, MD: Rowman and Littlefield, 1998.

Wolfe, Christopher. *The Rise of Modern Judicial Review: From Constitutional Interpretation to Judge-Made Law.* New York: Basic Books, 1986.

Precedent and Prologue

By Jeffrey Toobin
The New Yorker, December 6, 2010

Momentous Supreme Court cases tend to move quickly into the slipstream of the Court's history. In the first ten years after *Brown v. Board of Education,* the 1954 decision that ended the doctrine of separate but equal in public education, the Justices cited the case more than twenty-five times. In the ten years after *Roe v. Wade,* the abortion-rights decision of 1973, there were more than sixty-five references to that landmark. This month marks ten years since the Court, by a vote of five-to-four, terminated the election of 2000 and delivered the Presidency to George W. Bush. Over that decade, the Justices have provided a verdict of sorts on *Bush v. Gore* by the number of times they have cited it: zero.

Both sides had their reasons for consigning the decision to history and leaving it there. In his concession speech on the day after the decision, Al Gore said simply, "It's time for me to go." He meant it, and he left politics for a life of entrepreneurship and good works. George W. Bush, for his part, found little reason to dwell on the controversial nature of his ascension to office, and in his memoir, *Decision Points,* he devotes less than a page to the Supreme Court decision. ("My first response was relief," he writes of his reaction.) In public appearances, Antonin Scalia, a member of the majority in *Bush v. Gore,* regularly offers this message to people who question him about the decision: "Get over it!"

Even at the time, *Bush v. Gore* was treated as a kind of novelty item, a one-off decision that applied only to the peculiar facts then before the Justices. The majority itself seemed to want it that way. In the most famous sentence from the decision, the Justices wrote, "Our consideration is limited to the present circumstances, for the problem of equal protection in election processes generally presents many complexities." (Unlike most weighty decisions, *Bush v. Gore* had no single author and was delineated "per curiam," or by the Court, a designation the Justices usually reserve for minor cases.) In light of all these admonitions to leave the case be, might getting over it be the best advice?

Actually, no. To return briefly to the distant world of chads, hanging and otherwise, it's worth recalling what *Bush v. Gore* was about. The pervasive uncertainty about the results of the election in Florida—at the time, Bush led by five hundred and thirty-seven votes out of nearly six million cast—prompted the Florida courts, interpreting Florida election law, to order a statewide recount of all undervotes and overvotes, that is, ballots that indicated no Presidential preference or more than one. (Chads were the tiny paper rectangles that voters were supposed to push through punch-card ballots.) That recount had already begun on Saturday, December 9th, when five Justices—Scalia, William H. Rehnquist, Sandra Day O'Connor, Anthony M. Kennedy, and Clarence Thomas—issued a stay, barring the Florida authorities from continuing their labors. Three days later, the same five issued the per-curiam decision that stopped the recount once and for all.

What made the decision in *Bush v. Gore* so startling was that it was the work of Justices who were considered, to greater or lesser extents, judicial conservatives. On many occasions, these Justices had said that they believed in the preëminence of states' rights, in a narrow conception of the equal-protection clause of the Fourteenth Amendment, and, above all, in judicial restraint. *Bush v. Gore* violated those principles. The Supreme Court stepped into the case even though the Florida Supreme Court had been interpreting Florida law; the majority found a violation of the rights of George W. Bush, a white man, to equal protection when these same Justices were becoming ever more stingy in finding violations of the rights of African-Americans; and the Court stopped the recount even before it was completed, and before the Florida courts had a chance to iron out any problems—a classic example of judicial activism, not judicial restraint, by the majority.

Bush v. Gore would resonate, in any case, because the Court prevented Florida from determining, as best it could, whether Gore or Bush really won. (Recounts of the ballots by media organizations produced ambiguous results; they suggest that Gore would have won a full statewide recount and Bush would have won the limited recount initially sought by the Gore forces.) But the case also represents a revealing prologue to what the Supreme Court has since become. As in *Bush v. Gore*, nominally conservative Justices no longer operate by the rules of traditional judicial conservatism.

The Court is now led, of course, by Chief Justice John G. Roberts, Jr., who was appointed by Bush in 2005 (and who, in 2000, travelled to Florida as a private lawyer working on Bush's behalf). Under Roberts, the Court has continued to use the equal-protection clause as a vehicle to protect white people. In 2007, in Roberts's first major opinion as Chief, he struck down the voluntary school-integration plans of Seattle and Louisville, which had been challenged by some white parents. Likewise, under Roberts the conservatives have abandoned their traditional concern with states' rights if, for example, the state is trying to protect the environment. In another 2007 case, Roberts, Scalia, Thomas, and Samuel A. Alito, Jr. (who replaced O'Connor), argued in dissent that states had no right to force the Environmental Protection Agency to address the issue of global warming.

The echoes of *Bush v. Gore* are clearest when it comes to judicial activism. Judicial conservatism was once principally defined as a philosophy of deference to the democratically elected branches of government. But the signature of the Roberts Court has been its willingness, even its eagerness, to overturn the work of legislatures. Brandishing a novel interpretation of the Second Amendment, the Court has either struck down or raised questions about virtually every state and local gun-control law in the nation. In *Citizens United v. Federal Election Commission,* decided earlier this year, the Court gutted the McCain-Feingold campaign-finance law in service of a legal theory that contradicts about a century of law at the Court. (*Citizens United* removed limits on corporate expenditures in political campaigns; the decision is, at its core, a boon for Republicans, just as *Bush v. Gore* was a decade ago.) When the Obama health-care plan reaches the high court for review, as it surely will, one can expect a similar lack of humility from the purported conservatives.

Many of the issues before the Supreme Court combine law and politics in ways that are impossible to separate. It is, moreover, unreasonable to expect the Justices to operate in a world hermetically cut off from the gritty motives of Democrats and Republicans. But the least we can expect from these men and women is that at politically charged moments—indeed, especially at those times—they apply the same principles that guide them in everyday cases. This, ultimately, is the tragedy of *Bush v. Gore.* The case didn't just scar the Court's record; it damaged the Court's honor.

2014 Election Confirms *Citizens United* Decision Based on Fundamentally Flawed Premises

By Fred Wertheimer
The Huffington Post, November 6, 2014

The 2014 congressional elections confirmed that the Supreme Court's decision in *Citizens United* was based on fundamentally flawed premises.

The Court majority in *Citizens United* explicitly based its misguided decision on two grounds: campaign expenditures by outside groups would be made independently from candidates and full disclosure of the campaign activities would provide accountability to citizens and shareholders.

Neither has happened.

The Court's premises turned out to be divorced from reality and instead provided false cover for the explosive growth in outside spending of unlimited contributions by super PACs and 501(c) nonprofit corporations.

"Independent" Expenditures

The Supreme Court held in *Citizens United* that corporations could make expenditures in elections as long as they were not coordinated with candidates. The Court, citing its *Buckley* decision, stated, "[t]he absence of coordination . . . alleviates the danger that expenditures will be given as a quid pro quo for improper commitments from a candidate."

The "independent" spending by outside groups that has actually occurred in the past two elections, however, turned out to be a figment of the Court's imagination.

There has been widespread coordination between outside spending groups and candidates. For example, in the 2012 presidential election, almost every candidate had an individual candidate super PAC functioning as an arm of the candidate's campaign. In the 2014 congressional races, there were 92 such super PACs, more than quadruple the number in the 2010 races and more than double the number in 2012, according to the Center for Responsive Politics.

Individual candidate super PACs generally are run by the candidate's close associates and often receive contributions raised by the candidate. They are anything but "independent" from the candidate.

These super PACs exist basically for one purpose: they serve as vehicles to eviscerate candidate contribution limits by permitting wealthy individuals, corporations and other moneyed interests to give unlimited contributions to directly support the candidate.

The widespread coordination abuses occurring in our elections can be curbed. Legislative provisions to accomplish this goal, within the parameters of the *Citizens United* decision, are contained in the Empowering Citizens Act, sponsored by Representatives David Price (D-NC) and Chris Van Hollen (D-MD).

The provisions would define single-candidate super PACs as coordinated with the candidates they support, which would in effect shut down the PACs. The provisions would also strengthen the rules prohibiting coordination between other outside spending groups and candidates.

Disclosure by Outside Spending Groups

Eight of nine Supreme Court Justices voted in *Citizens United* to uphold the constitutionality of disclosure requirements for outside spending groups. The Court made clear that disclosure was an integral part of its decision to strike down the ban on corporate spending in elections.

The Court stated:

With the advent of the Internet, prompt disclosure of expenditures can provide shareholders and citizens with the information needed to hold corporations and elected officials accountable for their positions and supporters. Shareholders can determine whether their corporation's political speech advances the corporation's interest in making profits, and citizens can see whether elected officials are "in the pocket of so-called moneyed interests."

The Court further stated, "A campaign finance system that pairs corporate independent expenditures with effective disclosure has not existed before today."

Turns out it still does not exist, almost five years after the *Citizens United* decision.

As a result, a combined half billion dollars in secret money contributions was spent in the 2012 and 2014 national elections, primarily by 501(c) nonprofit corporations. This has brought back to our national elections the same kind of secret money that played a key role in the Watergate scandals, although now the amounts are far greater.

As in the case of coordination, this fundamental flaw in the *Citizens United* decision can be solved.

The DISCLOSE Act, legislation to provide comprehensive real time disclosure by outside spending groups, has been introduced by Representative Van Hollen in the House and by Senator Sheldon Whitehouse (D-RI) in the Senate.

Polls have shown that disclosure is overwhelmingly supported by the American people.

Nevertheless, since the *Citizens United* decision, congressional Republicans have blocked the enactment of new disclosure requirements to close the gaping loopholes that exist for outside spending groups. The challenge now is to restore the bipartisan support in Congress for disclosure that had existed for four decades until the *Citizens United* in 2010.

Other less comprehensive remedies are also being pursued to achieve disclosure by outside spending groups. They include a pending IRS rulemaking to revise flawed regulations that fail to properly limit the role that 501(c) groups can play in elections; an SEC petition to require public corporations to disclose their campaign activities to their shareholders and the public; and an FCC petition to improve disclosure by outside spending groups running campaign ads.

The Supreme Court based the *Citizens United* decision on "independent" expenditures and "effective" disclosure. Instead we ended up with coordinated expenditures; secret money; and a small number of the wealthiest people in America, major corporations, and others buying the opportunity to corrupt government decisions and exercising extraordinary influence over our elections.

Obama Wins the Battle,
Roberts Wins the War

By Tom Scocca
Slate, June 28, 2012

There were two battles being fought in the Supreme Court over the Affordable Care Act. Chief Justice John Roberts—and Justice Anthony Kennedy—delivered victory to the right in the one that mattered.

Yes, Roberts voted to uphold the individual mandate, joining the court's liberal wing to give President Obama a 5–4 victory on his signature piece of legislation. Right-wing partisans are crying treason; left-wing partisans saw their predictions of a bitter, party-line defeat undone.

But the health care law was, ultimately, a pretext. This was a test case for the long-standing—but previously fringe—campaign to rewrite Congress' regulatory powers under the Commerce Clause.

This is why the challenge to the ACA, and its progress through the courts, came as a surprise to Democrats and to mainstream constitutional scholars: Three years ago, there was no serious doubt that Congress had the power to impose the individual mandate.

A Bloomberg story last week nicely captured the stakes: "Obama Health Law Seen Valid, Scholars Expect Rejection":

> The U.S. Supreme Court should uphold a law requiring most Americans to have health insurance if the justices follow legal precedent, according to 19 of 21 constitutional law professors who ventured an opinion on the most-anticipated ruling in years.

> Only eight of them predicted the court would do so.

The scholars expected to see the court gut existing Commerce Clause precedent and overturn the individual mandate in a partisan decision: Five Republican-appointed justices voting to rewrite doctrine and reject Obamacare; four Democratic-appointed justices dissenting.

Roberts was smarter than that. By ruling that the individual mandate was permissible as a tax, he joined the Democratic appointees to uphold the law—while joining the Republican wing to gut the Commerce Clause (and push back against the necessary-and-proper clause as well). Here's the Chief Justice's opinion (italics in original):

Construing the Commerce Clause to permit Congress to regulate individuals precisely *because* they are doing nothing would open a new and potentially vast domain to congressional authority. Congress already possesses expansive power to regulate what people do. Upholding the Affordable Care Act under the Commerce Clause would give Congress the same license to regulate what people do not do. The Framers knew the difference between doing something and doing nothing. They gave Congress the power to *regulate* commerce, not to *compel* it. Ignoring that distinction would undermine the principle that the Federal Government is a government of limited and enumerated powers. The individual mandate thus cannot be sustained under Congress's power to "regulate Commerce."

The business about "new and potentially vast" authority is a fig leaf. This is a substantial rollback of Congress' regulatory powers, and the chief justice knows it. It is what Roberts has been pursuing ever since he signed up with the Federalist Society. In 2005, Sen. Barack Obama spoke in opposition to Roberts' nomination, saying he did not trust his political philosophy on tough questions such as "whether the Commerce Clause empowers Congress to speak on those issues of broad national concern that may be only tangentially related to what is easily defined as interstate commerce." Today, Roberts did what Obama predicted he would do.

Roberts' genius was in pushing this health care decision through without attaching it to the coattails of an ugly, narrow partisan victory. Obama wins on policy, this time. And Roberts rewrites Congress' power to regulate, opening the door for countless future challenges. In the long term, supporters of curtailing the federal government should be glad to have made that trade.

Supreme Court's Silence on Marriage Rights Speaks Volumes

By Marcia Coyle
The National Law Journal, October 6, 2014

By declining to take up any of the same-sex marriage cases pending before it on Monday, the U.S. Supreme Court defied the conventional wisdom that it finally would resolve the debate over the constitutionality of state bans on those marriages.

Experienced high court practitioners hesitate to speculate about why the justices take certain actions. But those advocating marriage equality tended to agree that, in denying review, the high court sent a clear signal that a majority thinks those bans are unconstitutional.

"The Supreme Court may feel the federal judges are all coming to the same conclusion and it's not necessary to intervene," Theodore Olson of Gibson, Dunn & Crutcher, colead counsel in one of two Virginia challenges, suggested. "It sends a fairly strong signal that federal judges who have ruled in favor of marriage equality are getting it right."

However, Byron Babione, senior counsel with Alliance Defending Freedom, defending bans in Virginia and Oklahoma, vowed that the marriage battle would continue.

"Several federal courts, including those in the Fifth, Sixth, Eighth and Eleventh circuits, still have cases working their way to the Supreme Court," he said. "The people should decide this issue, not the courts."

Evan Wolfson, founder of Freedom to Marry, the national campaign for marriage equality, agreed the battle is not over. Still, he said, the high court's inaction amounted to a "huge step forward" for the cause, because it effectively opens the door to same-sex marriage in five to 11 states that represent 60 percent of the American people.

"We have a national majority and soon we'll have a super national majority," Wolfson said. "But it's not a done deal until it's done. A glass 60 percent full is a good thing but if in 40 percent it's empty, you're not treated fairly. We want the Supreme Court to finish the job."

The court, without comment, refused to hear any of seven petitions from five states whose bans on marriage equality federal appellate courts had struck down. The denials mean same-sex marriages are legal in Indiana, Oklahoma, Utah, Virginia and Wisconsin and where federal appeals courts had ruled such prohibitions unconstitutional.

"Because the Supreme Court let the decisions of the Fourth, Seventh and Tenth circuits stand, that means the lower courts where there are cases pending in those circuits will soon issue orders allowing same-sex couples to marry," said Jon Davidson of Lambda Legal, cocounsel in another of the Virginia cases.

The other states covered by those three circuits are Colorado, Kansas, Illinois, Maryland, New Mexico, North Carolina, South Carolina, West Virginia and Wyoming. Counting those states, marriage equality would be the law in 30 states and the District of Columbia.

Predictions that the justices would hear a case this term were based partly on the fact that they had issued temporary stays blocking the rulings by the Fourth and Tenth circuits. Those stays generally indicate that the high court is interested in taking a case on the merits.

But those assumptions also were based on the fact that federal courts had stricken five state laws or constitutional amendments; under the circumstances, even without a split among the circuits, the justices seemed likely to step into the controversy.

"The court typically has been very hesitant to get ahead of the public will, but has done so when striking down segregation (*Brown v. Board of Education*) and the ban on interracial marriage (*Loving v. Virginia*)," Elizabeth Cooper, faculty director of the Feerick Center for Social Justice at Fordham University School of Law, said via email.

Now that a majority of Americans support marriage equality, she added, "The court's decision to not step in and to let these marriage rights stand, is, perhaps, a recognition of this growing support."

Jenner & Block's Paul Smith, cocounsel in Virginia's marriage class action, suggested a strategic move by the some of the justices. "I do think if the four dissenters in [*United States v.*] *Windsor* had any reason to think they could get five votes [against marriage equality] they would have granted cert," he said, referring to the 2013 ruling striking down the federal Defense of Marriage Act's narrow definition of marriage. The dissenters were Chief Justice John Roberts Jr. and Justices Antonin Scalia, Clarence Thomas and Samuel Alito Jr.

"Then the question is: Do the rest of the justices have reasons to grant cert now. And I guess they concluded it would be better to let things go for awhile, as long as there is no compelling reason to take a case," he said.

Justice Ruth Bader Ginsburg had suggested in some earlier interviews that the court might wait for a circuit split to develop. During recent arguments in the Sixth Circuit, a three-judge panel appeared likely to uphold state bans and thus create such a split.

Court scholar Erwin Chemerinsky, dean of the University of California, Irvine School of Law, believes the justices will wait for a split. But, he added, "It is hard to understand what the court thinks is gained by waiting for a circuit split here rather than it resolving the issue for the nation."

And as additional weddings go forward, Jenner & Block's Smith said, "It's going to be very difficult for the court to come along in some later case and reverse course. I think it would be a severe impingement on people's fundamental liberties to un-marry them."

Opponents of same-sex marriage remain undeterred by the court's inaction.

"The good news is that time is not on the side of those who want to redefine marriage," Family Research Council President Tony Perkins said. "As more states are forced to redefine marriage, contrary to nature and directly in conflict with the will of millions, more Americans will see and experience attacks on their religious freedom."

Perkins urged Congress to enact the State Marriage Defense Act, which, he said, "ensures that the federal government in its definition of marriage respects the duly enacted marriage laws of the states."

Why the Supreme Court May Finally Protect Your Privacy in the Cloud

By Andy Greenberg
Wired, June 26, 2014

When the Supreme Court ruled yesterday in the case of *Riley v. California*, it definitively told the government to keep its warrantless fingers off your cell phone. But as the full impact of that opinion has rippled through the privacy community, some SCOTUS-watchers say it could also signal a shift in how the Court sees the privacy of data in general—not just when it's stored on your physical handset, but also when it's kept somewhere far more vulnerable: in the servers of faraway Internet and phone companies.

In the Riley decision, which dealt with the post-arrest searches of an accused drug dealer in Boston and an alleged gang member in California, the court unanimously ruled that police need a warrant to search a suspect's phone. The 28-page opinion penned by Chief Justice John Roberts explicitly avoids addressing a larger question about what's known as the "third-party doctrine," the notion that any data kept by a third party such as Verizon, AT&T, Google or Microsoft is fair game for a warrantless search. But even so, legal analysts reading between the opinion's lines say they see evidence that the court is shifting its view on that long-stewing issue for online privacy. The results, if they're right, could be future rulings from America's highest court that seriously restrict both law enforcement's and even the NSA's abilities to siphon Americans' data from the cloud.

Digital Is Different

The key realization in Roberts' ruling, according to Open Technology Institute attorney Kevin Bankston, can be summarized as "digital is different." Modern phones generate a volume of private data that means they require greater protection than other non-digital sources of personal information. "Easy analogies of digital to traditional analog surveillance won't cut it," Bankston says.

Daniel Solove, a law professor at George Washington Law School, echoes that sentiment in a blog post and points to this passage in the opinion:

> First, a cell phone collects in one place many distinct types of information—an address, a note, a prescription, a bank statement, a video—that reveal much more in combination than any isolated record. Second, a cell phone's capacity allows even just one type of information to convey far more than previously possible. The sum of an individual's

private life can be reconstructed through a thousand photographs labeled with dates, locations, and descriptions.

That argument about the nature of digital collections of personal data seems to apply just as much to information held by a third–party company as it does to information held in the palm of an arrested person's hand. And Solove argues that could spell trouble for the third-party doctrine when it next comes before the Court. "The Court's reasoning in *Riley* suggests that perhaps the Court is finally recognizing that old physical considerations—location, size, etc.—are no longer as relevant in light of modern technology. What matters is the data involved and how much it reveals about a person's private life," he writes. "If this is the larger principle the Court is recognizing today, then it strongly undermines some of the reasoning behind the third party doctrine."

The Court's opinion was careful not to make any overt reference to the third–party doctrine. In fact, it includes a tersely worded footnote cautioning that the ruling's arguments about physical search of phones "do not implicate the question whether the collection or inspection of aggregated digital information amounts to a search under other circumstances."

But despite the Court's caveat, its central argument—that the notions of privacy applied to analog data are no longer sufficient to protect digital data from warrantless searches—doesn't limit itself to physical access to devices. And the opinion seems to hint at the Court's thoughts on protecting one sort of remotely stored phone data in particular: location data.

The Logic of Location Data

The *Riley* ruling cites an opinion written by Justice Sonia Sotomayor in the case of *US vs. Jones,* another landmark Supreme Court decision in 2012 that ended warrantless use of GPS devices to track criminal suspects' cars. GPS devices, Sotomayor wrote at the time, create "a precise, comprehensive record of a person's public movements that reflects a wealth of detail about her familial, political, professional, religious, and sexual associations." Roberts' reference to that opinion in Tuesday's ruling seems to acknowledge that the sensitivity of GPS device data extends to phone location data too. And there's little logical reason to believe that phone data becomes less sensitive when it's stored by AT&T instead of in an iPhone's flash memory.

With *Riley* and *Jones,* "we've now seen two indications that the Supreme Court is rethinking privacy for stored data," says Alex Abdo, a staff attorney at the American Civil Liberties Union. "Neither raises the question directly, but they both contain clues into the mindset of the court, and they both suggest that there's another victory for privacy in the waiting."

"If I were to guess," Abdo adds, "I would predict that the Supreme Court will make good on its suggestion that the third-party doctrine doesn't make sense in the context of cloud storage."

The ripples from Riley may extend to the NSA's surveillance practices, too, says Jennifer Granick, director of Civil Liberties at Stanford Law School's Center for Internet and Society. She points out that the NSA has used the same third-party doctrine arguments to justify its collection of Americans' phone data under section 215 of the Patriot Act. "What will this mean for the NSA's bulk collection of call detail records and other so-called 'metadata'?" she asks in a blog post ["SCOTUS & Cell Phone Searches: Digital is Different, Just Security, June 25, 2014]. "The opinion suggests that when the Court has that question before it, the government's approach may not win the day."

Thanks to the caveat footnote limiting its significance to physical searches of phones, the *Riley* ruling likely won't set any precedent useful for privacy activists just yet. But the OTI's Kevin Bankston says it hints that the Supreme Court has acknowledged the need for new privacy protections in the age of mobile computing. "The Court is clearly concerned with allowing access to data in the cloud or on cell phones without a warrant. And that's likely indicative about how they'll approach things like cell phone location tracking and NSA surveillance in the future," Bankston says. "The fourth amendment for the 21st century will be quite different from the fourth amendment in the 20th century."

Dawn Patrol

By Richard L. Hasen
Slate, October 19, 2014

On the surface, Supreme Court justices seem to have it pretty easy: They decide only around 70 cases per year with a written opinion, meaning each of the nine justices on average gets assigned to write fewer than nine majority opinions per year. They do not sit for regular argument in July, August, or September; and some justices use part of those summer months to moonlight as guest law professors in exotic locations.

But every so often court watchers are reminded that these justices are working very hard behind the scenes by reading briefs, exchanging memos, and debating outcomes. Case in point: The justices issued an order and a dissent in a Texas voting rights case at 5 a.m. Saturday morning. Supreme Court reporters stood by all night for the ruling. The holdup apparently was Justice Ruth Bader Ginsburg's six-page dissent, joined by Justices Elena Kagan and Sonia Sotomayor.

The Supreme Court allowed Texas to use its voter ID law in the upcoming election, even though a federal court decided a few weeks ago that Texas' law violated both the Constitution and the Voting Rights Act, and that Texas engaged in intentional racial discrimination in voting. The trial court had barred Texas from using its law this election, but the United States Court of Appeals for the 5th Circuit reversed that decision last week, and the law's challengers went to the Supreme Court, where, as expected, the court sided with Texas.

The Supreme Court's order was consistent with some of its other recent orders indicating that lower courts should not change the rules of running an election shortly before voting begins. I have dubbed this rule the *"Purcell* Principle," for a 2006 Supreme Court case so concluding.

The court had to decide the emergency request very quickly—early voting begins in Texas on Monday morning—but Justice Ginsburg did not need to write her extensive dissent. The week before, when Justices Samuel Alito, Antonin Scalia, and Clarence Thomas dissented from a Supreme Court order putting Wisconsin's voter ID law on hold, their entire dissent was only a few sentences. It was a dissent which disturbingly treated the right to vote as less important than deference to the Court of Appeals judgment, kind of an Anti-Purcell Principle.

Sometimes justices disagree with emergency court orders such as these and do not even bother to write a formal dissent. And recently, as Slate's Dahlia Lithwick has noted, the majority has not been explaining its various orders in cases from voting rights, to abortion, to same sex marriage, at all.

So why did Justice Ginsburg keep the court and court-watchers up all night for a relatively lengthy dissent from an order issued with no majority opinion? There is no way to know from the outside, but my guess is that she wanted to make an important statement about how the Supreme Court should handle these voting cases going forward and to publicly flag where she believes the court is going wrong. Like a rare oral dissent from the bench after a written opinion, this middle-of-the-night dissent calls attention to what Justice Ginsburg likely sees as a grave injustice.

To begin with, Justice Ginsburg pushed back against the Purcell Principle. Sure, it is important to make sure that courts do not change election rules at the last minute, but there were other issues at stake in deciding on the Texas stay. For example, the trial court—after a full trial on the merits—found that Texas was intentionally discriminating against minority voters. It appears to be unprecedented to let a law that was deemed racially discriminatory go into effect simply to avoid the risk of voter confusion and election administration inefficiency.

Further, Justice Ginsburg highlighted the large discriminatory effects of the law. Texas had what Justice Ginsburg called "the strictest regime in the country," with many forms of identification such as college student ID cards unacceptable. Unlike other states, Texas did not have an exemption in the law for those who were too poor to afford the certified birth certificate or other documents necessary to get the "free" ID card—a card which Justice Ginsburg said Texas did not let people know was widely available.

Justice Ginsburg also highlighted the trial court's findings that there were hundreds of thousands of voters potentially unable to get IDs because they were hours away from the government offices issuing IDs. The state had not made reasonable efforts to get IDs into the hands of everyone who wanted them.

Importantly, Ginsburg concluded that the effect of the law in its entirety would be to diminish voter confidence in the system. "The greatest threat to public confidence in elections in this case is the prospect of enforcing a purposefully discriminatory law, one that likely imposes an unconstitutional poll tax and risks denying the right to vote to hundreds of thousands of eligible voters," she wrote. The Texas case will likely make it back to the Supreme Court, perhaps next year, after the 5th Circuit takes a full look at the case. While the Supreme Court's vote on the stay order in the Texas case does not tell us for sure how things will go when the court gets to the constitutional merits of the challenge, the five conservative justices on the Supreme Court are likely to let Texas put its ID law in place because of their general view of the scope of the Constitution and the Voting Rights Act. No doubt Justice Ginsburg knows this.

But she's not going down without a fight, and if this dissent stands for anything, it's for the proposition that even if the court opts to erode the right to vote by way of unsigned orders at dawn, Ruth Bader Ginsburg will not let it be invisible to the rest of us.

Supreme Court Deals Major Blow to Patent Trolls

By Klint Finley
Wired, June 19, 2014

The Supreme Court just dealt a major blow to patent trolls.

On Thursday, the court upheld the notion that an idea alone can't be patented, deciding unanimously that merely implementing an idea on a computer isn't enough to transform it into a patentable invention. Published on the Supreme Court website, the decision does leave room for patenting specific ways of implementing an idea, but it could prevent some of the most frivolous patent cases from moving forward.

Such cases have become an enormous problem in recent years, particularly in the tech industry. The industry is plagued by an increasing number of "patent trolls," companies that exist solely to force money out of others using patents, and many large companies now spend an enormous amount of time and money defending themselves from patents that should never have been granted in the first place. Legislators and activists have long pushed for new patent laws in an effort to solve this problem, but recent efforts have stalled, and today's court decision can help limit the problem while other bills are penned.

The case in question was *Alice Corporation vs. CLS Bank*. Alice Corporation, a financial company based in Australia, holds a number of patents for facilitating financial exchanges between two parties by using a computer as a third party. CLS Bank, a foreign currency exchange company, filed a claim that the patents were "invalid, unenforceable, or not infringed," and then Alice countered with a claim that CLS was infringing its patents. The court ruled in favor of CLS, reasoning that third party intermediation is a fundamental building block of the economy, and not a novel invention and that "merely requiring generic computer implementation fails to transform that abstract idea into a patent-eligible invention."

The decision is important because many software patent cases are based on ideas rather than implementations, says Julie Samuels, executive director at the public policy think tank and research outfit Engine. "Most of the troll cases involve software patents of dubious quality," she says. "What the Supreme Court did in the *Alice vs CLS* case is give parties dealing with those various patents a very important tool to fight back by invalidating those patents and, going forward, gives the patent office instruction about what it can and cannot issue patents on."

For example, online advertising company Ultramercial is currently suing video streaming company Hulu. Ultramercial is alleging that Hulu violates its patent on forcing viewers to watch a commercial before playing copyrighted content. *Alice vs. CLS* establishes that the mere idea of showing ads before content isn't patentable—only the specific implementation.

But other patent reforms are still necessary to protect companies from frivolous patent suits. The *Alice vs. CLS* ruling may help prevent dubious patents from being granted in the future, but it won't stop patent trolls from filing suits with their existing software patent portfolios. And because of the high cost of fighting litigation, many companies may continue to shy away from fighting such suits, even if they are likely to win.

Legislators have tried to resolve the cost issue, but they've hit political road blocks. Last December, the House of Representatives passed a bill that addressed the matter in part by requiring the loser in a patent suit to pay the legal fees for the winner, which would, in theory, discourage frivolous claims and encourage wrongfully targeted companies and individuals to fight back. It was widely expected to pass in the Senate as well, but Senator Patrick Leahy, a Democrat from Vermont, killed the bill in during committee last month.

Samuels says the patent reform bill is still needed, but [*Alice vs. CLS* is] an important victory. It's yet another example of the Supreme Court reining in patent decisions made by circuit courts. And it solves a problem that was unlikely to be resolved by Congress. "Neither the House nor the Senate had the political will to address the patent quality issue," she says. "This decision deals with the issue Congress wasn't willing to, even if the law had passed."

The Trap in the Supreme Court's "Narrow" Decisions

By Jeffrey Toobin
The New Yorker, June 30, 2014

The Supreme Court concluded its term today with a pair of decisions widely described as "narrow"—that is, of limited application except to the parties in the lawsuits. Don't believe it.

In fact, the Court's decisions in *Burwell v. Hobby Lobby* and *Harris v. Quinn* conform to an established pattern for the Roberts Court. It's generally a two-step process: in confronting a politically charged issue, the court first decides a case in a "narrow" way, but then uses that decision as a precedent to move in a more dramatic, conservative direction in a subsequent case.

Harris, about the rights of workers and their unions, provides a classic example of the process in action. The larger issue here concerns government workers who are covered by a union contract but don't want to pay dues. Excusing these employees from contributing to union coffers would cripple the political and economic power of unions. This particular case concerned home-health-care workers in Illinois. By a vote of five-to-four, the five Republican appointees to the court allowed these workers—and only these workers—to avoid contributing to the union. But in his opinion Justice Samuel Alito, joined by Antonin Scalia, Anthony Kennedy, Clarence Thomas, and John Roberts, clearly indicates that the majority would have been willing extend its judgment to all government workers—and wound unions even more deeply.

The *Hobby Lobby* decision follows the same pattern. Again, Justice Alito's opinion (for the same five-to-four majority) expressed its ruling in narrow terms. Alito asserted that the case concerned only a single "closely held" private company whose owners had religious objections to providing certain forms of birth control. According to the court, federal law required that those wishes be honored.

But, as Justice Ruth Bader Ginsburg pointed out in her dissent, there is almost no limitation on the logic of the majority's view. Almost any closely held companies—which make up a substantial chunk of the American economy—can now claim a religious orientation, and they can now seek to excuse themselves from all sorts of obligations, including honoring certain anti-discrimination laws. And after today's "narrow" rulings, those cases will come.

From "The Trap in the Supreme Court's 'Narrow' Decisions" by Jeffrey Toobin, The New Yorker, 6/30/2014. Jeffrey Toobin/ The New Yorker/© Condé Nast.

The template here is the court's voting-rights jurisprudence. In the 2009 case of *Northwest Austin Municipal Utility District Number One v. Holder,* the court upheld a challenge to an application of Section 5 of the Voting Rights Act. Chief Justice Roberts's decision was "narrow," and it even drew the votes of the court's more liberal members. Four years later, though, Roberts used the *Northwest Austin* precedent as a wedge to destroy both Section 4 and Section 5 of the Voting Rights Act, as well as much of its effectiveness, in the case of *Shelby County, Alabama v. Holder.* The liberals who signed on to the *Northwest Austin* decision howled that they'd been betrayed. But it was too late.

The liberals have seemingly learned their lesson. None signed on to today's "narrow" majority opinions. They will not be surprised when the conservative quintet uses these decisions to rewrite the laws in profound ways. We shouldn't be surprised, either.

Without Actually Issuing Opinions, SCOTUS Has Already Decided a Lot

By Erwin Chemerinsky
ABA Journal, November 4, 2014

In the first few weeks of October Term 2014, the U.S. Supreme Court repeatedly made headlines through a series of unsigned orders and denials of certiorari. These actions, all of which occurred without explanation from the justices, are going to have an enormous effect on people's lives across the country. I cannot think of another time when so much happened through Supreme Court actions that occurred without judicial opinions.

Several unsigned orders involved state laws restricting voting. On Sept. 29, the justices allowed an Ohio law that limited early voting to go into effect. Federal District Judge Peter C. Economus had issued a preliminary injunction against the law's implementation, and the Cincinnati-based 6th U.S. Circuit Court of Appeals affirmed. But the Supreme Court, by a 5–4 margin, issued a stay in an unsigned order and allowed the restrictive Ohio law to go into effect. Justices Ruth Bader Ginsburg, Stephen G. Breyer, Sonia Sotomayor, and Elena Kagan dissented.

On Oct. 8, the court allowed a North Carolina law that restricted voting to go into effect. The Richmond, Virginia–based 4th U.S. Circuit Court of Appeals had found two provisions of the law likely to be a violation of the Voting Rights Act: barring voters from registering and casting their ballots on the same day, and refusing to count votes that were cast in the wrong polling places. The court, without explanation, permitted the law to be implemented. Justice Ginsburg, joined by Justice Sotomayor, dissented and argued that the two restrictions at issue, as well as others in the law, likely violated the Voting Rights Act.

By contrast, on Oct. 9, the Supreme Court, by a 6–3 margin, blocked a Wisconsin law requiring photo identification for voting from going into effect. The Wisconsin law was challenged on the ground that it would have a disproportionate effect against minority voters and thus violate the Voting Rights Act. Again, a federal district judge issued a preliminary injunction, concluding that the law would keep tens of thousands from being able to vote because of their lacking the proper identification. A three-judge panel of the Chicago-based 7th U.S. Circuit Court of Appeals reversed, and the circuit split 5–5 in an en banc vote. The Supreme Court, without explanation, stopped the Wisconsin law from going into effect, with Justice Samuel

A. Alito Jr. writing a short dissent joined by Justices Antonin Scalia and Clarence Thomas.

Most dramatically, just after 5 a.m. on Saturday, Oct. 18, the justices in a 6–3 decision allowed Texas's restrictive voter identification law to go into effect. A federal district court in Texas held a nine-day trial and issued a 143-page opinion declaring the Texas law an "unconstitutional burden on the right to vote" and the equivalent of an unconstitutional poll tax.

The Texas law, as Justice Ginsburg noted in her dissent, is "the strictest regime in the country." For example, unlike restrictive laws adopted in other states, such as Wisconsin, Texas will not accept student identification from in-state universities or identification cards issued by Native American tribes. Obtaining the permissible forms of identification requires obtaining a state-issued birth certificate for $22. The Supreme Court long ago ruled that a state cannot charge even a $1 fee for voting.

The federal district judge concluded that the effect of the Texas law will be that about 600,000 voters, primarily African-American and Latino, will be kept from voting. The district court agreed with the U.S. Justice Department and other challengers that the Texas law violated Section 2 of the Voting Rights Act of 1965 because it was enacted with a racially discriminatory purpose and would yield a prohibited discriminatory result.

Despite these findings, the Supreme Court issued its order to allow Texas to put its restrictive law into effect for the November elections. The court did so without any explanation and in an unsigned order. Justice Ginsburg filed a dissent, joined by Justices Sotomayor and Kagan. Justice Ginsburg lamented: "The greatest threat to public confidence in elections in this case is the prospect of enforcing a purposefully discriminatory law, one that likely imposes an unconstitutional poll tax and risks denying the right to vote to hundreds of thousands of eligible voters."

The court's unsigned orders have not just been in voting cases. On Oct. 14, the court, by a 6–3 margin, kept a Texas law from going into effect that would have closed many facilities where abortions were performed. The Texas law would have required that all clinics in the state upgrade their facilities to be hospital-like surgical centers, even when they perform abortions through the use of drugs. It also kept a requirement from going into effect in two areas that would have insisted that all doctors performing abortions have privileges to admit patients to a hospital within 30 miles of the clinic. Those two provisions had the effect of reducing the number of clinics still operating in the state to seven, compared with the 41 that recently had operated.

Again, the court gave no explanation for its order. Justices Scalia, Thomas, and Alito dissented and would have allowed the Texas law to go into effect. They, too, gave no explanation.

This practice of law by unsigned orders without opinions is troubling. A crucial aspect of the judicial process is that judges give reasons for their rulings. This explains the basis of the decisions to the litigants, provides guidance for lower courts, and makes the rulings seem more than arbitrary exercises of power. Even though the court needed to act quickly, there is no reason for not writing at least brief opinions explaining its decisions. There are many instances of justices acting very quickly when necessary, including with judicial opinions, such as in *Bush v. Gore* and the Pentagon Papers Case (*New York Times v. United States*). The court's orders will have a great effect on those who can vote and those who can't, on those who get elected and those who don't, and those on who can receive an abortion and those who can't. Yet the court gave no explanations for its actions.

There also is a more technical, serious problem with many of the court's recent actions: Appellate courts are supposed to overturn preliminary injunctions issued by trial courts only if there is an abuse of discretion. Also, appellate courts, including the Supreme Court, are supposed to defer to the fact-finding of the trial courts. In the Texas voting case, for example, there were detailed findings of fact by the federal district court, and it is inconceivable that the Supreme Court could conclude that its decision was an abuse of discretion, especially when a three-judge federal district court earlier had come to the same conclusion in blocking the law under the preclearance requirement of the Voting Rights Act.

So without issuing a single opinion in the first few weeks of the new term, the Supreme Court has decided a lot. And that is without even mentioning that Monday, Oct. 6, the court denied certiorari to review decisions of the 4th, 7th, and 10th Circuits declaring unconstitutional laws prohibiting marriage equality in Indiana, Oklahoma, Utah, Virginia, and Wisconsin. The result is to allow same-sex marriage in these states and ultimately all of the states within these circuits, effectively adding Colorado, Kansas, North Carolina, South Carolina, West Virginia, and Wyoming to the list of states where there will be marriage equality.

It has been an amazing start to October Term 2014.

How the Justices Move the Law

By Richard L. Hasen
SCOTUSblog, October 24, 2012

Without doubt, the Supreme Court's most prominent decision so far under the leadership of Chief Justice John Roberts has been *Citizens United v. FEC*. This five-to-four decision, striking down corporate campaign spending limits against a First Amendment challenge and overruling two earlier Supreme Court precedents, has been the subject not only of sustained academic commentary and editorial criticism but also of controversial criticism from President Obama in his 2010 State of the Union speech in the presence of a number of Supreme Court Justices. Critics have condemned *Citizens United* as the decision of an "activist" Supreme Court, while supporters have cheered the Court for correcting earlier errant precedent in conflict with the First Amendment.

As Barry Friedman has pointed out in a recent *Georgetown Law Journal* article ["The Wages of Stealth Overruling (With Particular Attention to *Miranda v. Arizona*)," July 23, 2010], the Supreme Court does not always move the law in such a prominent fashion. Despite the *Citizens United* ruling, and maybe now more because of the public reaction to it, express overrulings of precedent are rare. The Roberts Court also has engaged in "stealth overruling." Stealth overruling occurs when the Court does not explicitly overrule an existing precedent. Instead, it "fail[s] to extend a precedent to the conclusion mandated by its rationale," or it "reduc[es] a precedent to nothing." Using the example of the Roberts Court's treatment of *Miranda v. Arizona*, Friedman demonstrates how the Court has been able to greatly reduce the precedential force of *Miranda* without incurring public scrutiny and criticism. Friedman is critical of stealth overruling on a number of grounds, most importantly because "stealth overruling obscures the path of constitutional law from public view, allowing the Court to alter constitutional meaning without public supervision."

I leave to others the question whether the Roberts Court empirically engages in more (stealth) overruling than earlier groups of Supreme Court Justices did and, even if it does so, whether a higher overruling rate is grounds for condemnation. Instead, the more modest aim of my Essay in the *Emory Law Journal* ["Anticipatory Overrulings, Invitations, Time Bombs, and Inadvertence: How Supreme Court Justices Move the Law," August 1, 2011] is to catalog additional tools that Supreme Court Justices can use beyond express and stealth overruling to move the law. I also explain why Justices might choose to use one, rather than another, of these tools to move the law.

In particular, I analyze four additional tools. "Anticipatory overruling" occurs when the Court does not overrule precedent but suggests its intention to do so in a future case. "Invitations" exist when one or more Justices invite (1) litigants to argue for the overruling of precedent in future cases or (2) Congress to overrule Supreme Court statutory precedent. "Time bombs" exist when Justices include within a case subtle dicta or analysis not necessary to decide it with an eye toward influencing how the Court will decide a future case. "Inadvertence" occurs when the Court changes the law without consciously attempting to do so, through attempts to re-state existing law in line with the writing Justice's values.

Anticipatory overrulings can be aimed at either Congress or the public. By giving advanced warning or suggestion as to what a Court is going to do in a future case, the Court can give Congress (or another legislative body, in an appropriate case) a chance to make a change in law to forestall overruling. In the case of the Voting Rights Act issue in *NAMUDNO v. Holder,* for example, election law scholars have read the Court's decision as implicitly urging Congress to change aspects of the Act so that the Court would not strike down the law as unconstitutional.

Invitations to litigants, such as the invitations issued by Justice Alito, may signal to a litigant that now is a good time to ask for the overturning of precedent. Although the Court cannot pick which cases come up for possible review, invitations to litigants may make it more likely for a Justice to shape the Court's docket. This may be especially true in challenges to federal campaign-finance laws, which, thanks to special jurisdictional provisions, often come to the Court on direct appeal, making it more likely that the Court will hear the case on the merits.

It is also no coincidence that Justice Ginsburg, a frequent liberal dissenter in five-four cases on a conservative Court, is inviting Congress to overturn the Court in statutory cases (rather than inviting litigants to bring more cases). Justice Ginsburg is less likely than Justice Alito to get her preferences approved by the current Supreme Court, and so it is unsurprising that she is signaling Congress when there is an especially worthy statutory decision by the Court for Congress to consider overruling.

Time bombs, because of their subtlety, work differently. They are aimed at stacking the deck, or boxing in the Justices, in future cases in which related issues arise. They are meant to be subtle enough to avoid attracting the attention of other Justices who may disagree with the future use of the language included in the Court's opinion. That the Supreme Court in the *Arizona Free Enterprise Club's Freedom Club PAC v. Bennett* case ultimately relied upon the oblique citation of *Day [v. Holahan]* in *Davis v. FEC* as authority for reversing the Ninth Circuit is some evidence that Justice Alito's potential time bomb paid off. Time bombs also may serve to diffuse public opposition to controversial rulings. A ruling that appears to follow from earlier precedent, as opposed to breaking from precedent, is apt to be less controversial. This is true even if the Court is merely following dicta or an off-handed comment in an earlier case. But time bombs have a disadvantage: they are easier to ignore or dismiss than the more direct means of influencing how the Court decides cases.

All of these tools send signals to the lower courts. While lower courts do not have authority to ignore binding Supreme Court authority, lower courts can interpret cases in ways that are equivalent to overruling or use procedural devices, such as standing, to reach results in line with what the judges predict to be current Supreme Court majority preference.

I conclude that Supreme Court Justices have more tools at their disposal to change the law than first appears. But the various tools for moving the law come with their own costs and benefits, and are aimed at different audiences. Not all tools are appropriate in each circumstance. Here [papers.ssrn.com/sol3/papers.cfm?abstract_id=1750398] is a chart describing the tools and their costs and benefits. Perhaps the most significant part of this analysis is the demonstration that the Court can move the law even when Justices do not intend to do so. The *eBay Inc. v. MercExchange, L.L.C.* example shows the importance for lawyers and law professors to keep up on cases in their fields and to offer amicus help aimed solely at assisting the Court in avoiding inadvertent major changes in the law. Whatever one thinks of the various devices Justices may use to move the law, the law should move only when the Justices want the law to move.

5

Public Perceptions of the Court

Police officer directs people lining up outside the U.S. Supreme Court building, hoping to be admitted to the courtroom to hear oral arguments in *Arizona v. Inter Tribal Council et al.*, March 18, 2013.

Judging the Bench

To become an American citizen, an applicant must pass a written examination on American history. The question most frequently missed on the exam: Name five of the nine members of the U.S. Supreme Court. Most applicants can name only two or three; most native-born Americans can't do much better.

For many Americans the Supreme Court of the United States—often, since the nineteenth century, referred to by the acronym SCOTUS—remains a distant entity. They know that the court is a powerful force that affects their day-to-day lives, but just how this occurs persists as something of a mystery. The court's decisions are arrived at out of the public eye, and from the perspective of the public in far-flung galleries from coast to coast, the court operates on the exalted plane of legend, tragedy, or comedy.

Still, poll after poll shows that Americans agree that the court is a political institution, perhaps the ultimate political institution. Most are aware of the court's role in controversial developments during particular periods of American history: on the question of slavery, state rights, labor unions, abortion, civic rights, social benefits, and the legality of everything from limits on free speech to abuse of the law. Is it because the Court is not elected that it regularly has perception problems with the public?

Despite the court's magisterial trappings, the justices are well aware of how the public perceives it. Current Supreme Court Chief Justice John Roberts has displayed an awareness of the dangers of the public's perception that the court has a political slant. In a 2006 interview, Roberts told court scholar Jeffrey Rosen that continual close 5–4 decisions tend to undermine the court's legitimacy in the eyes of the public. Conversely, unanimity in decision remains quite powerful; unanimity also operates as a public confidence mechanism. As Rosen explains ("Roberts's Rules," *The Atlantic*, January/February 2007), "Unanimous, or nearly unanimous, decisions are hard to overturn and contribute to the stability of the law and the continuity of the Court; by contrast, closely divided, 5–4 decisions make it harder for the public to respect the Court as an impartial institution that transcends partisan politics." Roberts, according to Rosen ("Big Chief," *The New Republic*, July 13, 2012) "cares deeply about the Court's image in the outside world."

Past courts have not always responded to public opinion. After all, once appointed, the justices may, unless they choose otherwise, remain on the court for the rest of their lives; they are not directly subject to the verdict of the voters. Yet as Roberts recognizes, to lose legitimacy in the eyes of the public creates hazards the court has proved unwilling to risk, particularly when direct confrontation with another of the branches of the federal government is involved.

The perceived intransigence of the Supreme Court in the face of President Franklin D. Roosevelt's attempts to implement his New Deal arguably made the court as unpopular as it has ever been and prompted Roosevelt to formulate his notorious "court-packing" plan. Historians and political scientists continue to debate whether Justice Owen Roberts's "switch in time that saved nine"—his decision to switch sides, as it were, voting to uphold the constitutionality of Roosevelt's New Deal measures after a number of votes cutting the other way—was a radical shift in the face of intense political pressure or the result of a more gradual internal evolution of court jurisprudence.

At first the justices had, in a series of 5–4 votes, upheld New Deal legislation. But in May 1935 the Hughes Court—so designated because the chief justice was then Charles Evans Hughes—handed down three unanimous decisions that, in Jill Lepore's words ("Benched, *The New Yorker*, June 18, 2012), "devastated the New Deal." The court proceeded, over 18 months, to strike down a dozen popular, legislatively enacted measures. Thus the court was put on a collision course with both Congress and the president. Public support for Roosevelt during this period was dramatically expressed in the record-breaking rout of the Republican candidate, Alf Landon, in the 1936 presidential election. A month into his second term, in February 1937, Roosevelt launched a plan to break the court's stranglehold on the New Deal by "packing" the court with additional justices who would overrule the court's existing conservative majority. This plan, however, met with strong resistance from both the Congress and the public.

In the midst of these perilous developments, Justice Owen Roberts voted in March 1937 to uphold the latest New Deal measure before the court, and with this 5–4 decision, the tide turned. The Senate Judiciary Committee voted in May to scuttle the court-packing plan, averting a constitutional crisis. Was Roberts's decision motivated by politics, that is, the weight of public opinion? Pointing out that the critical decision (*West Coast Hotel v. Parrish*) was arrived at before the broaching of the court-packing plan, legal scholars Daniel E. Ho and Kevin M. Quinn cite a shift leftward in Roberts's thought over 1936, especially after Roosevelt's landslide electoral victory. In any case, in succeeding years Roosevelt made five new appointments to the court, eventually leaving Roberts as the court's most conservative member. (In all, Roosevelt—who served as president for three terms and part of a fourth—appointed eight justices to the Supreme Court, more than any other president except George Washington.)

One line of attack on the Hughes Court of the New Deal era rested on the justices' ages: six were 70 or over, including Charles Evans Hughes himself; Roosevelt argued that they were no longer equal to their task. Today the Roberts Court is assailed by some critics on similar grounds, particularly with regard to the aging justices' familiarity with emerging technology. But as Selina MacLaren has pointed out ["The Supreme Court's Baffling Tech Illiteracy Is Becoming a Problem," Salon, June 28, 2014] in one of the following articles, there is no easy correlation between the justices' ages and their technological "competence," as she puts it. MacLaren thinks that the real problem is not age per se but rather "that the justices were groomed in a field that emphasizes reasoning by analogy," and increasingly the justices' analogies are hardly recognizable to the public.

Moreover, the court's continued refusal to permit television cameras in the courtroom has led to a pervasive public image of secrecy. Although the court does release voice recordings of oral arguments, in an era in which instantaneous communication is the norm, the public's inability to watch the court in action (except for the very limited number of people who can attend court sessions) has made its work incomprehensible to many. Predictably, the justices are accused of elitism and lack of transparency, thus intensifying frustration with the justices' lack of direct accountability to the people.

Public perception of the Supreme Court may also be influenced by how the justices behave in public. For the most part, justices traditionally have kept a modest public profile and maintained a notable personal reserve. More recently, in speaking engagements, at conferences, and in other public forums—and even in memoirs such as Justice Clarence Thomas's *My Grandfather's Son* (2007) and Justice Sonia Sotomayor's *My Beloved World* (2012)—the justices have forthrightly revealed quite a bit about their backgrounds and personal lives, and some have acquired (or cultivated) a bolder and more outspoken reputation with both media and public. Partisan positions, or views perceived as such, taken by members of the court undoubtedly attract attention—as well as stoke various controversies—and thereby raise the general profile of the court. One result has been increased public scrutiny of the court and its constitutional role.

Is public perception of any branch of government a serious concern or does public perception merely mirror passing political trends? As many commentators have pointed out, the United States is a republic, not a direct democracy. The nation's founders, in fact, deeply distrusted direct democracy, fearing the whims of the mob. The public would do well to remember that the court functions as the conscience of the country's Constitution. As Laurence Tribe has pointed out, insofar as it is rooted in partisan politics, public perception of the court often does not take account of the difficulty of the issues before it, which are grounded in their own peculiar, gritty circumstances but in their broad implications transcend run-of-the-mill politics.

The justices remain individuals with their own personal, philosophical, and political views, and these views may offer a window on how they think about the issues that come before the court as well as on how the court approaches its work. But when the justices act in good faith, mindful of their primary allegiance to the Constitution, they may cast votes not predicted even by expert court watchers.

The public's view of the court in any era revolves around the public's approval of or frustration at the court's rulings—manipulated, often, by media, pundits, and politicians. The public's interest remains confined to political and social issues rather than encompassing the troublesome technicalities of law and precedent that the court must grapple with. That the justices are appointed rather than elected and that their rulings are, for immediate intents and purposes, final, perpetually leads to problems of public perception.

Owing to lamentable security concerns concerning vandalism and terrorism, the public is now permitted to enter the Supreme Court building only on the ground floor, where all those who pass into the building are subject to the security apparatus that now governs so much of Americans' public lives. In "The Supreme Court Steps: An Architectural Dissent," Paul Goldberger writes eloquently on what it is to walk up those steps and what this change means for the public's perception of the court. No longer can citizens ascend those marvelous steps meant to glorify the ascent to justice.

Postscript: On December 31, 2014, Chief Justice John Roberts announced in his 2014 year-end report that by 2016, the Supreme Court will make all its documents and rulings—including briefs filed by litigants—publicly available on the Internet. Thus the court has boldly responded to criticism from legal experts as well as from media outlets that have emphasized the public's perception of a technologically antiquated institution. In his report Chief Justice Roberts also defended the court's view of the need for caution in the face of technological developments that could disrupt its proceedings. Still, the court has opened the door to a new digital era and perhaps a new conception of its responsibility to the public.

—Kevin T. McEneaney

Bibliography

Chemerinsky, Erwin. *The Case against the Supreme Court.* New York: Viking, 2014.

Coyle, Marcia. *The Roberts Court: The Struggle for the Constitution.* New York: Simon & Schuster, 2013.

Epps, Garrett. *American Justice 2014: Nine Clashing Visions on the Supreme Court.* Philadelphia: University of Pennsylvania Press, 2014.

Feldman, Noah. *Scorpions: The Battles and Triumphs of FDR's Great Supreme Court Justices.* New York: Twelve Books, 2010.

Perry, Barbara. *The Priestly Tribe: The Supreme Court's Image in the American Mind.* Westport, CT: Praeger, 1999.

Root, Damon. *Overruled: The Long War for Control of the U.S. Supreme Court.* New York: Palgrave Macmillan, 2014.

Stevens, John Paul. *Five Chiefs: A Supreme Court Memoir.* Boston: Little Brown, 2011.

Toobin, Jeffrey. *The Nine: Inside the Secret World of the Supreme Court.* New York: Doubleday, 2004.

Toobin, Jeffrey. *The Oath: The Obama White House and the Supreme Court.* New York: Doubleday, 2012.

Tribe, Laurence H. *Uncertain Justice: The Roberts Court and the Constitution.* Boston: H. Holt, 2014.

Tushnet, Mark. *In the Balance: Law and Politics on the Roberts Court.* New York: Norton, 2013.

Woodward, Bob, and Scott Armstrong. *The Brethren: Inside the Supreme Court.* New York: Simon & Schuster, 2005.

Why the Supreme Court Needs Term Limits

By Norm Ornstein
The Atlantic, May 22, 2014

This has been quite a time for anniversaries: the 50th of the 1964 Civil Rights Act, the 50th of the Great Society, the 60th of *Brown v. Board of Education*. Each has produced a flurry of celebrations and analyses, including the latest, on *Brown*. Here's one more.

Ten years ago, on the occasion of the 50th anniversary of *Brown,* I attended one of the most interesting and moving panels ever. Yale Law School brought together six luminaries who had been clerks to Supreme Court justices during the deliberations over the *Brown* decision. They talked about the internal discussions and struggles to reach agreement, and the fact that the decision actually took two years. The justices—including Chief Justice Earl Warren and Justices Hugo Black, Felix Frankfurter, Sherman Minton, and others—tried mightily to build a consensus. Whatever their ideological predispositions, they all understood that this decision would alter the fabric of American society. They also knew it would reverberate for a long time, exacerbating some deep-seated societal divisions even as it would heal so many others and right so many wrongs.

The two terms allowed the justices to reach a unanimous conclusion. Afterward, Frankfurter penned a handwritten note to Warren that read: "Dear Chief: This is a day that will live in glory. It is also a great day in the history of the Court, and not in the least for the course of deliberation which brought about the result. I congratulate you."

As I read that letter, I thought about what would have happened if the current Supreme Court were transported back to decide *Brown*. Two years of deliberation? No way. Unanimous or even near-unanimous decision? Forget it. The decision would have been 5–4 the other way, with Chief Justice John Roberts writing for the majority, "The way to stop discrimination on the basis of race is to stop discriminating on the basis of race"—leaving separate but equal as the standard. The idea that finding unanimity or near-unanimity was important for the fabric of the society would never have come up.

Recent analyses have underscored the new reality of today's Supreme Court: It is polarized along partisan lines in a way that parallels other political institutions and the rest of society, in a fashion we have never seen. A couple of years ago, David Paul Kuhn, [in "The Incredible Polarization and Politicization of the Supreme Court," *The Atlantic,* June 29, 2012], noted that the percentage of rulings by one-vote margins is higher under Roberts than any previous chief justice in American history. Of course, many decisions are unanimous—but it is the tough, divisive, and most important ones that end up with the one-vote margins.

The *New York Times*'s Adam Liptak weighed in recently with a piece called "The Polarized Court," in which he said, "For the first time, the Supreme Court is closely divided along party lines." Scott Lemieux, in *The Week,* noted further that the polarization on the Court, like the polarization in Congress, is asymmetric; conservative justices have moved very sharply to the right, liberals a bit more modestly to the left. Much of the movement did occur before Roberts was elevated to the Supreme Court, but his leadership has sharpened the divisions much more, on issues ranging from race and voting rights to campaign finance and corporate power.

How did we get here? As politics have become polarized and as two-party competition intensified, control of the courts—which are increasingly making major policy decisions—became more important. With lifetime appointments, a party in power for two or four years could have sway over policy for decades after it left power. But to ensure that sway meant picking judges who were virtual locks to rule the way the party in power wanted. That meant track records in judicial opinions, and that in turn meant choosing sitting judges to move up to the Supreme Court. It also meant choosing younger individuals with more ideology and less seasoning; better to have a justice serving for 30 years or more than for 20 or less.

The Warren Court that decided *Brown* had five members who had been elected to office—three former U.S. senators, one of whom had also been mayor of Cleveland; one state legislator; and one governor. They were mature, they understood the law, but also understood politics and the impact of their decisions on society. As a consequence, they did not always vote in predictable fashion. Only one of the justices, Sherman Minton, had served on a U.S. appellate court—and he had been a senator before that appointment.

Now, zero members of the Supreme Court have served in elective office, and only Stephen Breyer has significant experience serving on a staff in Congress. Eight of the nine justices previously were on U.S. courts of appeal. Few have had real-world experience outside of the legal and judicial realm. And few of their opinions and decisions come as surprises. That is not to say that all the justices are naïve (although Anthony Kennedy's opinion in *Citizens United,* blithely dismissing the idea that there could be any corruption in campaign money spent "independently" in campaigns, was the epitome of naiveté). Roberts is political in the most Machiavellian sense; he understood the zeitgeist enough to repeatedly assure the Senate during his confirmation hearings that he would strive to issue narrow opinions that respected stare decisis and achieved 9–0 or 8–1 consensus, even as he lay the groundwork during his tenure for the opposite. His surprising ruling on the Affordable Care Act was clearly done with an eye toward softening the criticism that was sure to come with the series of 5–4 decisions on campaign finance and voting rights that lay ahead.

With a Court that is increasingly active in overturning laws passed by Congress and checking presidential authority when there is a president of the opposite party, that means nominations both to appeals courts and to the Supreme Court have become increasingly divisive and polarized, for both parties. And the policy future of the country depends as much on the actuarial tables and the luck of the draw for presidents as it does on the larger trends in politics and society. We could have one one-term president shaping the Court for decades, and another two-term president having zero appointments. And we could end up with a Supreme Court dramatically out of step for decades with the larger shape of the society, and likely losing much of its prestige and sense of legitimacy as an impartial arbiter, creating in turn a serious crisis of confidence in the rule of law.

For more than a decade, I have strongly advocated moving toward term limits for appellate judges and Supreme Court justices. I would like to have single, 18-year terms, staggered so that each president in a term would have two vacancies to fill. Doing so would open opportunities for men and women in their 60s, given modern life expectancies, and not just those in their 40s. It would to some degree lower the temperature on confirmation battles by making the stakes a bit lower. And it would mean a Court that more accurately reflects the changes and judgments of the society.

If we could combine term limits for justices with a sensitivity by presidents to find some judges who actually understand the real world of politics and life, and not just the cloistered one of the bench, we might get somewhere.

Cameras and the Courtroom Dynamic

By Nancy Marder
JURIST, February 24, 2012

Illinois, which has allowed cameras in its appellate courts and its supreme court since 1983, recently opened up its trial courts to cameras as part of a pilot program. Illinois is part of a growing movement to have cameras in the courtroom. This movement can be seen on the state level, not only in Illinois, but also in Pennsylvania, Minnesota and South Dakota. These states have amended their procedures to make them more accessible to cameras. All 50 states now permit cameras in their courts, albeit with various restrictions. On the federal level, the Judicial Conference recently approved a pilot program, which is being conducted by the Federal Judicial Center, in which 14 district courts are experimenting with cameras in the courtroom. Although the US Supreme Court has resisted permitting cameras during oral argument, Congress has been working on legislation that would allow cameras in the Supreme Court. On February 9, 2012, the Senate Judiciary Committee voted 11–7 in favor of having cameras in the US Supreme Court. A similar bill, the Cameras in the Courtroom Act of 2011, is still pending in the House Judiciary Committee.

Leaving aside the constitutional question of one branch taking an action that does not respect the judgment of a coordinate branch, is permitting cameras in the courtroom a wise policy decision? Making courts accessible to citizens is important, but courts can do this in different ways, such as making audio and written transcripts available as quickly as possible. Cameras are not the only answer. Admittedly, the trend has been toward allowing cameras in courtrooms, but there are good policy reasons to stop short of having cameras in the courtroom, particularly in trial courts. At the very least, state and federal courts need to proceed cautiously and consider what is at stake.

Proponents of cameras in the courtroom rely primarily on three arguments: education, transparency and accountability. They argue that cameras in the courtroom will teach citizens about the work of judges and courts. They point out that ordinary citizens know little about this branch of government, and that televising courtroom proceedings will allow people to watch and learn.

Proponents also argue that cameras in the courtroom will make the work of judges more transparent to the citizenry, and that government transparency is important in a democracy. Indeed, Illinois Chief Justice Thomas Kilbride, in explaining why cameras should be permitted in trial courts in Illinois, said: "This is another step to bring more transparency and more accountability to the Illinois court system."

Proponents also claim that cameras in the courtroom will make judges more accountable to the people. Citizens will be able to watch their judges in action, and decide whether they are performing adequately or not. The underlying assumptions are that if judges know they are being watched, they might treat lawyers and parties better than they now do.

Although these arguments have appeal, they are not supported by any evidence, and they focus only on the public, not the parties. Judges also need to ensure that the parties receive a fair trial. What gets lost in the debate on cameras in the courtroom, is that there are competing rights at stake and that there are many ways to ensure that a courtroom proceeding is public, and cameras are not the only way. Proponents' concerns about education, transparency and accountability are also met in other ways.

Although many states have permitted cameras in their courtrooms since 1978, and the US Supreme Court in *Chandler v. Florida* endorsed such state experimentation as long as it did not create a carnival atmosphere in the courtroom, there have been no studies showing that the citizenry has become more educated about courts as a result of these efforts. After almost 35 years with cameras in state courts, Americans' lack of knowledge of state judges and cases persists. Thus, the claim that cameras promote education is one that has not been systematically studied or borne out by the states' experience.

Similarly, the claims that cameras promote transparency and accountability have not been systematically studied or supported by the states' experience. Moreover, state court judges' work is already transparent in that courtrooms are open to the public, proceedings are conducted on the record, and judges write opinions in which they give reasons for their decisions. Many state judges are accountable in that they are elected to office and can remain only if the voters choose to keep them in office.

Before federal courts start following the states' lead and permitting cameras in the courtroom, it is worth considering what the trade-offs are. One concern, particularly in trial courts, is that judges, lawyers, witnesses and jurors can be affected by the presence of the cameras. In a 1994 study of cameras in federal courts, undertaken by the Federal Judicial Center, there were some judges, witnesses and jurors who felt that their behavior was affected by the presence of cameras during the pilot program. Proponents of cameras say that cameras do not affect behavior, but some trial participants in the federal pilot program felt otherwise.

If cameras are to be tried anywhere in the court system, the least likely place would be trial courts, where there are concerns about jurors and witnesses; appellate courts do not raise these same concerns. However, even appellate courts run the risk of attorneys and judges acting differently during oral argument because of cameras. Several of the Supreme Court justices have expressed this concern. They worry that they might not push a particular argument or hypothetical as far as they do now because of how it would be perceived on television. For every judge in a state appellate court who says his or her behavior was not affected by the cameras, there are some who felt that their behavior was. When that happens, the exchange between judge and lawyer suffers, which undermines the role of oral argument.

One solution, then, is to keep cameras out of courtrooms, but to make sure that the proceedings in addition to being open to the public are available online via audio and written transcript. The public gets to learn about the case and the judge's handling of it, without running the risk of adversely affecting the parties. This approach also avoids the power that images have to distract or to be misused. In an audio or transcript, the words remain the focal point, whereas in a televised proceeding, the images and personalities assume center-stage. The focus should be on the argument, not on what the judge or justice is wearing. Cameras in the courtroom, whether in the trial court or the Supreme Court, have the potential to turn courtrooms into just another form of entertainment. The OJ Simpson case, for example, was transformed from a murder trial into a drama about the personalities of the judge, attorneys and witnesses. Although the Simpson trial was an outlier, the harm that it did to public perceptions about courts and judges was enormous.

In this age where every citizen has a cell phone camera and images go viral on the Internet, the damage to courts could be irreparable. Far better, at least for now, is to keep cameras out of courtrooms and to keep citizens informed through other means, such as audio and transcripts, which are far less distracting to participants and observers alike.

At Supreme Court, Secretiveness Attracts Snoops

By Richard Wolf
USA Today, November 12, 2014

WASHINGTON — "Most powerful. Least accountable."

That's the catchphrase for a media campaign being unveiled Wednesday that targets the Supreme Court—not for what the justices do but for what they don't do.

As in: They don't publicize their schedules. They don't state their conflicts when recusing themselves from cases. They don't put their financial disclosures online. They don't bind themselves to a code of conduct. And they don't let cameras in the courtroom.

"The Supreme Court has taken on a larger role in American life in recent years. With that increased power comes the need for increased accountability," says Gabe Roth, former manager of the Coalition for Court Transparency, which has focused largely on the need for greater video and audio coverage of the court.

The new effort, to be called "Fix the Court," is intended to bring more media and advertising firepower to what has been a diffused effort on the part of liberal, conservative and government watchdog groups concerned about the high court's renowned seclusion.

It opens Wednesday with a six-figure advertising campaign aimed at politically active fans of Fox and MSNBC, as well as online sites. Funding comes from the non-partisan New Venture Fund.

"They told us where we can pray, picked our president, allowed billionaires to buy elections and made choices of life and death," the ad intones. "Nine judges, appointed for life to a court that makes its own rules and has disdain for openness and transparency—the Supreme Court, the most powerful and least accountable branch of government."

The campaign will open with five goals:

• It wants the justices to specify why they recuse themselves from cases, so the public can gauge their potential conflicts of interest.

• It wants annual financial disclosures filed online, with more details about the justices' benefactors.

• It wants them to abide by the same code of conduct that applies to other federal judges.

• It wants advance notice of their public appearances.
• It wants improved media and public access to their courtroom and plaza.

The justices' elusiveness has baffled reporters for years, inspiring outside efforts to track their travels in advance. The latest is a Twitter-based service called "SCOTUS Map" that collates future appearances on a map of the world.

"They're public figures. What they say makes news," Roth says. "They shouldn't be hiding their public appearances."

That's all the more important when the president and Congress become enmeshed in government gridlock, Roth says, leaving the court to decide issues such as who can vote, who can marry, who can afford health insurance—even matters of life and death.

The justices try to have it both ways, Roth says—guarding their privacy but hawking their books, asserting transparency but not explaining many rulings, claiming to be non-partisan but headlining events for the liberal American Constitution Society or conservative Federalist Society (where Justice Samuel Alito will appear Thursday).

Several watchdog groups that have been trying to coerce the high court into the 21st century will coordinate their efforts with Roth's organization.

"There's so much that happens behind closed doors," says Michelle Schwartz of the liberal Alliance for Justice. "We're going to be educating the public more, getting them to take notice."

A Modest Proposal

By Christopher Schmidt
ISCOTUS, November 12, 2014

Supreme Court justices love to talk about the importance of public engagement. The American people, they insist, need to understand what the Court does and why. They write books and articles, deliver lectures, and give interviews, often with the express intention of informing the public about the Court's work. Yet when it comes to actually reforming the way the Court operates to better serve these goals, the members of the Supreme Court sing a different tune. They hold tight to traditional practices, such as their process of releasing opinions, that make press coverage of the Court a uniquely challenging task. Not only do the justices refuse to allow cameras in the courtroom, but they delay release of audio of oral arguments until the end of each week and audio of opinion announcements until the beginning of the following Term.

While I think all of these practices should be reconsidered, for most of them I can see that there are some arguments on the side of tradition. (For a terrific discussion of these issues, see the video of this year's Constitution Day event [2014] at Chicago-Kent.) But that last one—the delay of releasing audio of opinion announcements for several months—is pretty much indefensible. What possible purpose does this policy serve? In justifying their refusal to allow any live broadcast (video or audio) of oral arguments, the justices often talk about their fear of the media reducing complex points to misleading sound bites or of grandstanding by lawyers and justices. The sound-bite concern is minimal in the context of opinion announcements, though. The justices are summarizing their written opinions, so they have already taken the sound-biting into their own hands. Any possible risk of selective quotation would seem to be the same, or even less, than the risk of improperly quoting an excerpt from their written opinion. As for judicial grandstanding, I just have trouble seeing this as a problem. If anything, as I have noted in previous ISCOTUS posts, the justices tend to tone down some of the more accusatory language from their written opinions when reading a dissent from the bench. Anyway, a bit of grandstanding would not be a bad thing if one of the goals of an opinion announcement is to convey the importance of the issues at stake.

Furthermore, as I have explored in a law review article and previous posts, the justices (or perhaps their clerks) seem to put a good deal of time and thought into distilling their complex, often technical written opinions into a more accessible, compelling product for general consumption. At their best, opinion summaries—and particularly oral dissents—are the product of a thoughtful abridging of the written opinion. Justices sometimes reorder key points. They amplify certain arguments while muting others. They often highlight more tangible or evocative examples. Sometimes they land upon a nice turn of phrase that was not in the written opinion. (One of the most memorable lines in Justice Breyer's oral dissent in *Parents Involved*—"It is not often in the law that so few have so quickly changed so much"— appears nowhere in his written dissent.) One would think the justices would want this live, condensed version of their opinion to be widely available. As it is now, the justices perform for a relatively miniscule audience in the courtroom. The best they can hope for is that a particularly notable performance might merit a mention in subsequent press accounts. This all makes little sense.

So here is my quite modest proposal: The Supreme Court should allow live broadcast of opinion announcements—preferably video, but audio would do. Or, if not live broadcast, then at least immediate release of video (or audio) recordings.

Bench announcements should be more important than they currently are. The voices of the justices, describing the reasoning behind their opinions in their own words, using language designed to appeal to the broader public, should be a part of the public debate that follows the release of a Court decision. They should be immediately available for teaching purposes as well. I have found bench announcements terrific teaching tools, particularly when working with audiences of non-lawyers. Not only do the justices do much of the work of condensing complex issues and highlighting key points, there is also something particularly engaging for students about hearing the opinions read in the justices' own words. Why should students and engaged citizens need to wait until the following Term to listen to these bench announcements?

If the Supreme Court justices have any interest at all in bringing the Court's public communications into the new century, and they certainly should, live video broadcast of opinion announcements would be a low-risk, high-benefit first step.

The Supreme Court's Baffling Tech Illiteracy Is Becoming a Problem

By Selina MacLaren
Salon, June 28, 2014

This week was a huge one for technology at the Supreme Court. The Court issued three opinions—*Riley v. California, United States v. Wurie,* and *American Broadcasting Companies, Inc. v. Aereo*—that taken together served as an endorsement of cell phone privacy and a condemnation of the online retransmission of TV shows to paid subscribers.

The months leading up to the decisions had been a rough ride for the justices. Following oral arguments for these cases, they were called "black-robed techno-fogeys." They were ranked based on technological incompetence. Their discussions of "the cloud" became the soundtrack for a comical YouTube video, and the blogosphere cringed when Chief Justice John Roberts learned, for the first time, that some people carry more than one cell phone. So, was all that nervous taunting warranted?

Well, yes, but not for the reasons we thought.

The problem isn't that the justices are old fogeys. The problem is that the justices were groomed in a field that emphasizes reasoning by analogy. And analogies were critical in these cases: The *Aereo* decision, for example, hinged on whether the company was more like an equipment provider or a cable company; the *Riley* and *Wurie* decisions addressed whether cell phones are sufficiently analogous to wallets. But emerging technology is, by definition, about breaking away from history. Perhaps reason by analogy hamstrings innovation, or perhaps it promotes impartial decision-making. In any event, it helps explain why the justices sometimes say such silly things.

Years of tortured analogies at oral arguments culminated most recently with this week's cases, but a look back at decisions from years past reveals an abundance of strained analogizing. In past arguments, computers were analogized to typewriters, phone books and calculators. Video games were compared to films, comic books and Grimm's fairy tales. Text messages were analogized to letters to the editor. A risk-hedging method was compared to horse-training and the alphabet. EBay was likened to a Ferris wheel, and also to the process of introducing a baker to a grocer. The list goes on.

"I think there are very, very few things that you cannot find an analogue to in pre-digital age searches," Justice Breyer said during the *Riley* oral argument. "And the problem in almost all instances is quantity and how far afield you're likely to be going." For the high court, a prior century or two apparently isn't too far afield.

The justices are tickled by these analogies. Justice Kennedy, for example, appears blissfully unaware of the new definition of "troll," and covered for his ignorance with a joke during oral argument for *eBay v. MercExchange*: "Is the troll the scary thing under the bridge, or is it a fishing technique?" This raised eyebrows in the patent industry, where "patent troll" is a stock phrase. Justice Breyer, during the *Riley* oral argument, interrupted a discussion about the GPS capabilities of smartphones with another analogy joke: "I don't want to admit it, but my wife might put a little note [with directions] in my pocket." (Is the smartphone supposed to be like his wife? Unclear.)

Justice Alito, arguably the most analogy-obsessed of the bunch, best summed up the Court's historical handicap when he teased Scalia in 2011, saying: "I think what Justice Scalia wants to know is what James Madison thought about video games. Did he enjoy them?"

But this fixation on technological analogies is more than just an idle curiosity. It has real-world implications that are not to be underestimated. Recent years have borne out that if a technology under scrutiny cannot be analogized to a historically protected invention, it may be doomed. In 2006, for example, Chief Justice Roberts doubted that eBay was an actual invention. He asked the lawyer, Seth Waxman, what the invention of eBay was, and when Waxman explained it as an electronic market, Chief Justice Roberts responded flippantly, saying, "I mean, it's not like he invented the internal combustion engine or anything. It's very vague."

When Waxman pushed back at Roberts, pointing out that "I'm not a software developer and I have reason to believe that neither is Your Honor," Roberts fully explicated his contempt for the technology. "I may not be a software developer, but as I read the invention [of eBay], it's displaying pictures of your wares on a computer network and, you know, picking which ones you want and buying them." He next said about the multibillion-dollar Internet corporation: "I might have been able to do that."

This came from the man who four years later asked the difference between a pager and an email.

So what should a lawyer do to prove an invention is truly an invention if there's no good historical analogy? Complicate things. In a recent oral argument about a computer-implemented, electronic escrow service, Justice Kennedy asked whether "a second-year college class in engineering" or "any computer group of people sitting around a coffee shop in Silicon Valley" could write the code for it "over a weekend." The lawyer said yes, to the dismay of many in the industry. No one directly challenged this point, but Justice Roberts referred to a flowchart in one of the briefs: "Just looking at it, it looks pretty complicated. There are a lot of arrows."

Granted, the justices are behind the times. Twenty-first-century technology has come to the Court, but the Court hasn't come to the twenty-first century. Justices still communicate by handwritten notes instead of email. The courthouse got its first photocopying machine in 1969, six decades after the machine was invented.

Oral arguments were first tape-recorded in 1955, nearly a hundred years after the first sound recording. At those arguments, blog reporters are denied press passes, tweeting is verboten, and justices thumb through hard copies of court documents. At the Supreme Court, every day is Throwback Thursday.

This might explain why the majority of Americans oppose life tenure for Supreme Court justices. Life tenure shields judicial independence and pays homage to the Founding Fathers' vision. At the time the Constitution was written, however, the average life expectancy was about 40 years. (Or 60 years if controlled for infant mortality.) Today, it's nearly twice as long. Clearly, life tenure meant something different for the founding generation.

Retirement has changed too. The average retirement age for the first 10 justices was 60, but since 1960 has been 75. Four of the nine current justices have passed that 75-year mark with no stated intent to leave. As this Court becomes older than any before it, some worry about mental decrepitude on the bench. Oral arguments, however, indicate no clear correlation between age and understanding technology.

I informally analyzed oral arguments for 10 recent technology cases, sorting the justices' questions into those that showed confusion and those that showed competence. Over half the time when Justice Scalia asks a tech-related question at oral argument, it is a question that indicates confusion. Justice Kennedy is a close second for most confused. Justice Alito asks about "predigital era" analogues more than any other justice. Justices Ginsburg and Scalia are uncharacteristically quiet in these cases, and Justices Roberts and Kennedy become more vocal. Justice Sotomayor mostly asks questions to show the other justices what she already knows about technology.

The justices can be roughly divided into two age groups: the 75-and-above justices (Ginsburg, Scalia, Kennedy and Breyer), and the 65-and-below justices (Thomas, Alito, Sotomayor, Roberts and Kagan). Justice Breyer is tech-savvy, Justice Alito is not. Justice Kagan is quiet, Justice Kennedy is not. The sample size is small, but the result is clear: When it comes to addressing technology, younger justices are not necessarily better. Instead, the flubs arise where analogies appear.

Before he joined the Court, Chief Justice Roberts suggested that "[s]etting a term of, say, fifteen years would ensure that federal judges would not lose all touch with reality through decades of ivory tower existence." Justice Scalia has voiced similar concerns about losing touch on the bench, confessing, "You always wonder whether you're losing your grip." But a looser grip on outdated analogies might be just what the Court needs.

The Supreme Court: The Last Bastion of American Leadership?

By Matt K. Lewis
The Week, July 8, 2014

Washington is broken. Congress can't seem to reach any decisions, much less achieve consensus on the big challenges facing our country. And over in the executive branch, President Obama has accomplished next to nothing in his second term. America has noticed, with approval ratings for both Obama and Congress in the cellar.

But there's one branch of government that's still doing stuff, whether you like it or not. Yes, the Supreme Court actually issues *decisions*—and, what's more, about two thirds of decisions in this recently concluded term were unanimous (including striking down President Obama's recess appointments and ruling that police need a warrant to search smartphones).

Now, it's not as if the Supreme Court is above the political fray. Nor is the Supreme Court particularly popular, with confidence in the institution at a middling 30 percent. As the *Los Angeles Times* recently noted, "people have more confidence in the court than in any other arm of government, but that may not be saying that much when confidence in the presidency stands at 29 percent and in the Congress at 7 percent."

While the Supreme Court and the presidency have roughly the same level of confidence from the public today, the presidency has plummeted far more in the last two decades. In 1991, Gallup said 72 percent of Americans had confidence in the presidency, versus 48 percent for the Supreme Court. Today they are essentially even.

So why is the court faring (relatively) better than the other two branches of government? Why is this institution (mostly) retaining its stature, while Congress and the president are so rapidly shedding theirs?

Here's one possibility: Supreme Court justices haven't been nearly as susceptible to the dangers and detriments of our nonstop digital world as congressmen and the president have.

For instance, because cameras aren't allowed in the courts, there is little chance for justices to showboat or fall prey to viral gaffes. There's little risk of them being overexposed, too. Ask yourself: Whose voice are you more familiar with—Barack Obama's, John Boehner's, or John Roberts'? Most of us rarely even hear the Supreme Court justices speak.

Transparency is generally positive. But there is a danger that technology has created a situation in which America is tipping too far toward direct democracy—an outcome the Founders feared. And the justices have been far less susceptible to this than congressmen and the president.

Lifetime appointments also help, granting them immunity from activists and lobbyists who increasingly try to "work the refs" (or, in some cases, urge their premature retirement for political purposes). There is no need to pander to one's base when one doesn't have to run for re-election—a stark contrast to the other two (elected) branches of government. They also don't need to raise *money* for re-election, so no need to pander to the outside groups, since there really is no outside game. The court of public opinion matters little here.

Supreme Court justices have only eight colleagues, and they know they are each going to be around for a long, long time. That is bound to change the way they all interact. Imagine if Ted Cruz knew he would never have another job, and that his key to success was to occasionally persuade at least four of his colleagues—say, John McCain, Rand Paul, Mitch McConnell, and Chuck Schumer—to join with him. "The court has institutional reasons to be collegial," said legal analyst and attorney Willy Jay on a recent episode of the Political Wire podcast.

Yes, a lot of these things have always been true of the Supreme Court. But that's the thing—as revolutions in culture, connectedness, technology, and politics have dramatically changed the way we scrutinize the legislative and executive branches, and the way each operates, the Supreme Court has been relatively sheltered, and thus relatively stable in the public's mind.

And let's not underestimate this, too: John Roberts is a good leader.

Roberts is keenly interested in preserving the integrity of the court (some go so far as to suggest Roberts ruled in favor of the Affordable Care Act's individual mandate as an intentional way to preserve the institution's legitimacy, and has probably had to exercise real leadership in corralling so many unanimous decisions. Agree with him or not, he is getting things done.

The presidency is not powerless, and Obama could surely have shown more leadership than he has in recent years. Instead, he has been ranked by voters to be the worst president since World War II. Meanwhile, being speaker of the House these days is tantamount to herding cats. So perhaps the Supreme Court really is America's final vestige of actual leadership—a group of adults who make up their minds about something, and then it happens.

Supreme Court's Ultimate Test: When Rights Collide

By Laurence H. Tribe
Los Angeles Times, June 24, 2014

Just as spring brings baseball and autumn means football, early summer is Supreme Court season. For a few weeks, all eyes turn to the Marble Palace, as the court tackles (or punts) many of the great legal issues of our time.

The latest string of landmark rulings, many handed down over forceful dissent, has inspired predictable commentary. The court is hopelessly divided, we're told. It is cravenly partisan, blind to reality and shockingly unprincipled. Except when we agree with it.

This kind of simple analysis captures the political imagination and fires up the talking heads.

Yet as tempting as it may be in this partisan age to see clarity in the law and malice in the views of others, it's not that tidy. The fiercely independent justices are too diverse, the court's role too complex and the Constitution too capacious to yield to such caricature.

"The Constitution is a pantheon of values, and a lot of hard cases are hard because the Constitution gives no simple rule of decision for the cases in which one of the values is truly at odds with another," retired Justice David H. Souter said in a 2010 Harvard commencement speech. "We want order and security, and we want liberty. And we want not only liberty but equality as well." (Not to mention privacy, transparency, accountability and efficiency.)

Such clashes of values force the justices to exercise judgment: to balance compelling and conflicting values, to forge law by matching shared principles and traditions with ever-changing circumstances and needs. Acting in good faith, reasonable people can disagree over these profoundly hard issues.

Rather than treating those with whom we disagree as fools or knaves (or both), we would be better served to recognize a fundamental truth of our Constitution and democracy: The most complex questions can never be answered once and for all, certainly not by nine black-robed men and women interpreting a centuries-old charter.

Consider the hotly anticipated decision in *McCullen vs. Coakley,* about a Massachusetts law that effectively banishes protesters from coming within 35 feet of an abortion clinic.

Where many see a case about women's rights to shape their own destinies, others see a case about the right to try to dissuade pregnant women from doing something horrible. In truth, two sets of rights are at issue, and the court must decide how best to respect them both. That issue is much harder than the standard liberal/conservative story acknowledges.

Another case the court will decide this term, *Harris vs. Quinn,* also involves a clash of values. That case asks whether a state may compel even those public employees who elect not to join a union to pay fees to the union, since they benefit from the collective bargaining agreements it negotiates.

A "yes" answer would compromise the rights of workers to disassociate themselves from a union, rights grounded in the freedoms of speech and association. A "no" answer would compromise the rights of workers to form a union that can robustly defend their most fundamental interests. Reducing the case to the familiar debate over public employee unions oversimplifies the issues.

Another of this term's cases, *National Labor Relations Board vs. Noel Canning,* also doesn't lend itself to such simplification. It asks the court to decide when the president can make "recess appointments" to federal agencies. Even in this brave new age of filibuster reform, the case could have major implications when the Senate and presidency are controlled by different political parties.

Although often viewed as a referendum on President Obama's aggressive use of the recess power, the *Noel Canning* case raises far deeper questions. It asks the court to decide whether and how to adapt the separation of powers to an age of partisan dysfunction. And any ruling will inevitably interact in uncertain ways with shifting partisan agendas and Senate rule reform.

Each of these cases marks another step in the court's unending quest to balance conflicting rights, to distill the meaning of U.S. history, to draw a map of constitutional guarantees even as the terrain shifts beneath its feet. They afford the justices, and all of us, a chance to revisit and reflect on what the Constitution ought to mean in our time.

This shared commitment to an ongoing constitutional dialogue unifies us, reminding us of our role as "We the People," even when we disagree with the court's ruling. Agreeing to live under the rule of law embodied in the court's necessarily temporary resolutions of the deepest conflicts is one of America's greatest strengths.

This is not to say we must live happily with whatever the court rules. We can and should express our disagreements, whether by legislating, voting, protesting, criticizing, calling for amendments or arguing that the dissenters' views should eventually become the law—as they sometimes do. But that process should respect, not dismiss, the clash of values embraced by our Constitution.

Laurence H. Tribe is the Carl M. Loeb University Professor and Professor of Constitutional Law at Harvard Law School. His most recent book is Uncertain Justice: The Roberts Court and the Constitution *(coauthored with Joshua Matz).*

The Supreme Court Steps: An Architectural Dissent

By Paul Goldberger
The New Yorker, May 5, 2010

Last year, at a panel discussion at the National Gallery in Washington sponsored by the Foundation for Art and Preservation in Embassies, Associate Justice of the Supreme Court Stephen G. Breyer recalled his experience in building the Federal courthouse in Boston, a project he oversaw in the nineteen-eighties, before he was appointed to the Supreme Court. It was clear from the way he spoke that Breyer was not a typical client, or a typical judge acting as an architectural client. He spoke with considerable passion about the role he wanted the building to play in the civic life of Boston, and he talked about how he had worked with the architect, Harry Cobb, to design every element of the courthouse in a way that would reflect the dignity and the symbolism of the law. So it was not that surprising that this week Justice Breyer produced what may be the first architectural dissent ever issued by a sitting Justice of the Supreme Court. It wasn't a legal opinion but a statement in which Justice Breyer (joined, let the record show, by Associate Justice Ruth Bader Ginsburg) took issue with the decision of Chief Justice John Roberts to make a significant change in the physical workings of Breyer's current courthouse, the Supreme Court of the United States, which, as of this week, the public will only be permitted to enter via the ground floor, where security matters presumably can be handled more efficiently. No longer will the public be able to walk up the majestic flight of forty-four steps designed by the architect Cass Gilbert and walk through a portico and under Gilbert's classical pediment, on which is carved the phrase "Equal Justice Under Law."

It's not a casual change, since everything Gilbert was trying to do in his design for the Supreme Court, one of the iconic buildings of the United States, is embodied in the processional movement you make to go into it. The greatness of the Supreme Court as a work of architecture is not in its interior space—the courtroom in which the nine Justices sit is dignified but not extraordinary—but in the way you approach it. The entrance of the Court isn't just a front door; it's more like the judges' bench, and you approach it in a carefully crafted sequence of space and movement, which Gilbert choreographed brilliantly. You feel humbled, and you feel elevated. He managed to make you feel at once the gravity of the past and the openness of the future. Here, as you walk up those white marble steps, classical architecture isn't an old, stuffy past weighing heavily on you; it is more a source of comfort, solace, and a sense of wisely considered possibility.

Of course, what wisdom the Supreme Court has, or doesn't have, doesn't come from its architecture, and if we can't enter the Supreme Court the way Cass Gilbert meant us to, it doesn't mean the Court will operate any differently. But we will see it differently, and Justice Breyer knew that. "The significance of the court's front entrance extends beyond its design and function," he wrote. "To many members of the public, this court's main entrance and front steps are not only a means to, but also a metaphor for, access to the court itself."

We won't lose all appreciation of the law; the effect of this change is subtler than that. But settings matter, and they matter particularly so far as institutions like the Supreme Court are concerned, because from now on people will approach the Supreme Court the way they approach any other government building, which is to say they will slip into it through an ordinary ground-floor doorway and be greeted by scanning and X-ray machines that resemble those in an airport concourse, and this remarkable place will feel more like any other place. It will feel like yet another part of the vast, amorphous, anxious bureaucracy, which is the one thing that we count on the Supreme Court not to be.

Bibliography

Balkin, Jack M. *Living Originalism*. Cambridge, MA: Belknap Press of Harvard University Press, 2011.

Baum, Lawrence. *The Supreme Court*, 11th ed. Thousand Oaks, CA: CQ Press, 2012.

Biskupic, Joan, and Elder Witt. *The Supreme Court at Work*, 2 vols. 2d ed. Washington, DC: CQ Press, 1997.

Bloch, Susan Low, Vicki C. Jackson, and Thomas G Krattenmaker. *Inside the Supreme Court: The Institution and Its Procedures*. St. Paul: Thomson/West, 2008.

Bloom, Lackland H., Jr. *Methods of Interpretation: How the Supreme Court Reads the Constitution*. New York: Oxford University Press, 2009.

Brenner, Saul, and Joseph M. Whitmeyer. *Strategy on the United States Supreme Court*. New York: Cambridge University Press, 2009.

Chemerinsky, Erwin. *The Case against the Supreme Court*. New York: Viking, 2014.

Clark, Thomas S. *The Limits of Judicial Independence*. New York: Cambridge University Press, 2011.

Collins, Paul M., Jr., and Lori A. Ringhand. *Supreme Court Confirmation Hearings and Constitutional Change*. New York: Cambridge University Press, 2013.

Cook, Tracy L. *First Amendment Religious Liberties: Supreme Court Decisions and Public Opinion, 1947–2013*. El Paso: LFB Scholarly Pub., 2014.

Cushman, Clare. *The Supreme Court Justices: Illustrated Biographies, 1789-2012*. 3d ed. Thousand Oaks, CA: CQ Press, 2013.

Davis, Richard. *Justices and Journalists: The U.S. Supreme Court and the Media*. New York: Cambridge University Press, 2011.

Davis, Richard, ed. *Covering the United States Supreme Court in the Digital Age*. New York: Cambridge University Press, 2014.

Devins, Neal, and Davison M. Douglas, eds. *A Year at the Supreme Court*. Durham, NC: Duke University Press, 2004.

Dowling, Shelley L., ed. *State of the Federal Judiciary: Annual Reports of the Chief Justice of the Supreme Court of the United States*. Buffalo: W. S. Hein, 2000.

Duffy, Jill, and Elizabeth Lambert. "Dissents from the Bench: A Compilation of Oral Dissents by U.S. Supreme Court Justices." *Law Library Journal* 102 (Winter 2010): 7 ff.

Epstein, Lee, et al. *The Supreme Court Compendium: Data, Decisions, and Developments*, 5th ed. Thousand Oaks, CA: CQ Press, 2012.

Finkelman, Paul, ed. *The Supreme Court: Controversies, Cases, and Characters from John Jay to John Roberts*, 4 vols. Santa Barbara, CA: ABC-CLIO, 2014.

Finkelman, Paul, and Melvin I. Urofsky. *Landmark Decisions of the United States Supreme Court,* 2d ed. Washington, DC: CQ Press, 2008.

Frank, Walter M. *Making Sense of the Constitution: A Primer on the Supreme Court and Its Struggle to Apply Our Fundamental Law.* Carbondale, IL: Southern Illinois University Press, 2012.

Frederick, David C. *Supreme Court and Appellate Advocacy,* 2d ed. St. Paul: Thomson/West, 2010.

Fried, Charles. *Saying What the Law Is: The Constitution in the Supreme Court.* Cambridge, MA: Harvard University Press, 2004.

Friedman, Barry. *The Will of the People: How Public Opinion Is Influenced the Supreme Court and Shaped the Meaning of the Constitution.* New York: Farrar, Straus, Giroux, 2009.

Friedman, Leon, ed. *Argument: The Oral Argument before the Court in Brown v. Board of Education of Topeka, 1952–55.* New York, Chelsea House, 1983.

Friedman, Leon, and Fred L. Israel. *The Justices of the United States Supreme Court, 1789–1978: Their Lives and Major Opinions,* 4 vols. 4th ed. New York: Facts on File, 2013.

Greenhouse, Linda *The U.S. Supreme Court: A Very Short Introduction.* New York: Oxford University Press, 2012.

Hall, Kermit L., ed. *The Oxford Companion to the Supreme Court of the United States,* 2d ed. New York: Oxford University Press, 2005.

Hall, Kermit L., and John J. Patrick. *The Pursuit of Justice: Supreme Court Decisions That Shaped America.* New York: Oxford University Press, 2006.

Hoffer, Peter C., Williamjames H. Hoffer, and N.E.H. Hull. *The Supreme Court: An Essential History.* Lawrence: University Press of Kansas, 2007.

Johnson, John W. ed. *Historic U.S. Court Cases: An Encyclopedia,* 2d ed., 2 vols. New York: Routledge, 2001.

Jost, Kenneth, ed. *The Supreme Court A to Z,* 5th ed. Thousand Oaks, CA: CQ Press, 2012.

Kahn, Ronald, and Ken I. Kersch, eds. *The Supreme Court and American Political Development.* Lawrence: University Press of Kansas, 2006.

Katz, Stanley N., gen. ed. *Oliver Wendell Holmes Devise History of the Supreme Court of the United States,* 13 vols. New York: Cambridge University Press, 2006–. [Originally published by Macmillan, 1971–2006.]

Kautz, Steven, et al., eds. *The Supreme Court and the Idea of Constitutionalism.* Philadelphia: University of Pennsylvania Press, 2009.

Leiter, Richard A., and Roy M. Mersky. *Landmark Supreme Court Cases: The Most Influential Decisions of the Supreme Court of the United States,* 2d ed. New York: Facts on File, 2012.

Lerner, Max. *Nine Scorpions in a Bottle: Great Judges and Cases of the Supreme Court,* ed. by Richard Cummings. New York, Arcade, 1994.

Lindquist, Stefanie A., and Frank B. Cross. *Measuring Judicial Activism.* New York: Oxford University Press, 2009.

Marcus, Maeva, James R. Perry, et al., eds. *The Documentary History of the*

Supreme Court of the United States, 1789–1800. 8 vols. New York: Columbia University Press, 1985–2006.

Marietta, Morgan. *A Citizen's Guide to the Constitution and the Supreme Court: Constitutional Conflict in American Politics.* New York: Routledge, 2014.

Martin, Fenton S., and Robert Goehlert. *How to Research the Supreme Court.* Washington, DC: Congressional Quarterly, 1992.

Martin, Fenton S., and Robert U. Goehlert. *The U.S. Supreme Court: A Bibliography.* Washington, DC: Congressional Quarterly, 1990.

McCloskey, Robert G. *The American Supreme Court,* 5th ed., rev. by Sanford Levinson. Chicago: University of Chicago Press, 2010.

Newmyer, R. Kent. *The Supreme Court under Marshall and Taney,* new ed. Wheeling, WV: H Davidson, 2006.

Peppers, Todd C., and Artemus Ward, eds. *In Chambers: Stories of Supreme Court Law Clerks and Their Justices.* Charlottesville: University of Virginia Press, 2012.

Posner, Richard A. *Breaking the Deadlock: The 2000 Election, the Constitution, and the Courts.* Princeton, NJ: Princeton University Press, 2001.

Posner, Richard A. *How Judges Think.* Cambridge, MA: Harvard University Press, 2008.

Rosen, Jeffrey. *The Most Democratic Branch: How the Courts Serve America.* New York: Oxford University Press, 2006.

Rosen, Jeffrey. *The Supreme Court: The Personalities and Rivalries That Defined America.* New York: Times Books, 2007.

Rutland, George H., ed. *The Supreme Court: A Bibliography with Indexes.* New York: Nova Science Publishers, 2006.

Savage, David G. *Guide to the U.S. Supreme Court,* 5th ed., 2 vols. Thousand Oaks, CA: CQ Press, 2010.

Savage, David G. *The Supreme Court and the Powers of the American Government,* 2d ed. Washington, DC: CQ Press, 2009.

Schwartz, Bernard. *A History of the Supreme Court.* New York: Oxford University Press, 1993.

Shapiro, Stephen M., et al. *Supreme Court Practice,* 10th ed. Edison, NJ: Bloomberg BNA, 2013.

Shaw, Stephen K., William D. Pederson, and Frank J. Williams, eds. *Franklin D. Roosevelt and the Transformation of the Supreme Court.* Armonk, NY: M.E. Sharpe, 2004.

Sloan, Cliff, and David McKean. *The Great Decision: Jefferson, Adams, Marshall, and the Battle for the Supreme Court.* New York: PublicAffairs, 2009.

Steamer, Robert J. *Chief Justice: Leadership and the Supreme Court.* Columbia: University of South Carolina Press, 1986.

Tanenhaus, David S., ed. in chief. *Encyclopedia of the Supreme Court of the United States,* 5 vols. Detroit : Macmillan Reference USA, 2008.

Toobin, Jeffrey. *The Nine: Inside the Secret World of the Supreme Court.* New York: Doubleday, 2007.

Toobin, Jeffrey. *The Oath: The Obama White House and the Supreme Court.* New York: Doubleday, 2012.

Tribe, Laurence H., and Joshua Matz. *Uncertain Justice: The Roberts Court and the Constitution.* New York: H. Holt, 2014.

Tushnet, Mark V., ed. *I Dissent: Great Opposing Opinions in Landmark Supreme Court Cases.* Boston: Beacon Press, 2008.

Tushnet, Mark V.. *Red, White, and Blue: A Critical Analysis of Constitutional Law.* 1988; reprint, with a new foreword and afterword, Lawrence: University Press of Kansas, 2015.

Urofsky, Melvin, ed. *Biographical Encyclopedia of the Supreme Court: The Lives and Legal Philosophies of the Justices.* Washington, DC: CQ Press, 2006.

Vile, John R. *Essential Supreme Court Decisions: Summaries of Leading Cases in U.S. Constitutional Law,* 16th ed. Lanham, MD: Rowman & Littlefield, 2014.

Ward, Artemus, and David L. Weiden. *Sorcerers' Apprentices: 100 Years of Law Clerks at the United States Supreme Court.* New York : New York University Press, 2006.

Whittington, Keith E. *Political Foundations of Judicial Supremacy: The Presidency, the Supreme Court, and Constitutional Leadership in U.S. History.* Princeton, NJ: Princeton University Press, 2007.

Websites

Federal Judicial Center
http://www.fjc.gov/

Established by Congress in 1967 on the recommendation of the Judicial Conference of the United States, the Federal Judicial Center is the "research and education agency of the federal judicial system," and its resources are primarily directed toward legal professionals and employees of the judiciary. The center's many "specific statutory duties," as presented at the site, are categorized as:
- conducting and promoting research on federal judicial procedures and court operations;
- conducting and promoting orientation and continuing education and training for federal judges, court employees, and others;
- conducting and fostering the study and preservation of federal judicial history; and
- providing information and advice to further improvement in the administration of justice in the courts of foreign countries and inform federal judicial personnel of developments in foreign court systems that could affect their work.

The site presents the results of the center's research on federal court operations and procedures and on court history, as well as selected educational materials produced for judges and court employees.

Institute on the Supreme Court of the United States (ISCOTUS)
http://www.kentlaw.iit.edu/institutes-centers/institute-on-the-supreme-court-of-the-united-states

The Institute on the Supreme Court of the United States (ISCOTUS) is a project of the Illinois Institute of Technology's Chicago-Kent College of Law offering information, educational resources, and scholarship on the Supreme Court. Currently the chief components of Chicago-Kent's ISCOTUS are the Oyez Project and the ISCOTUSnow blog. The Oyez Project is a "complete and authoritative source for all audio recorded in the Court since the installation of a recording system in October 1955." The ISCOTUSnow blog houses explanatory videos on Supreme Court news and decisions since the 2011 term, a Weekly Roundup of the court's activities, and lively commentary on matters that have come (or soon will come) before the court. ISCOTUS offers two apps, for iPhone, iPad, and Android devices. ISCOTUSnow (free) features recent Supreme Court oral arguments and opinion announcements, along with ISCOTUSnow blog posts. PocketJustice (paid) accesses more than 600 cases and 300 hours of audio.

JURIST

http://www.jurist.org/

JURIST is a "Web-based legal news and real-time legal research service" produced by University of Pittsburgh law faculty and more than 60 law student reporters, editors, and Web developers—most of them volunteers—as a public service. The intention is to "track important legal news stories and materials and present them rapidly, objectively and intelligibly in an accessible, ad-free format," with a particular focus on primary sources such as judicial decisions, legislation, testimony, reports, and press releases. The site maintains a legal archive and offers detailed legal backgrounders on important news story. "Legal scholars, leading policymakers and key legal practitioners from the US and abroad" contribute commentary. The coverage is international.

Justia

https://www.justia.com/

The Justia website focuses on making primary legal materials and community resources free and easy to find on the Internet: case law, codes, regulations, legal articles, and legal blog and twitterer databases, as well as a directory of lawyers, legal forms, and "legal answers" in various areas, of the law, by state. Justia works with educational, public interest and other socially focused organizations (such as the Oyez Project). The Justia site hosts two blogs: Justia.Blog, on law, technology and legal marketing, and Verdict, devoted to legal analysis and commentary.

Legal Information Institute's Supreme Court Collection, Cornell University

http://www.law.cornell.edu/supct/supremes.htm

The Legal Information Institute (LII) maintains two collections of decisions by the US Supreme Court: (1) Current decisions, distributed through Project Hermes, the court's program for distributing decisions electronically since 1990. Until January 1997, the LII did not archive decisions at Cornell but instead built finding aids on top of the existing collection at Case Western Reserve University. Thereafter LII received direct Hermes distribution and also converted the entire CWRU "backlist" into richly crosslinked HTML for mounting at the LII site, together with caselists and finding aids. (2) The LII Collection of Historic Decisions, comprising more than 600 of the court's most important decisions from its founding to the present, accompanied by a variety of finding aids. The site also offers opinions, orders, calendars, and case updates (including oral argument previews). The LII publishes a biography and decision list for each of the justices, the court's schedule of oral arguments, the text of court rules, information about the court's authority and jurisdiction, and a glossary of terms used in decisions.

National Archives and Records Administration

http://www.archives.gov/research/guide-fed-records/groups/267.html

All audio recordings of opinion announcements recorded and transmitted to the National Archives and Records Administration (NARA) from 1955 to the present are available at the National Archives in College Park, Maryland. Note that opinion announcement recordings are not available to the general public during the current term; they are transmitted from the Supreme Court of the United States to the National Archives at the beginning of the following term. For more information on opinion announcement recordings at the National Archives, contact the Motion Picture, Sound, and Video Records Section at (301) 837-3540. For information on accessing records online, visit http://www.archives.gov/research/start/online-tools.html

Office of the Solicitor General

http://www.justice.gov/osg

The Solicitor General "supervise[s] and conduct[s] government litigation in the United States Supreme Court." The Office of the Solicitor General is a page at the website of the United Sates Department of Justice. It provides Supreme Court briefs filed by the Solicitor General from 1985 to the present, searchable by caption, docket number, term, type, and subject.

SCOTUSblog

http://www.scotusblog.com/

SCOTUSblog presents daily news round-ups and commentary about the Supreme Court as well as blog posts and a trove of court-related resources. The Term Snapshot section includes a preview feature, This Week at the Court; major cases; upcoming oral arguments and petitions; pending major petitions; recent decisions; special features such as symposia on current issues before the court; court statistics; a court calendar; and, embedded in its own window, the SCOTUSblog Twitter feed. A daily Petitions We're Watching selection highlights a petition anticipated to be of particular interest to the justices. The most recent blog posts appear in the "Latest" section, while a "Featured Posts" section singles out significant posts for more sustained exposure. There are case pages on merits cases, and an archives section preserves everything written at the site and all the materials that have been collected on every case. There are sortable and searchable tables of all the Merits

Cases and Petitions We're Watching. A "mobile" version of the blog is available for readers accessing the site via smartphone.

Supreme Court Historical Society
http://www.supremecourthistory.org/

Founded by Chief Justice Warren E. Burger, the Supreme Court Historical Society is a private nonprofit organization devoted to the collection and preservation of the history of the Supreme Court of the United States. The website provides information about the history of the Court, a timeline of the justices from the beginning of the court to the present, a page on each justice with an audio clip of the justice speaking, multimedia historical documentaries on President Franklin D. Roosevelt's court-packing scheme and on the Grand Commission that decided the 1876 election, a feature on the successive "homes" of the Supreme Court; a list of the most significant oral arguments heard by the Supreme Court from 1955 to 1993, and a history of oral argument focusing on female advocates. The court's traditions and protocols are covered under the rubric How the Court Works. Sample texts are provided for some of the society's publications, such as the *Journal of Supreme Court History* and the society's newsletter, *SCHS Quarterly*. Teachers will find lesson plans and textbook excerpts at the Learning Center page.

Supreme Court of the United States
http://www.supremecourt.gov/

The official web site of the Court. Offers pages on opinions, oral arguments, case documents, rules and guidance, information for the press, and About the Court, a page that provides information about the court building itself and about the sitting justices as well as a timeline and table of all of the justices who have served on the court. The News Media page presents not only press releases, media advisories, and a selection of the justices' speeches but the full text of the Chief Justice's Year-End Report on the State of the Judiciary, both from 2000 to the present. Other resources include same-day slip opinions; the current docket; oral argument transcripts; merit briefs, via the American Bar Association; calendars and schedules; and public and visitor information. Opinions are available beginning with the October 1991 Term. Provides PDFs of the *United States Reports*.

The U.S. Supreme Court Database
http://supremecourtdatabase.org/

This public database contains data on every case decided by the Supreme Court, organized in six categories: identification variables, such as citations and docket numbers; background variables, such as the origin of the case and the reason the court agreed to accept it; chronological variables, such as the date of decision and the

Supreme Court; substantive variables, such as legal provisions and issues; outcome variables, such as disposition of the case, formal alteration of precedent, declaration of unconstitutionality; and voting and opinion variables, such as how the individual justices voted, their opinions, their concurrences and dissents. Currently there are 247 variables in all. Data may be downloaded and analyzed with SPSS, Stata, and Excel, or the analysis may be performed online without any specialized software. Online tutorial demonstrates how to use the site's analytical tools and provides examples of the kinds of questions that the database can answer. In the current version, an individual justice's vote can be the unit of analysis rather than the case. so that a user may, for example, easily compare the behavior of one or more of the justices with that of others. The site houses the earlier versions of the Database, users are now able to replicate any analysis conducted with earlier versions.

The Volokh Conspiracy
http://www.washingtonpost.com/news/volokh-conspiracy/

An influential "group blog" cofounded in 2002 by Eugene Volokh and Alexander Volokh, the Volokh Conspiracy is a classic blog on law and public policy written for the most part by law professors from across the country. The bloggers post freely on any subject that interests them, and although their general orientation is on a spectrum from libertarian to conservative to centrist, they "don't toe a party line and sometimes disagree even with each other." Posts vary widely in type; they may be technical observations addressed to fellow law professionals; thoughts on the law, news, or politics for colleagues and the general public; or idiosyncratic commentary on cultural issues or the poster's personal interests. Formerly freely available on the Internet, the blog migrated to the *Washington Post* in January 2014, and in June 2014 it was put behind the *Post*'s paywall. Visitors may access the current blog ten times in a month without paying for a *Post* subscription, and the blog's substantial archive (2002–2014) is still accessible for free.

Index